ICON CRITICAL GUIDES

William Shakespeare

King Lear

EDITED BY SUSAN BRUCE

Series editor: Richard Beynon

Published in 1997 by Icon Books Ltd.,
Grange Road, Duxford, Cambridge CB2 4QF
e-mail: icon@mistral.co.uk

Distributed in the UK, Europe, Canada, South Africa and Asia by the
Penguin Group: Penguin Books Ltd., 27 Wrights Lane, London W8 5TZ

Published in Australia in 1997 by Allen & Unwin Pty. Ltd.,
PO Box 8500, 9 Atchison Street, St. Leonards, NSW 2065

Series editor: Richard Beynon
Series devised by: Christopher Cox
Cover design: Christos Kondeatis
Typesetting: Wayzgoose

ISBN 1 874166 71 4

Printed and bound in Great Britain by
Caledonian International Book Manufacturing Ltd., Glasgow

Contents

Realism

The introduction to this chapter excerpts Dickens' account of Macready's restoration to the English stage of the original *King Lear*, and then uses this essay to chart some differences between Dickens' reading of the Fool, and those of his Romantic peers. Part One of this chapter (p. 89) covers 'Character Criticism and the Redemption of King Lear': A.C. Bradley's account of the play, still influential amongst students of English Literature today. Also included in this section of the chapter are extracts from Anna Jameson, on Cordelia. Part Two (p. 101) treats those who were among the very few pre-1960s critics to read the play from a position motivated at least in part by concern about social injustice; extracts here are from Swinburne, Tolstoy, and Orwell.

From Christianity to Chaos

A brief introduction to this chapter explains that the period from 1904 until the early 1960s was dominated by redemptionist, Christian, readings of *King Lear*; Part One (p. 117) extracts two such readings, Wilson Knight's and L.C. Knights', and explains the New Critical theory which lay beneath both the content and the method of those readings. Part Two (p. 132) covers two treatments of the text which stand out as interestingly anomalous in this period, Freud's, and William Empson's: both of these, in different ways, concern the text's meditation on renunciation (as had Orwell's essay on the play). Part Three (p. 143) takes us up to the 1960s, with extracts from Jan Kott's *Shakespeare Our Contemporary* (which saw the play as absurdist), and a short description of Peter Brook's 1962 production of *King Lear* (which interpreted it as nihilistic).

Contemporary Criticism of *King Lear*

This chapter attempts, through extract more than explication, to offer some sense of the variety of the criticism which has proliferated since the 1960s, and especially in the last decade; it also attempts to illustrate the degree to which historicisms, of various forms, now dominate readings of *King Lear*. Critics extracted here are: Stanley Cavell, Jonathan Goldberg, Kathleen McLuskie, Coppélia Kahn, Stephen Greenblatt, Lisa Jardine and Richard Halpern.

INTRODUCTION

The Question of Value

L ET US begin with three assessments of *King Lear*. The first is an example of an early eighteenth-century response to the play. Here is Lewis Theobald (1688–1744), editor of Shakespeare, on the character of Lear himself:

■ Now when the Poet has . . . work'd up . . . his Audience to a full Compassion of the King's Misfortunes, to give a finishing stroke to that Passion he makes his Sorrows to have turn'd his Brain. In which Madness . . . *Shakespeare* has wrought with such Spirit and so true a Knowledge of Nature that he . . . [never] will be equall'd in it by any succeeding Poet. . . .

I must conclude with some short Remarks on the . . . Artful Preservation of *Lear*'s Character. Had *Shakespeare* read all that *Aristotle*, *Horace* and the Criticks have wrote on this Score he could not have wrought more happily. . . . I cannot sufficiently admire [Lear's] Struggles with his Testy Humour; his seeming Desire of restraining it, and the Force with which it resists his Endeavours and flies out into Rage and Imprecations. To quote instances of half these Beauties were to copy Speeches out of every Scene where *Lear* either is with his Daughters or Discoursing of them. The Charms of the *Sentiments*, and *Diction*, are too numerous to come under the Observation of a single Paper . . . □

Lewis Theobald, from *The Censor*, no.10 (2 May 1715).[1]

The second extract was written almost 200 years later, in 1906. This is Leo Tolstoy, recounting his experience of Shakespeare, and in particular, of *King Lear*:

■ I remember the astonishment I felt when I first read Shakespeare. I expected to receive a powerful aesthetic pleasure, but . . . I felt an irresistible repulsion and tedium, and doubted as to whether I was senseless in feeling works regarded as the summit of perfection by the whole of the civilized world to be trivial and positively bad, or whether the significance which this civilized world attributes to the works of Shakespeare was itself senseless. . . .

I will endeavour to show why I believe that Shakespeare cannot be recognized either as a great genius, or even as an average author. . . . [At this point Tolstoy surveys the general critical consensus on *Lear*, from Dr Johnson to Brandes, and then begins to attack the play scene by scene.]

The second act [of *King Lear* is] full of unnatural events, and yet more unnatural speeches, not flowing from the position of the characters, and finishing with a scene between Lear and his daughters which might have been powerful if it had not been permeated with the most absurdly foolish, unnatural speeches . . . put into the mouth of Lear. Lear's vacillations . . . would be exceedingly touching if they were not spoiled by the verbose absurdities to which he gives vent . . .

[Shakespeare's] characters continually do and say what is not only unnatural to them, but utterly unnecessary . . . It is sufficient to read *King Lear* alone, with its insanity, murders, plucking out of eyes, Gloucester's jump, its poisonings, and wranglings . . . to be convinced of this. . . .

Nothing demonstrates so clearly the complete absence of aesthetic feeling in Shakespeare as comparison between him and Homer. The works which we call the works of Homer are artistic, poetic, original works, lived through by the author or authors; whereas the works of Shakespeare . . . have nothing whatever in common with art and poetry. □

Leo Nikolayevich Tolstoy, 'Shakespeare and the Drama'[2]

Our third extract needs some introduction. One of the difficulties we have in talking about *King Lear* is that the version of the text which students, and many academics, generally read, is not one which would have been familiar to a seventeenth-century audience. All of Shakespeare's works were produced in various editions in the late sixteenth and early seventeenth centuries, generally in at least one Quarto version of the individual play, as well as in the 1623 Folio, which reprinted all the plays together ('Quarto' and 'Folio' refer to the size of the books). In the case of some plays, these two (or more) editions are very similar, varying only in relatively insignificant respects, such as individual words and phrases, or speech prefixes. But in the case of *King Lear* there are some very substantial differences between the 1608 Quarto edition of the play (sometimes called the 'Pied Bull Quarto') and the version which appears in the Folio collected works (see the appendix to this book for a sample of these differences). The Quarto edition, for instance, contains 300 lines which do not appear in the Folio, the Folio 100 absent from the Quarto. Act 4, scene 3, wherein is related to Kent Cordelia's reaction to the news of Lear's strife ('her smiles and tears/ Were like, a better way') appears only in the Quarto version. The last lines of the play are given to Edgar in the Folio, and to Albany in the Quarto, and there are other changes: the role of the Fool, for instance, has been argued to be different in the two texts, as have those of Albany, of Edgar, and of Kent.[3] But due to a widely held editorial conviction that nothing written, or probably written, by Shakespeare, should be lost to the reader of the play, almost all editions of *King Lear* conflate the two early editions of *King Lear*, to produce a composite version of the text (which, as several recent writers have remarked, has no authority at all).[4]

Many explanations have been offered for the inconsistencies between the two early versions of the play: that the Quarto is an early, pre-production version of the play, taken from Shakespeare's 'foul papers' (or first draft), and the Folio a later version used as an acting text; that both versions derive from a manuscript, or a transcript of a manuscript; that the Quarto version was reconstructed from memory, perhaps by the company of actors. Since the early 1980s, however, a growing number of academics have proposed that Shakespeare revised the earlier version of the play to offer us, instead, the later Folio version. (The theory of revision, it should be noted, is not in itself entirely new, although the degree to which it is now accepted is.) My third extract comes from Gary Taylor's *Reinventing Shakespeare* (1990), and concerns a debate which took place at a conference in Williamstown, Massachusetts, between G.K. Hunter, who was defending the composite version of the text which is generally reprinted as *'King Lear'*, and Steven Urkowitz, who was arguing the 'revisionist' case, claiming that we must understand the Quarto and Folio versions as radically distinct entities. Urkowitz', obviously, is the position with which Taylor agrees:

■ In contending that Shakespeare revised his work, these scholars themselves revise the accepted paradigms of editorial and critical practice. Their collective challenge to 250 years of Shakespeare texts does more than alter or displace hundreds of lines and stage directions in a dozen plays. Revisionism insists that texts are made; they become – they do not flash instantaneously into perfect and unalterable being. Over a certain period an author makes a text; during a later period . . . the author remakes the same text; the revised version results from a kind of posthumous collaboration between a deceased younger self and a living older self. Later, the text is remade again, by eighteenth-century editors. Thereafter, the text is continually remade, in small ways, although the received structure remains intact. Now we see that text being remade again, fundamentally.

Whatever the cogency of Hunter's arguments, the very fact that he is here – in Williamstown, debating Urkowitz – strengthens Urkowitz' position. The audience can see for itself that there are now at least two texts of *King Lear*: Hunter's and Urkowitz'. The debate itself demonstrates that Shakespeare's text is a contested site, that what we read must be decided by the likes of Hunter or the likes of Urkowitz. The text, which had been taken for granted, has now become a matter . . . of choice; therefore it will always remain a matter of choice. Shakespeare himself cannot walk onto the platform at the end of the session and declare in favour of Urkowitz or Hunter. So it is we, the audience, who make the decision. The nature of the occasion demonstrates to everyone present that Shakespeare's text is a contemporary communal construct. □

Gary Taylor, *Reinventing Shakespeare*[5]

We have here then, three very different assessments of *King Lear*, and indeed of Shakespeare's *oeuvre*. Theobald sees Shakespeare as the apotheosis of the literary artist, unequalled by any other writer in his ability to manipulate his audience to sympathise with his hero, in the 'charms' of his 'sentiments' and 'diction', and in his 'knowledge' of 'nature'. Tolstoy, by contrast, sees no such charms in *King Lear*, and, moreover, dislikes precisely what Theobald applauds. Where Theobald sees beauty of diction, Tolstoy sees only 'verbose absurdities'; where Theobald extols Shakespeare's consummate knowledge of nature, Tolstoy condemns him for ubiquitous unnaturalness; what Theobald sees as the play's crowning glory or 'finishing stroke' heads Tolstoy's list of the play's manifold implausibilities. *King Lear*, like all of Shakespeare's plays, is for Tolstoy repulsive, tedious, 'trivial and positively bad'.

In Theobald and Tolstoy, then, we have two diametrically opposed responses to *King Lear*. Gary Taylor's reaction to the play shares more in common with Tolstoy's than with Theobald's: Tolstoy, he maintains, '[struggles] against the idolatries of [his] day, . . . [and sets] up the emotional honesty of [his] own responses against the cant and convention [he] hears all around [him] and in Shakespeare himself' (Taylor p. 399). Taylor believes that we ought to rebel against a literary tradition which sees *King Lear* as one of the greatest, if not the greatest, of all works of literature: 'for the English Romantics' he claims earlier in *Reinventing Shakespeare*, 'one of the revolutions that *King Lear* imagines and forecloses is a revolution against *King Lear* itself. Shakespeare had become one of the venerable authorities, one of the colossal father-kings, that his play defends' (Taylor p. 161). But in the longer extract that I have quoted above, Taylor is saying something rather different, not that *King Lear* is 'good', or 'bad', but that *King Lear* does not actually exist. For Taylor here, different ages remake Shakespeare in their own image, seeing in him what they want to see, making up a *King Lear* to suit their own peculiar cultural prejudices and predilections. We are not simply talking about different interpretations of, or responses to, the text here, nor even of different interpretations of and responses to two texts, Quarto and Folio, but of a multitude of texts, befitting a multitude of ages.

Is *King Lear* a great play? Is it 'positively bad'? Or is it merely a 'contemporary communal construct'? It is not the purpose of this book to answer this question, or indeed to offer explicit judgement on the relative merits of the criticism on the play that I will be reproducing in the pages which follow, although, for the record, I will say here that my own opinion on the text's aesthetic value shares more in common with Theobald's than it does with either of the other two critics I have quoted so far, even if I would not express my admiration for *King Lear* in the same terms as does Theobald, nor ascribe it to the same qualities of the text; and that Taylor's position seems to me to be inconsistent: if there is no 'real' *King Lear*, there is nothing either to praise or to attack, and therefore to speak longingly of a 'revolution against *King Lear* itself' becomes, in Taylor's own terms, as meaningless as it would be to praise the play's virtues.

It will seem to some readers perverse, even reactionary, to begin this volume with an introduction which raises, if not directly addresses, the question of literary value. For perhaps one of the most notable differences between contemporary literary criticism and almost all of the critical writing which precedes it is that practising literary critics today almost never address the question of value, whereas critics of the past almost always did (and generally sought to defend their perceptions of the greatness of Shakespeare, if not always of *King Lear*: Tolstoy, if not in a minority of one, was a fairly lone voice). It would take an entire volume fully to account for the contemporary reluctance explicitly to address questions of value, but here are some brief suggestions. One explanation might lie in a shift in the conception of what a critic should do, a shift which has its origin in the gradual institutionalisation of writing about literature. Pre-twentieth-century critics wrote, by and large, for an (admittedly highly educated and therefore elite) general public, and they saw their task as one of explaining to that public the virtues and failings of the text that they took as their subject matter. For Pope, for example, in 1725, the most excellent criticism was a matter of asterisking the 'most shining Passages', which, in his edition of Shakespeare's works, 'are distinguish'd by comma's in the margin, and where the beauty lay not in the particulars but in the whole a star is prefix'd to the scene'. 'This seems to me,' he goes on, 'a shorter and less ostentatious method of performing the better half of Criticism (namely the pointing out an Author's excellencies) than to fill a whole paper with citations of fine passages, with *General Applauses* or *empty Exclamations* at the tail of them'.[6]

Many earlier critics, one hastens to add, and even, at times Pope himself, did more than this. But for most, appreciation – or sometimes denigration – was seen as the principal role of the critic. This started to change with the creation of English as a subject of university study towards the end of the nineteenth century.[7] With this development, writing about English literature increasingly became produced within universities, and directed towards those working within those institutions. In the early years of this century the audience for such writing was the student and the scholar. More recently, coexistent with an ever increasing pressure within the academic world to increased specialisation (academics now specialise in a given period, such as 'The Renaissance' or 'Romanticism', and few now possess the general range of knowledge owned, say, by an Auerbach) the audience for critical writing has bifurcated. Books about English literature tend now to be addressed in the first instance either to students or to academics: we are, in short, reaching the point where 'textbooks' for English Literature are as conceivable, and even as necessary, as are textbooks for chemistry or the biological sciences.

At first, the growing 'professionalisation' of English Literature proceeded on the assumption that with the exception of very recent literary works 'we' (i.e. university teachers) knew which works were great, which only good, and which not worth bothering about. Thus for I.A. Richards, writing in 1925,

■ The qualifications of a good critic are three. He must be adept at experiencing, without eccentricities, the state of mind relevant to the work he is judging. Secondly, he must be able to distinguish experiences from one another as regards their less superficial features. Thirdly, he must be a sound judge of values.[8] □

The unspoken object of critical production, then, became not an assessment of the value of a text (for that, it was assumed, a good critic should already know), but an explanation of how a text achieved its 'effects', how it 'works'. And this conception of the critic's 'work' (interpretation, not appreciation) has only been exacerbated by the explosion of literary theory that has occurred over the last two or three decades, to which we will return in the final chapter of this book.

Critics writing on Shakespeare today, then, do not generally extol his virtues as they did prior to the twentieth century (it is, indeed, a misconception common amongst students that appreciation is what is required in their essays: it is not, and nothing is gained by telling your reader how wonderful a speech is 'reason not the need' – even if you think, as I do, that it is really pretty good). This, however, does not mean that the debate about value is dead (although it may have been buried for a time), for it has resurfaced over the past two or three decades in debates about the canon, and Shakespeare's place in it, a debate into which Taylor is entering in *Reinventing Shakespeare*. But this is a debate conducted in very different terms from those which we will see adopted in Chapters One and Two of this book. In fact, we have now arrived at a situation in which critics who do admire Shakespeare, and *King Lear*, sometimes struggle to find the terms in which to express that admiration, partly because admiration is neither new nor original, and partly because to express admiration is to enter into a political minefield. This paradoxical situation, in which expressions of positive value are contained at once because such admiration is traditional, because it is passé, and because it is now counter to the dominant critical orthodoxy, has resulted in an odd state of affairs in which, insofar as explicit value-judgements are concerned, the voices which are audible are likely to be those of denigration: if expressions of admiration were initially buried under the sense that they were redundant because to express such admiration would be to state what everyone already knew, they are now submerged under the perception that to express aesthetic or emotional approval of the text, however qualified, is to risk accusations of, or indeed descent into, political naïvety. For the student, this can be confusing. *King Lear* occupies so deep, and so high, a place in our literary culture that it is impossible to 'come to it fresh'. And it is certainly true that students, who read the play for the first time (something a little different from coming to it fresh) are likely, given its place in our literary culture, to expect, as did Tolstoy, to find it a masterpiece. Unthinking adherence to a dogma of adulation is a bad thing in literary study, as it is in any other walk of life. But adherence to a dogma of scorn is equally undesirable. Perhaps knowing a little of the history of these contrasting positions might enable you to make up your own minds on the questions that underlie this very complex argument.

Whether or not Taylor is correct in his assumptions about the literary merit, or lack thereof, of *King Lear*, or in his contention that the text is a cultural mirage, it is undoubtedly true that the *King Lear* which most of us read today is far from identical with the *King Lear* which most people who knew the play at all would have recognised prior to the mid-nineteenth century. This is not only because, as we have seen, editors have traditionally conflated the Quarto and the Folio versions of the text of *King Lear*, but also because, as we shall see in much more detail in Chapter One of this book, the version of *King Lear* which held sway in the English Theatre for a very long time was Nahum Tate's 1681 adaptation of the play, which changes it very substantially indeed. This is the play that the theatre-going public would have known: the *Lear* of the Quarto/Folio, although still read, was not performed in England until the mid-nineteenth century (the tragic ending was restored in 1823, but the Fool did not reappear until 1838). *King Lear*, in other words, was not staged in anything like its original form for more than one hundred and fifty years, and if, today, most of those who read Tate's version find it a travesty of the original text, the same cannot be said for many of those who wrote about the play before 1800, for whom Shakespeare's *Lear* was inferior to Tate's adaptation (for reasons we will examine more fully later in this book). Suffice it to say here that if it is true that literary value is not, at least explicitly, a compelling concern to most literary critics today, it did dog the reception of *King Lear* for many years after its original appearance.

The extracts with which I began this introduction, then, are not necessarily 'representative' of their respective ages. Theobald extols the virtues of *King Lear* during a period in which every production of the play used an adaptation of it far removed from whatever version of the play one assumes that Shakespeare actually wrote, or preferred. Tolstoy attacks the play when, in his own words, Shakespeare is the object of 'universal adulation' and *King Lear* regarded as one of the best of his works. And although Taylor's championing of the revision theory is increasingly shared by critics writing on the play, his implication that 'we' would do well to take up our intellectual cudgels against a critical tradition which has thus far 'foreclosed a revolution against *King Lear* itself' appears at a juncture in literary critical history wherein, perhaps for the first time since the height of Romanticism (although for different reasons), *King Lear* has taken on a cultural precedence against which virtually all other texts pale into insignificance. Not all – perhaps not many – writers today would express this in the kind of terms Stanley Wells uses when he states that '*King Lear* is widely regarded as the greatest tragedy written by the greatest dramatist of the post-classical world, and as one of the monuments of Western civilisation':[9] few today would nail their colours to the mast in terms so unabashedly value-laden. Yet even those who, like Taylor, want to challenge the assumption that Shakespeare is England's greatest literary practitioner would probably agree that amongst all of his works, *King Lear* is the text whose toppling would be most significant. *King Lear*, in other words, is seen as supremely important even by those who would be the most staunch in their denial that it possesses any intrinsic literary merit. To topple *Lear* would be more significant than to topple *The Winter's Tale*, more significant than to topple *As You Like It*, more significant, even, than to topple *Hamlet*.

If most critics today would shy away from explicitly describing *King Lear* as 'great', (still less attempt to levy judgement on whether it is 'greater' than *Twelfth Night*, or *Coriolanus*, or *Hamlet*), then why would its toppling be so significant? Toppling, indeed, from what? One answer to this question has been offered by R. A. Foakes. As he explains, *King Lear*'s current status as Shakespeare's most important, or most central, text, is a relatively recent phenomenon. He begins his *Hamlet Versus Lear* with a neat synopsis of recent shifts in the assessment of these two plays (I have, for reasons of space, condensed Foakes' list; his original is more complex):

■ (a) *Hamlet*

'*Hamlet* – the noblest and greatest of all [Shakespeare's] tragedies' (John Keble, 1830)

. . .

'*Hamlet* is the greatest creation in literature that I know of' (Alfred, Lord Tennyson, . . . 1883)

. . .

'. . .[*Hamlet*] is almost universally considered to be the chief master-piece of one of the greatest minds the world has known' (Ernest Jones, 1949)

. . .

(b) *King Lear*

'[*King Lear*] is the best of all Shakespeare's plays' (William Hazlitt, 1817)

. . .

'In the twentieth century *Hamlet* has yielded to *King Lear* the distinc-tion of being the play in which the age most finds itself' (L. C. Knights, 1960)

. . .

'The play that has come to be regarded as the definitive achievement of Shakespearean tragedy' (Howard Felperin, 1977)

. . .

'The tragedy of *Lear*, deservedly celebrated among the dramas of Shakespeare, is commonly regarded as his greatest achievement' (Stephen Booth, 1983)[10] □

As Foakes goes on to explain:

■ *Hamlet* and *King Lear* . . . have always challenged for regard as Shakespeare's greatest work . . . *Hamlet* . . . remained the central . . . work of Shakespeare until the 1950s. About 1960, however, an intriguing double shift took place. On the one hand, *King Lear* regained its ascen-dancy in critical esteem . . . On the other hand, *King Lear* changed its nature almost overnight: the main tradition of criticism up to the 1950s had interpreted the play as concerned with Lear's pilgrimage to redemption, . . . but in the 1960s the play became Shakespeare's bleakest and most despairing vision of suffering, all hints of consola-tion undermined or denied. (Foakes pp. 3–4) □

We shall return to this shift in interpretation of the text later in this book.

Here, I want to use a final quotation to introduce a few brief pointers about how to use the criticism included in the pages that follow. In the concluding paragraph of *Hamlet Versus Lear*, Foakes re-addresses the question from which his book began: that of which play is 'the greatest' of Shakespeare's works. 'When critics claim the status of "greatest" for one play or the other', Foakes remarks, they are:

■ in effect asserting that the play concerned is the one he or she finds most significant for the time, and most relevant to himself or herself at a particular historical moment . . . I suspect that for the immediate future *King Lear* will continue to be regarded as the central achievement of Shakespeare, if only because it speaks more largely than the other tragedies to the anxieties and problems of the modern world. □

(Foakes, p. 224)

Students, as well as some critics, sometimes assume that literary criticism gets better the closer one gets to our own age. But the principle of progress is a poor model, even a pernicious one, for our thinking about the humanities. Literary criticism, like literature itself, is not teleological. Rather, literature and criticism alike speak to the 'anxieties and problems' of the worlds from which they emerge, and the historical circumstances which surround the consideration of those problems and anxieties. And although *King Lear* has not always been 'the play in which the age most finds itself' it has held a considerable claim to that status for rather a long time now, and is, as R. A. Foakes remarks, likely to continue to do so.

. . .

It remains only to add a few, more 'technical', notes. In this book I have attempted, in relatively limited space, to reproduce as wide a range as possible of a vast critical corpus. This has meant that almost all of the material I have reproduced here is cut, sometimes quite brutally. My strategy for cutting was to preserve content at the expense of form (when such a choice was necessary). So I deleted lengthy analogies, comparisons, similes, and meta-commentary, and almost all internal footnotes (unless they were absolutely necessary to the meaning of the extract). Although I have never left an essay out because it has already been widely reproduced, I have on some occasions reproduced a shorter excerpt from it than I would otherwise have done in order to leave room for the representation of other, less well-known and/or widely available material. I have concentrated explication around material which I think students of the period might find difficult or unfamiliar, or which (in my experience, at least) they often invoke, but don't fully understand (A. C. Bradley, for instance).

CHAPTER ONE

Neo-Classicism

Introduction

■ I, therefore will begin. Soule of the Age!
   The applause! delight! the wonder of our Stage!
My *Shakespeare*, rise; I will not lodge thee by
   Chaucer, or *Spenser*, or bid *Beaumont* lye
A little further, to make thee a roome:
   Thou art a Moniment, without a tombe,
And art alive still, while thy Booke doth live,
   And we have wits to read, and praise to give.[1] □

'Triumph, my Britaine, thou hast one to showe,/ To whom all scenes of
Europe homage owe,' remarks Ben Jonson a little later in the poem from
which the above lines are extracted; Shakespeare, he maintains, 'was not
of an age, but for all time'. For Jonson here, Shakespeare is eternal because
he speaks for all that is important and valuable in human nature, and
expresses eternal truths that transcend any notion of historical specificity.
Yet at the same time, Jonson wants Shakespeare to be the spokesman for
what is, after all, a very small minority within the human race.

   Shakespeare is eternal, but he's also very British; Shakespeare speaks
to everyone, but he's the spokesman for only a few. Conceptually, these
two propositions may make uneasy bedfellows, but they are nevertheless frequently conjoined in the popular, and indeed critical, account
of what Shakespeare stands for. Thus Edward Capell, one of the greatest
early editors of Shakespeare's plays, wrote in 1768 that literary works
are the kingdom's 'estate in fame, that fame which letters confer upon
her'; 'the worth and value of which', he goes on,

■ sinks or raises her in the opinion of foreign nations, and she takes her
rank among them according to the esteem which these are held in. It is then
an object of national concern that they should be sent into the world with

all the advantage which they are in their own nature capable of receiving; and who performs this office rightly is in this a benefactor to his country, and somewhat entitled to her good will. [Shakespeare's works] . . . stand foremost in the list of these literary possessions; are talk'd of wherever the name of *Britain* is talk'd of, that is . . . wherever there are men. □
Edward Capell, dedication to his edition of *Mr. WILLIAM SHAKESPEARE his Comedies, Histories, and Tragedies*[2]

In many ways, these writers were correct in both of their apparently inconsistent assumptions: Shakespeare has, so far, certainly proved to be the most enduring cultural export that Great Britain has ever produced, his works sustaining, in the late twentieth century, a veritable industry of which this book is only an infinitesimally small part. But Jonson's confident assumption of the intrinsic coherence of Shakespeare's *oeuvre* (in speaking of one 'Booke' he represents that *oeuvre* as itself a monument, as solid, tangible, and unchanging as stone) belies the actual nature of Shakespeare's texts (especially *King Lear*), which, as we have seen, have to be reconstructed from early editions whose reliability is questionable.[3] And although he surely did not intend it this way, Jonson's reference to 'My Shakespeare' implicitly presupposes the possibility that 'Jonson's Shakespeare' might be different from somebody else's. Whose Shakespeare are we talking about in the seventeenth and eighteenth centuries? And in particular, whose *King Lear*?

Part One: Nahum Tate's Adaptation of *King Lear*

The short answer to this question is that for the most part we are not talking about Shakespeare's *King Lear* at all in this period; nor, indeed, were most contemporary commentators on the play. The sixteenth and seventeenth centuries saw adaptations of many of Shakespeare's plays take precedence on the English stage over the original versions; 'from a Catalogue annexed to the last Edition of Shakespeare,' George Steevens remarked scathingly in 1779, 'it appears that only Six of his Plays have escaped the Ravages of critical Temerity, or theatrical Presumption'.[4] Now all dramatic productions of a text are, of course, reconstructions of it (it is a cliché that no two performances, let alone productions, of the same play are ever the same). And most dramatic productions of Shakespearean texts are in some sense adaptations of them: it is a very rare performance of *King Lear* or of *Hamlet* which plays the text uncut. But Restoration adaptations of Shakespeare's texts revised their originals much more radically than does a twentieth-century production which cuts a scene from here, and fifty lines from there. Nahum Tate's adaptation of *King Lear* was no exception to this rule: the degree to which it differs from Shakespeare's original text will be evident from the extracts from it which follow.

From *The HISTORY of King LEAR: A Tragedy, Acted at the Duke's Theatre.*
Reviv'd with Alterations. By N. Tate

■ Act I

Enter Bastard *solus.*

Bast. THOU Nature art my Goddess, to thy Law
My Services are bound; why am I then
Depriv'd of a Son's Right, because I came not
In the dull Road that Custom has prescrib'd?
Why Bastard, wherefore Base, when I can boast
A Mind as gen'rous, and a Shape as true
As honest Madam's Issue? Why are we
Held Base, who in the lusty Stealth of Nature
Take fiercer Qualities than what compound
The scanted Births of the stale Marriage-bed;
Well then, legitimate *Edgar*, to thy Right
Of Law I will oppose a Bastard's Cunning.
Our Father's Love is to the Bastard *Edmund*
As to legitimate *Edgar*; with Success
I've practis'd yet on both their easy Natures:
Here comes the old Man chaf't with th' Information
Which last I forg'd against my Brother *Edgar*,
A Tale so plausible, so boldly utter'd,
And heightned by such lucky Accidents,
That now the slightest Circumstance confirms him,
And Base-born *Edmund* spight of Law inherits.

Enter Kent *and* Gloster.

Glost. Nay, good my Lord, your Charity
O'er shoots it self to plead in his Behalf;
You are your self a Father, and may feel
The Sting of Disobedience from a Son
First-born and best-Belov'd: Oh Villain *Edgar*!

Kent Be not too rash, all may be Forgery,
And Time yet clear the Duty of your Son.

Glost. Plead with the Seas, and reason down the Winds,
Yet shall thou ne'er convince me, I have seen
His foul Designs through all a Father's Fondness:
But be this Light and thou my Witnesses,

That I discard him here from my Possessions,
Divorce him from my Heart, my Blood, and Name.

Bast. It works as I cou'd wish; I'll shew my self.

Glost. Ha! *Edmund!* welcome Boy; O *Kent!* see here.
Inverted Nature, *Gloster's* Shame and Glory,
This By-born, the wild sally of my Youth,
Pursues me with all filial Offices,
Whilst *Edgar,* beg'd of Heaven, and born in Honour,
Draws Plagues on my white Head, that urge me still
To curse in Age the Pleasure of my Youth.
Nay, weep not, *Edmund,* for thy Brother's Crimes;
O gen'rous Boy! thou shar'st but half his Blood,
Yet lov'st beyond the Kindness of a Brother:
But I'll reward thy Vertue. Follow me.
My Lord, you wait the King, who comes resolv'd
To quit the Toils of Empire, and divide
His Realms amongst his Daughters; Heaven succeed
But much I fear the Change.

Kent I grieve to see him
With such wild Starts of Passion hourly seiz'd,
As render Majesty between itself.

Glost. Alas! 'tis the Infirmity of his Age,
Yet has his Temper even been unfixt,
Chol'rick and sudden; hark, They approach.

Exeunt Gloster *and* Bastard.

Flourish. Enter Lear, Cornwall, Albany, Burgundy, Edgar, Goneril,
Regan, Cordelia, Edgar *speaking to* Cordelia *at Entrance.*

Edg. *Cordelia,* Royal Fair, turn yet once more,
And e'er successful *Burgundy* receive
The Treasure of thy Beauties from the King,
E'er happy *Burgundy* for ever fold Thee,
Cast back one pitying Look on wretched *Edgar.*

Cord. Alas! What wou'd the wretched *Edgar* with
The more unfortunate *Cordelia?*
Who in Obedience to a Father's Will
Flies from her *Edgar's* Arms to *Burgundy's?*

Lear   Attend my Lords of *Albany* and *Cornwall*,
        With Princely *Burgundy*.

[Here follows a condensed version of the love-test] . . .

Lear   [to *Regan*] Therefore to thee and thine Hereditary
        Remain this ample Third of our fair Kingdom.

Cord. [*Aside*] Now comes my Trial, how am I distrest,
        That must with cold Speech tempt'the Chol'rick King
        Rather to leave me Dowerless, then condemn me
        To loath'd Embraces.

Lear   Speak now Our last, not least in Our dear Love,
        So ends my Task of State, – *Cordelia*, speak?
        What canst thou say to win a richer Third
        Than what thy Sisters gain'd?

Cord. Now must my Love, in Words, fall short of theirs
        As much as it exceeds in Truth, – Nothing, my Lord.

Lear   Nothing can come of Nothing, speak agen.

[Here follows Lear's banishment of Cordelia and Kent, and Burgundy's rejection of Cordelia dowerless.]

Manent Edgar *and* Cordelia.

Edg.   Has Heaven then weigh'd the Merit of my Love,
        Or is't the Raving of my sickly Thought?
        Cou'd *Burgundy* forgo so rich a Prize,
        And leave her to despairing *Edgar's* Arms?
        Have I thy Hand *Cordelia*? Do I clasp it?
        The Hand that was this Minute to have join'd
        My hated Rival's? Do I kneel before thee,
        And offer at thy Feet my panting Heart?
        Smile, Princess, and convince me; for as yet
        I doubt, and dare not trust the dazling Joy.

Cord. Some Comfort yet, that 'twas no vicious Blot
        That has depriv'd me of a Father's Grace,
        But meerly want of that which makes me Rich
        In wanting it; a smooth professing Tongue:
        O Sisters! I am loth to call your Fault

As it deserves; but use our Father well,
And wrong'd *Cordelia* never shall repine.

Edg.   O heav'nly Maid! that art thyself thy Dow'r,
Richer in Vertue than the Stars in Light,
If *Edgar's* humble Fortunes may be grac't
With thy Acceptance, at thy Feet he lays 'em.
Ha, my *Cordelia*! dost thou turn away?
What have I done t' offend thee?

Cord.   Talk't of Love.

Edg.   Then I've offended oft, *Cordelia* too
Has oft permitted me so to offend.

Cord.   When, *Edgar*, I permitted your Addresses,
I was the darling daughter of a King,
Nor can I now forget my Royal Birth,
And live dependant on my Lover's Fortune;
I cannot to so low a Fate submit;
And therefore study to forget your Passion,
And trouble me upon this Theam no more.

Edg.   Thus Majesty takes most State in Distress!
How are we tost on Fortune's fickle Flood!
The Wave that with surprizing Kindness brought
The dear Wreck to my Arms, has snatcht it back,
And left me mourning on the barren Shoar.

Cord.   [*Aside*] This baseness of th' ignoble *Burgundy*,
Draws just Suspicion on the Race of Men;
His Love was Int'rest, so may *Edgar's* be
And He, but with more Complement, dissemble;
If so, I shall oblige him by denying:
But if his Love be fixt, such constant Flame
As warms our Breasts, if such I find his Passion,
My Heart as grateful to his Truth shall be,
And Cold *Cordelia* prove as kind as He.   *Exit*.[5] □

From this extract we can note some of the innumerable changes that
Tate makes in his adaptation (another, not apparent here, is the cutting
of the Fool). The plot and subplot are condensed and compacted right
from the start, with Edmund playing a much more central role in the
drama, as the transposition of his 'Bastard' speech indicates. In Tate's

version Kent's reference to Lear's 'wild starts of Passion' and Gloster's to his 'unfixt,/ Chol'rick and sudden' 'Temper' prepares us for Lear's behaviour before ever we see him; Lear's madness, moreover, is even explained to us prior to our experience of it, in Gloster's diagnosis of senile dementia, 'the Infirmity of his Age'. Finally, of course, we can see in this opening scene one of the most striking elements of Tate's adaptation: the creation of a 'love interest' between Cordelia and Edgar, which necessitates the cutting of France, provides a romantic explanation for Cordelia's refusal to play the love-test and – bizarrely – results in Cordelia conducting her own test of Edgar's affections. But perhaps the most major change of all lies in Tate's rewriting of the end of the play, as an extract from the last scene will show:

■ (*From* Act 5)

Alb. The Troops, by *Edmund* rais'd, I have disbanded;
Those that remain are under my Command.
What Comfort may be brought to chear your Age,
And heal your savage Wrongs, shall be apply'd,
For to your Majesty we do resign
Your Kingdom, save what Part your self conferr'd
On us in Marriage.

Kent Hear you that, my Liege?

Cord. Then there are Gods, and Vertue is their Care.

Lear Is't Possible?
Let the Spheres stop their Course, the Sun make Hault,
The Winds be husht, the Seas and Fountains rest;
All Nature pause, and listen to the Change.
Where is my *Kent*, my *Cajus*?

Kent Here, my Liege.

Lear Why I have News that will recal thy Youth;
Ha! Didst thou hear't, or did th' inspiring Gods
Whisper to me alone? Old *Lear* shall be
A King again.

Kent The Prince, that like a God has Pow'r, has said it.

Lear *Cordelia* then shall be a Queen, mark that:
Cordelia shall be a Queen; Winds catch the Sound,
And bear it on your rosie Wings to Heav'n.
Cordelia is a Queen.

Re-enter *Edgar* with *Gloster.*

[Here follows Lear's reconciliation with Gloucester and the news of the deaths of Edmund, Goneril and Regan.] . . .

Lear   . . . *Edgar*, I defer thy Joys too long:
      Thou serv'dst distrest *Cordelia*; take her Crown'd;
      Th' imperial Grace fresh blooming on her Brow;
      Nay, *Gloster*, thou hast here a Father's Right,
      Thy helping Hand t'heap Blessings on their Heads.

Kent   Old *Kent* throws in his hearty Wishes too.

Edg.   The Gods and you too largely Recompence
      What I have done: the Gift strikes Merit dumb.

Cord.   Nor do I blush to own my Self o'erpaid
      For all my Suff'rings past.

Glost.   Now, gentle Gods, give *Gloster* his Discharge.

Lear   No, *Gloster*, thou hast Business yet for Life;
      Thou, *Kent*, and I, retir'd to some cool Cell
      Will gently pass our short Reserves of Time
      In calm Reflections on our Fortunes past,
      Cheer'd with Relation of the prosperous Reign
      Of this celestial Pair; thus our Remains
      Shall in an even Course of Thoughts be past,
      Enjoy the present Hour, nor fear the last.

Edg.   Our drooping Country now erects her Head,
      Peace spreads her balmy Wings, and Plenty blooms.
      Divine *Cordelia*, all the Gods can witness
      How much thy Love to Empire I prefer!
      Thy bright Example shall convince the World
      (Whatever Storms of Fortune are decreed)
      That Truth and Vertue shall at last succeed.

Exeunt Omnes. □

(Summers, pp. 251–3)

What lay behind Tate's decision to make these changes in his adaptation of the Shakespearean text? And why did Tate's version of the play prove so popular on the English stage? For popular it certainly was: from the spring of 1681 when it was first performed, to 1838, when Macready revived the Shakespearean text, every performance of *King Lear* used Tate's adaptation of the play. Tate himself offered some explanations for his decisions in a prefatory letter to the printed version of his adaptation:

From Tate's Prefatory Letter

■ To My Esteem'd FRIEND THOMAS BOTELER, Esq

Sir,

YOU have a natural Right to this Piece, since by your Advice I attempted the Revival of it with Alterations. . . . I found that the New-modelling of this Story, wou'd force me sometimes on the difficult Task of making the chiefest Persons speak something like their Characters, on Matter whereof I had no Ground in my Author. Lear's real and Edgar's *pretended Madness have so much of extravagant* Nature, *(I know not how else to express it,) as cou'd never have started, but from our* Shakespear's *Creating Fancy. The Images and Languages are so odd and surprizing, and yet so agreeable and proper, that whilst we grant that none but* Shakespear *cou'd have form'd such Conceptions; yet we are satisfied that they were the only Things in the World that ought to be said on these Occasions. I found the Whole to answer your Account of it, a Heap of Jewels, unstrung, and unpolish'd; yet so dazzling in their Disorder, that I soon perceiv'd I had seiz'd a Treasure. 'Twas my good Fortune to light on one Expedient to rectifie what was wanting in the Regularity and Probability of the Tale, which was to run through the Whole, as* Love betwixt Edgar *and* Cordelia; *that never chang'd Word with each other in the Original. This renders* Cordelia's *Indifference, and her Father's Passion in the first Scene, probable. It likewise gives Countenance to* Edgar's *Disguise, making that a generous Design that was before a poor Shift to save his Life. . . . This Method necessarily threw me on making the Tale conclude in a Success to the innocent destrest Persons: Otherwise I must have incumbered the Stage with dead Bodies . . .*

I have one Thing more to Apologize for, which is that I have us'd less Quaintness of Expression even in the newest Parts of this Play. I confess, 'twas Design in me, partly to comply with my Author's Style, to make Scenes of a Piece, and partly to give it some Resemblance of the Time and Persons here represented . . .

Your obliged Friend

and humble Servant,

N.Tate. □

(Summers, pp. 177–8)

From Tate's prefatory letter we can begin to excavate some of the critical tenets which motivated the changes that he made to the text. Tate finds Shakespearean 'Images and language', both 'odd and surprizing' and 'agreeable and proper' at the same time; his (disingenuous) assertion that he has endeavoured to 'comply with my author's style' is belied by his consistent simplification of Shakespeare's language, as well as by his intention to 'make scenes of a piece'. Like many readers of *King Lear*, he is disturbed by the lack of explicit motivation for some of the main actions of the principal characters. There are no easy answers to questions such as 'Why does the king fly into such a rage in Act I of the play?' or 'Why does Cordelia refuse to speak her love when questioned on it by her father?' But whereas the play's refusal to offer straightforward elucidation to questions like these is something which has intrigued many twentieth-century critics, some of whom might argue that it is precisely within this opacity and difficulty that the play's richness resides, for Tate, Cordelia's 'indifference' and Lear's 'passion' are aesthetic shortcomings, rendering the 'Tale' of the original play irregular and improbable.

Tate is not only unhappy with the 'improbability' of some of the characters' motivations. He is also disturbed by what he considers to be transgressions of decorum in the original text. Tate wants the 'chiefest Persons' in the tale to 'speak something like their characters', and to act, always, according to a very strict conception of what that 'character' 'ought' to be. Thus Edgar, being noble, should have higher motives for his disguise than that of saving his own skin (the understanding that in certain circumstances discretion may be the better part of valour does not seem to have crossed Tate's mind). Being 'noble' (both in terms of action and in terms of social status) apparently renders Edgar a fit partner for Cordelia: the social distinctions between royalty and nobility which underlie Shakespeare's text are, for Tate, insignificant – Tate, indeed, seems unaware that the fact that the two 'never chang'd Word with each other in the original' might say something about Shakespeare's conception of proper social hierarchy. This 'happily imagined' liaison, moreover, affords a way in which the plot and subplot can be intrinsically linked. (That Tate and his audiences look for such explicit ways to draw the two plots together, incidentally, speaks also to their blindness to the subtler links between plot and subplot in the original text.) The responses to Tate's *Lear* which follow indicate how strongly his audience was in agreement with him.

Responses to Tate's *Lear*

■ The King and *Cordelia* ought by no means to have dy'd, and . . . Mr *Tate* has very justly alter'd that particular which must disgust the . . . Audience, to have Vertue and Piety meet so unjust a Reward. So that this Plot, tho' of so celebrated a Play, has none of the Ends of Tragedy, moving neither Fear not Pity. We rejoice at the Death of the *Bastard* and the two Sisters, as of Monsters in Nature under whom the very Earth must groan. And we see with horror and Indignation the Death of the King, *Cordelia* and *Kent*. □

Charles Gildon, *Remarks on the Plays of Shakespeare* (1710).[6]

■ The plot [of *King Lear*] is rather disjointed, and the scenes frequently intrude upon the unities of time and place. But the catastrophe,[7] so happily conceived by TATE, atones for all the unreformed irregularities; and we may venture to say that from his hands the public have received a dramatic piece which appeals so powerfully to the passions that when performed with suitable abilities it proves rather a degree of painful pleasure, and shrinks nature back upon herself. □

Francis Gentleman, from *The Dramatic Censor; or Critical Companion* (2 vols, 1770), Vickers, 5:406

■ The morals of Shakespeare's plays are in general extremely natural and just; yet why must innocence unnecessarily suffer? why must the hoary, the venerable Lear be brought with sorrow to the grave? Why must Cordelia perish by an untimely fate? the amiable, the dutiful, the innocent Cordelia! She that had already felt the heart-rending anger of a much beloved but hasty mistaken father! She that could receive, protect, and cherish a poor, infirm, weak, and despised old man although he had showered down curses on her undeserving head! That such a melancholy catastrophe was by no means necessary is sufficiently evinced by the manner in which the same play is now performed. Ingratitude now meets with its proper punishment, and the audience now retire exulting in the mutual happiness of paternal affection and filial piety. Such, if practicable, should be the winding up of all dramatic representations, that mankind may have the most persuasive allurements to all good actions . . . □

William Richardson, *A Philosophical Analysis and Illustration of some of Shakespeare's remarkable Characters* (1774), Vickers, 6:131

■ . . . The passion of Edgar and Cordelia is happily imagined; it strongly connects to the main plot of the play and renders it more interesting to the spectators; without this, and the consequent happy catastrophe, the alteration of *Lear* would have been of little worth. Besides, after these turbulent scenes of resentment, violence, disobedience, ingratitude, and rage between Lear and his two eldest daughters, with the king's consequent agony and distraction, the unexpected interview of Cordelia and Edgar in Act III gives a pause of relief to the harassed and distressed minds of the audience. It is a gleam of sunshine and a promise of fair weather in the midst of storm and tempest. . . . the spectators always dismissed the two lovers with the most rapturous applause. □

Thomas Davies, from *Dramatic Miscellanies* (1784), Vickers, 6:377

Part Two: Neo-Classicism: the Theory behind Tate's Practice

It is perhaps in the metaphor which we saw Tate adopt to describe the original *King Lear* that the main key to these responses to the original text really lies. 'A Heap of Jewels, unstrung and unpolish'd: yet so dazzling in their disorder. . .': it is in their sense of what is 'orderly' and 'decorous' that the late seventeenth- and eighteenth-century readers of Shakespeare often found him so lacking. In the introduction to volume 1 of his *Shakespeare: The Critical Heritage* Brian Vickers details some of the reasons people gave for adapting Shakespeare's plays: these include the simplification of the language of the text (often through the removal of metaphors) to make it more comprehensible and the removal of violations of various kinds of decorum (of action, as in deaths on stage; of social position, either formally as in heroes speaking in prose, or in terms of content, as in nobles running away; and of genre, as in the mixing of comedy and tragedy – hence Tate's eradication of the Fool).[8] Seventeenth- and eighteenth-century audiences were also unwilling to put up with violations of the unities, and of poetic justice, and they very much wanted their literature to embody a clear moral message: as Tate says in the prologue to his adaptation, 'Morals were always proper for the Stage,/ But are ev'n necessary in this Age'. Expressions of many of these aesthetic requirements can be noted in the extracts we have just read: Gentleman objects to Shakespeare's failure to observe the unities of time and place; Richardson thinks the original ending of the play immoral; and Gildon considers that it is tasteless and has 'none of the Ends of Tragedy, moving neither Fear not Pity'.

Gildon's reference to fear and to pity alludes to Aristotle's theory of tragedy, for it was Aristotelian theory – or, at least, a version of it – which underlay most of the writing about tragedy, and tragedies, during the period covered by this chapter.[9] Towards the end of that period, attachment to these Neo-Classical (sometimes also called 'Neo-Aristotelian') principles began, finally, to wane. But for the most part, it was Shakespeare's failure to conform to a strict Neo-Classical conception of the 'Rules' for drama which motivated some of the profoundest dissatisfaction with him. The extracts which follow are designed to indicate more precisely what some of these 'Rules' were, and to lay out some of the theoretical debates and presuppositions which underlay most of the criticism of *King Lear* during this period and motivated Tate's adaptation of the play.

From John Dryden, preface to his adaptation, *Troilus and Cressida, or Truth Found Too Late* (1679)

■   The Grounds of Criticism in Tragedy

Tragedy is thus defined by *Aristotle*, (omitting what I thought unnecessary in his Definition). 'Tis an imitation of one intire, great, and probable action; not told but represented, which by moving in us fear and pity, is conducive to the purging of those two passions in our minds. [Tragic] . . . Action . . . must be . . . single, that is, it must not be a History of one Mans life: Suppose of . . . *Julius Caesar*, but one single action of theirs. This condemns all . . . double action[10] of Plays. . . .

The natural reason of this Rule is plain, for two different independent actions, distract the attention . . . of the Audience, and consequently destroy the intention of the Poet: If his business be to move terror and pity and one of his Actions be Comical, the other Tragical, the former will divert the people, and . . . make void his greater purpose. Therefore as in Perspective so in Tragedy there must be a point of sight in which all the lines terminate: Otherwise the eye wanders, and the work is false . . .

Action . . . ought to be probable, as well as admirable and great. 'Tis . . . always necessary that there should be a likeness of truth, something that is more than barely possible . . . To invent therefore a probability and to make it wonderfull, is the most difficult undertaking in the Art of Poetry: for that which is not wonderfull, is not great, and that which is not probable, will not delight a reasonable Audience. . . .

To instruct delightfully is the general end of all Poetry. . . . To purge the passions by Example, is . . . the particular instruction which belongs to Tragedy. . . . Pride and want of commiseration are the most predominant vices in Mankinde: therefore to cure us of these two, the inventors of Tragedy have chosen to work upon two other passions, which are fear and pity. We are wrought to fear, by their seting before our eyes some terrible example of misfortune, which hapned to persons of the highest Quality; for such an action demonstrates to us, that no condition is privileg'd from the turns of Fortune: this must of necessity cause terror in us and consequently abate our pride. But when we see that the most virtuous as well as the greatest are not exempt from such misfortunes, that consideration moves pity in us: and insensibly works us to be helpfull to, and tender over the distress'd, which is the noblest . . . of moral virtues. Here 'tis observable that it is absolutely necessary to make a man virtuous if we desire he should be pity'd: We lament not, but detest a wicked man, we are glad when we behold his crimes are punish'd and that Poetical justice is done upon him. . . .

The first Rule . . . is to make the moral of the work; that is to lay down to your self what that precept of morality shall be, which you would insinuate into the people: . . . 'Tis the Moral that directs the whole action of the Play to one center; and that action or Fable, is the example built upon the moral, which confirms the truth of it to our experience . . .

The manners . . . are . . . those inclinations . . . which move and carry us to actions . . . in a Play; or which incline the persons to such, or such actions: . . . To produce a Villain, without other reason than a natural inclination to villany, is in Poetry to produce an effect without a cause . . .

. . . [T]he manners . . . must be apparent, that is in every character of the Play, some inclinations of the Person must appear: and these are shown in the actions and discourse. Secondly the manners must be suitable or agreeing to the Persons; that is to the Age, Sex, dignity and the other general heads of Manners: thus when a Poet has given the Dignity of a King to one of his persons, in all his actions and speeches, that person must discover Majesty, Magnanimity, and jealousy of power; because these are suitable to the general manners of a King. . . .

. . . If the inclinations [of a character] be obscure, 'tis a sign the Poet is in the dark, and knows not what manner of man he presents to you; and consequently you can have no Idea . . . of that man: nor can judge what resolutions he ought to take; or what words or actions are proper for him. . . . □

Vickers, 1:252–9

Dryden believed that the manners, or motivations, of Shakespeare's persons are 'generally apparent', but as we have seen, Tate had difficulties with Edgar's flight (which he thought denoted a lamentable lack of noble character), with Cordelia's silence (which he considered in need of a proper explanation,) and with Lear's sudden shift from magnanimity to wrath (which he makes efforts both to explain and to forewarn us of). Other writers were so enamoured of the idea that manners ought always to be consistent that they had problems with the madness of Lear, considering it inappropriate to the dignity of a king to crown himself with straw. But perhaps the most interesting aspect of the debate over the 'Rules' during this period, and one of the most relevant to an understanding of the reception of *King Lear*, were the arguments which took place over the morality of drama, and in particular, over the supposed duty of tragedy to instruct its audience in the workings of Divine justice.

Neo-Classical theory did not simply lay down strictures concerning the appropriate formal characteristics of 'good' literature (that, for example, genres – like comedy and tragedy – or language – as in verse and prose – ought not to be mixed). These formal requirements, like those concerning content, were invoked in the service of what Gildon calls the 'Ends' of literary art. For the Neo-Classicists, art should both entertain and instruct, but these two functions lie, according to them, in a hierarchical relation to each other, entertainment being subordinate to, and operating in the service of, instruction. Thus the mixing of generic modes is for Dryden wrong because comic action within something purporting to be a tragedy will 'divert the people and . . . make void [the dramatist's] greater purpose', that 'greater purpose' being the 'insinu[ation] into the people' of 'the noblest of moral virtues'.

Neo-Classical theory commandeered the Aristotelian notion of catharsis, and used it to serve the ends of a theory of aesthetic merit which was moralistic in the extreme. Great art for the Neo-Classicists had an intensely pedagogical role to play; 'Finding in History, the same *end* happen to the *riteous* and to the *unjust, vertue* often opprest, and *wickedness* on the throne,' Thomas Rymer claims, the classical tragedians

■ saw these particular *yesterday-truths* were imperfect . . . to illustrate the *universal* and *eternal truths* by them intended. Finding also that this *unequal* distribution of rewards and punishments did perplex the wisest and by The *Atheist* was made a scandal to the *Divine Providence*. They concluded, that a *Poet* must of necessity see *justice* exactly administred, if he intended to please. □

Thomas Rymer, *The Tragedies of the Last Age*, in Zimansky, pp. 22–3

For Rymer, the entertainment that great poetry must afford is contingent on its capacity to impart a more readily comprehensible vision of justice than the one which actual history has so far been able to offer. Rymer believes that rewards and punishments should be respectively the fates of virtue and villainy in tragedy; only then can tragedy communicate an unambiguous moral message. It was, in fact, Rymer himself who first coined the term 'poetical justice'. The debate over 'poetic justice' is not one which is confined to the period covered in this chapter (we come across very similar presuppositions today when we read critics who argue, or assume, that tragic closure effects some kind of 'punishment' on its protagonists). But never has the debate over poetic justice been more explicit than it was during this period, nor the concept of poetic justice quite so widely accepted.

As the responses of Charles Gildon and William Richardson to Tate's *Lear* indicate, many writers in the seventeenth and eighteenth century endorsed Rymer's position on the desirability of poetic justice. The following exchange, between Addison and Dennis, offers some sense of the terms in which the debate on poetic justice was conducted in the period:

Joseph Addison and John Dennis on Poetical Justice (1711–12)

■ The English Writers of Tragedy are possessed with a Notion that when they represent a virtuous . . . Person in Distress they ought not to leave him till they have delivered him out of his Troubles . . . . This Errour they have been led into by a ridiculous Doctrine in modern Criticism, that they are obliged to an equal Distribution of Rewards and Punishments and an impartial Execution of poetical Justice. Who were the first that established this Rule I know not; but I am sure it has no Foundation in Nature, in Reason, or in the Practice of the Ancients. We find that Good and Evil happen alike to all Men on this Side the Grave; and as the principal Design of Tragedy is to raise Commiseration and Terrour in the Minds of the Audience we shall defeat this Great End if we always make Vertue and Innocence happy and successful. Whatever Crosses and Disappointments a good Man suffers in the Body of the Tragedy, they will make but small Impression on our Minds when we know that in the last Act he is to arrive at the end of his . . . Desires. When we see him engaged in . . . his Afflictions we are apt to comfort ourselves because we are sure . . . that his Grief . . . will soon terminate in Gladness. For this Reason the ancient Writers of Tragedy treated Men in their Plays as they are dealt with in the World, by making Virtue sometimes happy and sometimes miserable . . . . Terrour and Commiseration leave a pleasing Anguish in the Mind and fix the Audience in such a serious Composure of Thought as is much more lasting and delightful than any little transient Starts of Joy and Satisfaction . . . *King Lear* is an Admirable Tragedy . . . as *Shakespeare* wrote it; but as it is reformed according to the chymerical Notion of poetical Justice in my humble Opinion it has lost half its Beauty . . . □

Joseph Addison, from the *Spectator*, No. 40, Vickers, 2:272–3

Addison's essay provoked the following reply from Dennis:

■ . . . what will this dogmatical Person say now, when we shew him that this . . . Doctrine of poetical Justice is not only founded in Reason and Nature, but is itself the Foundation of all the Rules, and ev'n of Tragedy itself? For what Tragedy can there be without a Fable? or what Fable without a Moral? or what Moral without poetical Justice? What Moral, where the Good and the Bad are confounded by Destiny, and perish alike promiscuously? Thus we see this Doctrine of poetical Justice is more founded in Reason and Nature than all the rest of the poetical Rules together. For what can be more natural, and more highly reasonable, than to employ that Rule in Tragedy without which that Poem cannot exist? . . .

Poetical Justice, says your Correspondent, *has no Foundation in Nature and Reason, because we find that good and evil happen alike to all Men on this side the Grave.* In answer to which [I] must . . . tell him that this is . . . a dangerous Assertion, that we neither know what Men really are, nor what they really suffer.

. . . [H]ow seldom do we know [men's] Passions . . . ? And as Passion is the Occasion of infinitely more Disorder in the World than Malice . . . can any thing be more just than that . . . Providence . . . should punish Men for indulging their Passions . . . ?

. . . [F]or ought we know, Good and Evil does not happen alike to all Men on this side the Grave. Because 'tis for the most part by their Passions that Men offend, and 'tis by their Passions, for the most part, that they are punish'd. . . . The Wicked take the utmost Care to . . . conceal [their passions] for which reason we neither know what our Neighbours are nor what they really suffer. Man is . . . too shallow . . . a Creature to know another Man throughly, to know the Creature of an infinite Creator; but dramatical Persons are Creatures of which a Poet is himself the Creator. And tho' a Mortal is not able to know the Almighty's Creatures he may be allow'd to know his own . . . and what they ought to suffer; nay, he must be allow'd not only to know this himself, but to make it manifest and unquestionable to all his Readers and Hearers. . . .

But suppose I should grant that there is not always an equal Distribution of Affliction and happiness here below? Man is a Creature who . . . will find Compensation in Futurity for any seeming Inequality in his Dealing here. But the Creatures of a poetical Creator are imaginary and transitory. They have no longer Duration than the Representation of their respective Fables, and consequently, if they offend they must be punish'd during that Representation. And therefore we are very far from pretending that poetical Justice is an equal Representation of the Justice of the Almighty. . . . □

From John Dennis, *An Essay upon the Genius and Writings of Shakespeare,* Vickers, 2:295–7

It may seem strange to us now, but Addison's was the voice of a small minority in this period, Dennis' the position endorsed by the majority. Not for the Neo-Classicists the measure of literature's greatness by the degree to which it encourages us to ask questions of the workings of the world. For those such as Dennis, the rules governing the nature of a properly ethical artistic work are at once stark and straightforward: 'The Good must never fail to prosper and the Bad must always be punish'd', as Dennis put it in an earlier essay (Vickers 2:284–5). The outcome of a play must be universally understood by its audience as being in accordance with a divine justice that transcends historical contingency. This understanding is possible since no doubt about a character's motivations is conceivable for the author of a tragedy and contingent upon no doubt about a character's motivations being left available to the audience: never should we have to 'seek for the cause' of a character's misfortunes. Nor should we be left assuming that characters will meet their just deserts in the great hereafter. Rewards and punishments must be absolute, unambiguous, and immediate. Dennis is unable, indeed, to imagine a tragedy which fails to observe these rules: his very definition of tragedy argues, circularly, that since Tragedy must communicate a moral, a moral is thus necessary in Tragedy.

The following two extracts show how deeply Neo-Classical theories inhabited responses to *King Lear*. The first essay concerns Tate's adaptation of the text, and indicates the hold which notions of poetic justice held on the public imagination, whilst the second, a criticism of Shakespeare's original text, attacks *King Lear* for the improbabilities and irregularities of its plot, and, in particular, the opacity of its principal characters' motivations.

From Thomas Cooke, *Considerations On the Stage* . . . (1730)

■ The Tragedy on which I . . . make my Remarks is *King Lear*, as altered from *Shakespeare* by *Tate*; because almost every Character in that Play is an Instance of Virtue being rewarded and Vice punished. . . .

WHILE *Lear* and the Companions of his Wretchedness are almost without Hopes, unerring Nature is pursuing her Course; the Vices of *Goneril, Regan*, and *Edmund* are working their own Ruin, and the Uprising of those whom their Cruelty had reduced to the lowest State of Misery. Here is a Lesson *that administers Comfort to the poor and the distressed*. From the Fortunes of *Lear* and his Followers Wretches whose Wretchedness was accomplished by the Crimes of other Persons may learn to hope that the same Propensity to Evil that urged their Enemys wrongfully to effect their Fall will impel them to such Actions as shall render them unable to preserve what they have unjustly acquired, and thereby be the Cause of restoring the injured to their Right. . . . While *Cordelia, Gloucester, Edgar* and *Kent* are in the most desperate Condition *Goneril, Regan, Edmund* and *Cornwall* are filling up the Measure of their Sins, which produce their own Punishment. . . .

NOW . . . let us sum up the moral Inferences which are to be made from [the play]. *Edmund, Cornwall, Goneril*, and *Regan* are disloyal to their Prince, undutyful to their Parents, and every Way false to their Trust. Their Crimes are attended with so many horrid Circumstances that their Punishment is scarcely adequate to their Guilt. *Lear* and *Gloucester* had offended, but more to Appearance thro an Error of the Judgement than the Will; they are punished. They are made sensible of their Errors, and are placed in a State of Tranquility and Ease agree-able to their Age and Condition, with *Kent* (whose Loyalty remained unshocked to the last), rejoicing at the Felicity of *Edgar* and *Cordelia*, whom they had wronged, and who forsaked them not in the Hour of Distress, and who cherished a virtuous Love each for the other.

I HAVE read many Sermons, but remember no one that contains so fine a Lesson of Morality as this Play. Here is Loyalty to a Prince, Duty to a Parent, Perseverance in a chast Love, and almost every exalted virtue of the Soul recommended in the lovelyest Colours; and the opposite vices are placed in the strongest Light in which Horror and Detestation can place them. . . . The Poet shews in this Tragedy that the vengeance of Heaven co-operates, as indeed it always does, with the natural Course of Things. And when virtue meets her due Reward we may say, with *Cordelia, there are Gods, and Virtue is their Care* . . . for the allwise Disposer of all Things has from the Beginning annexed Rewards to Virtue and Punishment to Vice; and in these we find Nature . . . consistent with herself . . . . What more profitable Lesson can the People be taught than this? Virtue is the inexhaustible Fountain of Joy, and Vice of Misery; and this Lesson the Stage more effectually teaches than a Sermon because the Spectators have before their Eyes the Actions and the Causes of them. They see the Effects, and how they operate, and are convinced that they are the natural Consequences of Such Causes; the Impression therefore that they must make in their Minds must cer-tainly be in Favour of what seems lovely in their Eyes, and fruitful of Happyness. And we cannot suppose that they will soon enter on any Action like what they were just before instructed to behold with Horror and Detestation, and which is attended with inevitable woe. □

Vickers, 2:465–8

From Charlotte Lennox, *Shakespear Illustrated* (1753–4)

■ This Fable, . . . drawn from the . . . History of *King Leir*[11] is so altered by *Shakespeare* . . . as to render it much more improbable than the Original. There we are sufficiently disgusted with the Folly of a Man who gives away one Half of his Kingdom to two of his Daughters because they flatter him with Professions of the most extravagant Love, and deprives his youngest Child of her Portion for no other Crime but confining her Expressions of Tenderness within the Bounds of plain and simple Truth. But *Shakespeare* has carried this Extravagance much farther. He shews us a King resigning his Kingdom, his Crown and Dignity to his two Daughters, reserving nothing to himself, not even a decent Maintenance, but submitting to a mean Dependance on the Bounty of his Children, whom, by promis-ing Rewards proportionable to the Degree of Flattery they lavish on him, he has stimulated to outvie each other in artful Flourishes on their Duty and Affection toward him . . .

Lear does not run mad till the third Act. Yet his Behaviour towards *Cordelia* in this first Scene has all the Appearance of a Judgment totally depraved: He asks *Cordelia* what she has to say to draw a Dowry more opulent than her Sisters. Thus he suggested to her a Motive for exceeding them in Expressions of Love. The noble Disinterestedness of her Answer afforded the strongest Conviction of her Sincerity, and that she possessed the highest Degree of filial Affection for him, who hazarded the Loss of all her Fortune to confine herself to simple Truth in her Professions of it. Yet for this *Lear* banishes her his Sight, consigns her over to Want, and loads her with the deepest Imprecations. . . . *Lear*, while in his Senses, acts like a mad Man, and from his first Appearance to his last seems to be wholly deprived of his Reason.

In the History *Lear* Disinherits *Cordelia*, but we read of no other kind of Severity exerted towards her. The King of *France*, as well in the History as the Play, charm'd with the Virtue and Beauty of the injured *Cordelia*, marries her without a Portion. *Shakespeare* does not introduce this Prince till after the absurd Trial *Lear* made of his Daughters' Affection is over. The Lover who is made to Marry the disinherited *Cordelia* on account of her Virtue is very injudiciously contrived to be Absent when she gave so glorious a Testimony of it, and is touch'd by a cold Justification of her Fame, and that from herself, when he might have been charm'd with a shining Instance of her Greatness of Soul and inviolable Regard to Truth.

So unartfully has the Poet managed this Incident that *Cordelia's* noble Disinterestedness is apparent to all but him who was to be the most influenced by it. In the Eyes of her Lover she is debased, not exalted; reduced to the abject Necessity of defending her own Character, and seeking rather to free herself from the Suspicion of Guilt than modestly enjoying the conscious Sense of superior Virtue.

Lear's Invective against her to the King of *France* is conceived in the most shocking Terms . . . Well might the King of *France* be startled at such Expressions as these from a Parent of his Child. Had he been present to have heard the Offence she gave him to occasion them, how must her exalted Merit have been endeared to him by the extream Injustice she suffered! . . . □

Vickers 4:142–3

Cooke's essay on Tate's adaptation speaks (in all of its convoluted prolixity) for itself. It follows the strictures of 'poetical justice' to the letter, exhibiting what can only be described as a strikingly naive conception of the capacity (and willingness) of an audience to be instructed by such moral principles as those Cooke sees in Tate's *Lear*. Lennox's piece is, like

Cooke's, firmly rooted in Neo-Classical principles: it is the motivation behind the character's actions that she finds most ridiculous in Shakespeare's play, and like Cooke, she objects to Shakespeare's transgression of poetic justice, as well as his deviations from proper decorum. But despite Lennox's blindness to many of the subtleties in the play, some of her observations bear comparison with far more recent treatments of the text. On the one hand, she is apparently unaware that her own objections to Lear's behaviour in Act I, scene i of the play are voiced in the same scene by Kent, and she is deaf to the play's sustained examination of the very questions about madness and sanity which she berates it for overlooking. But on the other hand, Lennox could be argued to anticipate some twentieth-century feminist treatments of the text, in her attack on King Lear for, in effect, inviting his daughters' hypocrisy, and for the 'shocking' violence of his invective against Cordelia, for instance, as well as in her discomfort with the way in which Shakespeare 'debases' Cordelia, reducing her to the 'abject Necessity of defending her own Character'.

There were, of course, some other voices. John Berkenhout, for example, scoffed at the demand that drama should observe the unities: 'If these *unities* had existed in Nature, Shakespeare was so well acquainted with her that I trust he would have found them out': he says, 'but Nature is so far from prescribing the *unities* to a dramatic writer that if he means to accomplish the principal design of the theatre, amusement, they must be carefully avoided.' (Vickers, 6:158) But few of these defences of Shakespeare were able to find positive terms of approbation to replace the onslaught of Neo-Classical denigration whose application to Shakespeare's plays they deplored. Either they tended to be merely bardolatrous, or they made reference to a kind of primitive natural genius, oddly coupled with historical ignorance, as did Rowe who argued that:

■ [A]s *Shakespeare* liv'd under a kind of mere Light of Nature, and had never been made acquainted with the Regularity of those . . . [Rules], so it would be hard to judge him by a Law he knew nothing of. We are to consider him as a Man that liv'd in a State of almost universal License and Ignorance. There was no establish'd Judge, but every one took the liberty to Write according to the Dictates of his own Fancy. □
(1709), Vickers 2:198

So too Pope on Shakespeare's characters:

■ His *Characters* are so much Nature her self that 'tis . . . injury to call them by so distant a name as Copies of her. . . . [E]very single character in *Shakespeare* is as much an Individual as those in Life itself; it is . . . impossible to find any two alike; . . .

To judge therefore of *Shakespeare* by *Aristotle's* rules is like trying a man by the Laws of one Country who acted under those of another. He writ to the *People*; and writ at first without patronage from the better sort, and therefore without aims of pleasing them; without assistance or advice from the Learned, as without the advantage of education or acquaintance among them; without that knowledge of the best models, the Ancients to inspire him with an emulation of them; in a word, without any views of Reputation, and of what Poets are pleas'd to call Immortality:[12] . . . □

Alexander Pope, from *The Works of Shakespeare, Collated and Corrected*, (1725) Vickers, 2:404

Even Dr Johnson's endnote on *Lear* resorts to the notion of historical barbarity to defend the text against accusations of improbability (in Lear's conduct and that of his daughters) and of transgressions of proper decorum (in the onstage representation of the putting out of Gloucester's eyes). And despite the account of the seductive power of the play which he gives in his opening paragraph, in his closing lines[13] he plumps, albeit guardedly, for Tate:

From Samuel Johnson's Endnote on *King Lear*

■ The tragedy of Lear is deservedly celebrated among the dramas of Shakespeare. There is perhaps no play which keeps the attention so strongly fixed; which so much agitates our passions and interests our curiosity. The artful involutions of distinct interests, the striking opposition of contrary characters, the sudden changes of fortune, and the quick succession of events, fill the mind with a perpetual tumult of indignation, pity, and hope. There is no scene which does not contribute to the aggravation of the distress or conduct of the action, and scarce a line which does not conduce to the progress of the scene. So powerful is the current of the poet's imagination, that the mind, which once ventures within it, is hurried irresistibly along.

On the seeming improbability of Lear's conduct it may be observed, that he is represented according to histories at that time vulgarly received as true. And perhaps if we turn our thoughts upon the barbarity and ignorance of the age to which this story is referred, it will not appear so unlikely as while we estimate Lear's manners by our own. Such preference of one daughter to another, or resignation of dominion on such conditions, would yet be credible, if told of a petty prince of Guinea or Madagascar. Shakespeare, indeed, by the mention of his earls and dukes, has given us the idea of times more civilised, and of life regulated by softer manners; and the truth is, that though he so nicely discriminates, and so minutely describes the characters of men, he commonly neglects and confounds the characters of ages, by mingling customs ancient and modern, English and foreign.

My learned friend Mr Warton, who has in the *Adventurer* very minutely criticised this play, remarks, that the instances of cruelty are too savage and shocking, and that the intervention of Edmund destroys the simplicity of the story. These objections may, I think, be answered, by repeating, that the cruelty of the daughters is an historical fact, to which the poet has added little, having only drawn it into a series by dialogue and action. But I am not able to apologise with equal plausibility for the extrusion of Gloucester's eyes, which seems an act too horrid to be endured in dramatick exhibition, and such as must always compel the mind to relieve its distress by incredulity. Yet let it be remembered that our authour well knew what would please the audience for which he wrote.

The injury done by Edmund to the simplicity of the action is abun-, dantly recompensed by the addition of variety, by the art with which he is made to co-operate with the chief design, and the opportunity which he gives the poet of combining perfidy with perfidy, and connecting the wicked son with the wicked daughters, to impress this important moral, that villainy is never at a stop, that crimes lead to crimes, and at last terminate in ruin.

But though this moral be incidentally enforced, Shakespeare has suffered the virtue of Cordelia to perish in a just cause, contrary to the natural ideas of justice, to the hope of the reader, and, what is yet more strange, to the faith of chronicles. Yet this conduct is justified by the Spectator, who blames Tate for giving Cordelia success and happiness in his alteration, and declares, that in his opinion, 'the tragedy has lost half its beauty' [see Addison above]. . . . A play in which the wicked prosper, and the virtuous miscarry, may doubtless be good, because it is a just representation of the common events of human life: but since all reasonable beings naturally love justice, I cannot easily be persuaded, that the observation of justice makes a play worse; or, that if other excellencies are equal, the audience will not always rise better pleased from the final triumph of persecuted virtue.

In the present case the publick has decided. Cordelia, from the time of Tate, has always retired with victory and felicity. And, if my sensations could add any thing to the general suffrage, I might relate, that I know not whether I ever endured to read again the last scenes of the play till I undertook to revise them as an editor . . .[14] □

Part Three: Other Critical Preoccupations

Perhaps one measure of the degree to which critical preoccupations have changed over the last two hundred years can be gauged by a brief (and far from exclusive) list of what early critics of the play did not address. As we have already mentioned, Tate cut from his adaptation the role of the Fool, which at once denoted and exacerbated a tendency to consider the role inconsequential and unimportant. There were a few isolated voices of dissent, but these tended still to read the importance of the Fool through an interest either in what the play had to say about madness, as in this defence of Shakespeare's mixing of the genres:

■ [Shakespeare's] Comedy and Tragedy are by no means forced into Union, but are engrafted on each other . . . [T]he Mirth of Lear's Fool . . . so far from being unseasonable, is placed in significant Opposition to the frensy of his Master. . . . □

George Steevens, from 'Observations on the plays altered from Shakespeare' (1779), Vickers, 6:206

or, again, on how the Fool expresses qualities of Lear's character, and facilitates the trajectory of the main character's tragic error, as in Capell's note here:

■ The king's tenderness for his fool . . . and that fool's faithfulness and love of his master, are great height'nings both of the daughters' unnaturalness and (consequently) of this play's effect as a tragedy; the first shewing the king's affectionate nature, the other the just returns to such nature and the almost constant effects of it. To this love of his master should be attributed the satire that runs through all the fool's songs, his riming moralities, and almost his every speech that has fallen from him 'till now; being all seemingly calculated to awaken that master (under shew of diverting him) to a sense of his error, and to spur him on to some remedy. □

Edward Capell, from *Notes and Various Readings to Shakespeare* (1780), Vickers, 6:225

With the exception of Lennox's remarks on Lear's diatribes against his daughters and Cordelia's abjection, there is very little on what we would now term the sexual politics of the play. Despite the fact that Tate centralises the role of Edmund in his adaptation of *King Lear*, using Edmund's 'Bastard' monologue as his opening speech, there is little examination of the discursive status that bastardy might hold in the drama: no-one, for instance (and as far as I know) draws any connections between the way in which both plot and subplot revolve around the issue of inheritance. Few, indeed, drew any connections between plot and subplot at all, and those that did tended, again, to focus on the issue of madness rather than on the sexual and other political concerns which would be more likely to characterise criticism of the play today. It was, then, madness and Lear's character which constituted the main focus of interest for critics in these (relatively) early years, as the following extract will indicate.[15]

From William Richardson, 'On the Dramatic Character of *King Lear*' (1783)

■ Those who are guided in their conduct by impetuous impulse, arising from sensibility and undirected by reflection, are liable to *extravagant* or *outrageous* excess. Transported by their own emotions they misapprehend the condition of others; they are prone to exaggeration; and even the good actions they perform excite amazement rather than approbation. Lear, . . . under the power of excessive affection, believed that his children were in every respect deserving. During this ardent . . . mood he ascribed to them such . . . sentiments as justified his extravagant fondness. . . . What condescension . . . could be a suitable reward for their filial piety? He divides his kingdom among them . . .

But he is not only extravagant in his love; he is no less outrageous in his displeasure.

The conduct proceeding from unguided feeling will be *capricious*. In minds where principles of regular and permanent influence have no authority every feeling has a right to command; and every impulse, how sudden soever, is regarded during the season of its power with entire approbation.

. . . Lear feels extreme pain . . . [at his daughters' actions]; he vents his resentment; but he has no power. Will he then become morose and retired? His . . . temper will not give him leave. . . . [A]ccustomed to authority, consequently of an unyielding nature, he would wreak his wrath, if he were able, in deeds of excessive violence. . . . He who could pronounce such imprecations against Goneril as, notwithstanding her guilt, appear shocking . . . would in the moment of his resentment have put her to death. If, without any ground of offence he could abandon Cordelia and cast off his favourite child, what would he not have done to the unnatural and pitiless Regan?

Here, then, we have a curious spectacle: a man accustomed to bear rule, suffering sore disappointment and grievous wrongs; high minded, impetuous, susceptible of extreme resentment, and incapable of yielding to splenetic silence or malignant retirement. What change can befal his spirit? For his condition is so altered that his spirit also must suffer change. What! but to have his understanding torn up by the hurricane of passion, to scorn consolation, to lose his reason! Shakespeare could not avoid making Lear distracted. Other poets exhibit madness because they chuse it, or for the sake of variety, or to deepen the distress: but Shakespeare has exhibited the madness of Lear as the natural effect of such suffering on such a character. It was an event in the progress of Lear's mind, driven by such feelings, desires, and passions as the poet ascribes to him, as could not be avoided.

. . . Lear, thus extravagant, . . . capricious, . . . irresolute, and impetuously vindictive, is almost an object of disapprobation. But our poet . . . blends the disagreeable qualities with such circumstances as correct this effect, and form one delightful assemblage. Lear, in his good intentions, was without deceit; his violence is not the effect of premeditated malignity; his weaknesses are not crimes but often the effects of misruled affections. This is not all: he is an old man; an old king; an aged father; and the instruments of his suffering are undutiful children. He is justly entitled to our compassion; . . . Add to all this that he becomes more and more interesting towards the close of the drama; not merely because he is more and more unhappy, but because he becomes really more deserving of our esteem. His misfortunes correct his misconduct; they rouse *reflection*, and lead him to that *reformation which we approve*. We see the commencement of this reformation after he has been dismissed by Goneril and meets with symptoms of disaffection in Regan. He who abandoned Cordelia . . . and banished Kent, . . . seeing his servant grossly maltreated, and his own arrival unwelcomed, has already sustained some chastisement: he does not express that ungoverned violence which his preceding conduct might lead us to expect. He restrains his emotion in its first ebullition, and reasons concerning the probable causes of what seemed so inauspicious. . . .

As his misfortunes increase we find him still more inclined to reflect on his situation. . . . Soon after we find him actually pronouncing censure upon himself. . . . At last he is in a state of perfect contrition, and expresses less resentment against Goneril and Regan than self-condemnation for his treatment of Cordelia, and a perfect, but not extravagant sense of her affection. □

Vickers, 6:358–61

Richardson here argues not that Lear's rage and his affection stand in an oppositional relation to each other, but that they are both manifestations of a deeper quality, that of extravagant or outrageous excess.[16] His essay is one of the few in the period to read the character of Lear as in some way intrinsically related to his social position: for Richardson, rashness is not simply a 'personal' characteristic of 'Lear the man', but a political characteristic of Lear the king. Richardson notes, though he does not elaborate, the fact that Lear is 'an old man; an old king; an aged father;' and he mentions several times that Lear has hitherto been used to being obeyed in authority. Even Richardson does not go so far as to argue that tragic causality in this play might lie in the fact that Lear's kingdom is already riven by potential divisions; that, in other words, Lear's errors might catalyse rather than cause the tragedy. This kind of approach, which would view Lear's character as one amongst many elements in a tragic world in which causality is overdetermined, was foreign to critics of the seventeenth and eighteenth centuries (we will meet it, finally, in our discussion of contemporary criticism). Like everyone else at this time, Richardson sees Lear's personality as the root cause, indeed, the only cause, of the tragic events in the play. Nevertheless, Richardson's implicit criticism of monarchical authority evinces an insight unusual for the period; a more common response to Lear is one which underplays his age and celebrates his authority.

Richardson's is also an interesting essay for the point that he makes about Lear's madness: that it is the 'natural effect of such suffering on such a character, . . . an event in the progress of Lear's mind'. His remark is notable in part for its insistence that madness is organic in the play, and that Shakespeare had no choice in its inclusion. This is quite different to the tenor of most of the debate over madness in the play during these years, which centred around its cause, and was phrased, more or less explicitly, in terms of Shakespeare's intention.

Two distinct views, one 'personal', the other 'political', emerge about the cause of Lear's madness during this period. The first held (in the words of Joseph Warton, sometime headmaster of Winchester) that Shakespeare 'judiciously represents the loss of royalty as the particular idea which has brought on the distraction of LEAR, and which perpetually recurs to his imagination and mixes itself with all his ramblings' (from the *Adventurer* no. 132, (5 January 1754), Vickers 4:78). The second maintained that Lear's madness was occasioned by the ingratitude of Lear's daughters, deriving, that is, from his position as a father. Thus Arthur Murphy, attacking Warton, argues that:

■ . . . Had [Lear] lost his reason on account of his abdicated throne the emotions of pity would not be so intense as they now are, when we see him driven to that extreme by the cruelty of his own children. A monarch voluntarily abdicating and afterwards in a fit of lunacy resuming his crown would, I fear, border upon the ridiculous. . . .

. . . [Lear] is full of the loss of his dignity only as it was the occasion of the ill treatment he met with, not from a thirst of rule. . . . □

Arthur Murphy, from the *Gray's Inn Journal* (1753–4),
Vickers, 4:95–108

Opinions were divided between these two explanations, partly because of a popular conception that, in the words of Joseph Warton, 'Madness [is] occasioned by a close and continued attention of the mind to a single object'. However much he disagrees with Warton on the cause of that madness, Murphy is in agreement with him on this point, insisting also that 'Lear's mind settles into a fixed attention to that single object'. This is a conception quite different, it will be noted, from our contemporary popular understanding of extreme psychological disturbance, which tends to ascribe it to a complex of psychological stresses; this attachment to the singular mirrors the way in which, as we have seen, seventeenth- and eighteenth-century commentators were impelled to seek for a single cause for the tragedy itself, and to find it in the character of Lear himself.

Part Four: Productions of *King Lear*

No discussion of the status of *King Lear* in this period would be complete without mentioning the actor with whom the figure of Lear was synonymous during the latter half of the eighteenth century. Other actors, such as Betterton, Robert Wilkes, and Spranger Barry, played the role during the period covered by this chapter, but no-one garnered to himself such popular acclaim for his interpretation of the role as did David Garrick. Garrick, of course, played Tate's *Lear* and not the original, although he did delete some of Tate's interpolations, restoring instead some of the original language. He considered, but rejected, as 'too bold an attempt'[17] the restoration of the Fool; other aspects of the text, such as the liaison between Edgar and Cordelia, and the happy ending, were kept by him entirely. Many accounts of Garrick's interpretation of the King Lear have been left to us; here follows one of the most interesting:

From Arthur Murphy, *The Life of David Garrick, Esq.* (1801)

■ It was in Lear's madness that Garrick's genius was remarkably distinguished. He had no sudden starts, no violent gesticulation; his movements were slow and feeble; misery was depicted in his countenance; he moved his head in the most deliberate manner; his eyes were fixed; or, if they turned to any one near him he made a pause, and fixed his look on the person after much delay; his features at the same time telling what he was going to say before he uttered a word. During the whole time he presented a sight of woe and misery, and a total alienation of mind from every idea but that of his unkind daughters. He was used to tell how he acquired the hints that guided him when he began to study this great and difficult part. He was acquainted with a worthy man, who lived in Leman-street, Goodman's Fields; this friend had an only daughter, about two years old. He stood at his dining-room window, fondling the child and dangling it in his arms,

when it was his misfortune to drop the infant into a flagged area, and killed it on the spot. He remained at his window screaming in agonies of grief. The neighbours flocked to the house, took up the child, and delivered it dead to the unhappy father, who wept bitterly, and filled the street with lamentations. He lost his senses, and from that moment never recovered his understanding. As he had a sufficient fortune his friends chose to let him remain in his house, under two keepers appointed by Dr. Monro. Garrick frequently went to see his distracted friend, who passed the remainder of his life in going to the window and there playing in fancy with his child. After some dalliance he dropped it, and, bursting into a flood of tears filled the house with shrieks of grief and bitter anguish. He then sat down, in a pensive mood, his eyes fixed on one object, at times looking slowly round him as if to implore compassion. Garrick was often present at this scene of misery, and was ever after used to say that it gave him the first idea of King Lear's madness. This writer has often seen him rise in company to give a representation of this unfortunate father. He leaned on the back of a chair, seeming with parental fondness to play with a child, and, after expressing the most heartfelt delight, he suddenly dropped the infant, and instantly broke out in a most violent agony of grief, so tender, so affecting and pathetic that every eye in company was moistened with a gush of tears. 'There it was,' said Garrick, '*that I learned to imitate madness*; I copied nature, and to that owed my success in *King Lear*'. □
(Vickers, 6:633–4)

There is a dubious morality behind the opportunistic use Garrick apparently made of his friend's personal tragedy, but the anecdote tells us a great deal about Garrick's understanding of the play. His interpretation of the role centres exclusively on a personal narrative; this narrative, moreover, is richly suggestive of the preconceptions about Lear which, as we have already seen, were frequently brought to the text. The literal fall represented in this narrative is a consequence of the father's love of his daughter, and the actions that lead to the tragic event are his alone, just as the 'tender expressions of [Lear's] great love to his children' (in Richard Roderick's phrase), as well as his less affectionate actions, were held by some entirely to motivate the tragedy in the text.[18] And, most saliently of all, it is in the narrative the loss of the man's daughter which occasions his descent into madness. Thus not merely in the manner of the man's madness, but also in its precipitating incident, this anecdote conforms to the dominant view of the cause of Lear's madness held by many late eighteenth-century critics.

Garrick's representation of Lear is an appropriate topic with which to end this chapter, for the exchange that follows raises many of the issues we have covered in the course of it, and also points us forward to the next stage in the reception of *King Lear* in England, which saw the revival of Shakespeare's text in English theatres. Here are two quite different responses to Garrick's production of Tate's *Lear*.

From Samuel Foote, *A Treatise on the Passions* (1747)

■ The Portrait that *Shakespeare* has given us of Lear is that of a good-hearted Man, easily provoked, impatient of Contradiction, and hasty in Resolution. The Poet himself, who seldom fails to direct the Actor, has thought an Apology necessary at the opening of the Play for what might appear immoral in the Conduct . . . of his Hero, by laying the Blame on a natural Habit, *"tis said that I am Choleric'*; and then, as a Testimony of the . . . innate Goodness of his Disposition, upon hearing the tragical End of his unnatural Daughters at the Close of the Play [having Lear say, 'Ungrateful as they were,/ Tho' the Wrongs they have heaped on me are numberless;/ I feel a Pang of Nature for them yet'] . . . This I take to be a Sketch of Lear's moral Character, a Circumstance that never ought to escape the View of the Actor.

And here sorry I am to set out with an Observation that Mr. G[arrick] seems quite regardless of . . . *Lear's* Attributes . . . the Curse at the End of the first Act . . . should be utter'd with a Rage almost equal to Phrenzy, . . . [with] no Premeditation, no Solemnity . . . Nor can I easily pardon the Tears shed at the Conclusion. The whole Passage is a Climax of Rage, that strange Mixture of Anger and Grief is to me highly unnatural; and besides, this unmanly Sniveling lowers the Consequence of Lear. . . .

. . . I would [Direct] the Actor to . . . [Enquire] into the Cause of the Madness he is to represent, that his Deportment may be conducted suitably therewith. For example, in *Lear* we find *Lear's* Mind at first entirely possess'd with the Thoughts of his Daughters Ingratitude, which was the immediate Cause of his Distress. To this he subjoins some Reflections on the State . . . of his Afflictions, and thus far his Reason holds. But when his Mind . . . looks back to the remote Cause, which was a voluntary Resignation of the Regal Power, then the Idea of his former Grandeur rises to his View; which, when he compares with his present Misery and observes the Impossibility of remounting the Throne he had quitted, then his Brains turn and his Reason forsakes him.

The Desire of Royalty, then, is the Point that distracts *Lear's* Judgment; . . . How, then, is this mad Monarch to be employed[?] in picking Straws, and boyish Trifling, or in Actions more . . . suitable to his imaginary Dignity, such as frequent Musings with the Finger on the Brow – as if the Welfare of Kingdoms depended on his Care . . . Every Motion, every Look should express an Extravagance of State and Majesty. And when mad *Tom* is consulted . . . *Lear* should not . . . play with his Straws, or betray the least mark of knowing the real Man. . . . No Sign of Equality, no Familiarity, no sitting down Cheek by Jowl; this might be a proper Representation of a mad Taylor, but by no means corresponds with my Idea of *King Lear* . . . □

Vickers, 3:212–14

Foote's foolishness in attributing to 'the poet himself' the words of Tate's adaptation (and of misquoting even that) made him an easy target for the anonymous author of *An Examen of the New Comedy*, who addressed an open letter to Garrick in the following terms:

From Anon, *An Examen of the New Comedy* (1747)

■ . . . [T]he Author of a late *Treatise upon the Passions* . . . has grossly mistook the Character of *Lear*, and either has not given himself the trouble to read the Original or . . . has only quoted a few inconsiderable Passages to serve his own Ends and mislead the Ignorant. He opens his Criticism of *Lear* with *a short Account of the Passions,* which . . . is unanswerable; . . . but . . . unfortunately . . . he imprudently discovers his weak Side, and lies open to the Attacks of every thinking Man in the Kingdom. In order to give us a Sketch of *Lear's* moral Character, . . . he quotes a Passage that is not in SHAKESPEARE. [Here the author reproduces Foote's (mis)quotation of Tate's 'I feel a Pang of Nature for 'em yet'.] Is it not surprizing that this great . . . Man of Taste should propose Lines for your Consideration which are in the vile Alterations by Tate? . . . [T]he Censor has not only injur'd *Shakespeare* by taking this Sketch from the unhallow'd Pencil of Tate but he has even injur'd poor Tate himself, for his Lines are thus:

Ungrateful as they were, my Heart feels yet

A Pang of Nature for their wretched Fall!

Where are our Critick's Ears, that he could not find out that his second Line (for it belongs to No-body else) is three Syllables too long, and is neither Prose or Poetry? He condemns you greatly for your Manner of uttering the Curse against *Goneril*; but had he look'd into *Shakespeare* he would not have been so severe upon *your Tears shed at the Conclusion,* or have said that the *strange Mixture of Grief and Passion was highly unnatural;* for this Speech immediately following the Curse is your Direction and Authority . . . [Here the author quotes Lear's reference to his 'hot Tears which break from [him] perforce', from Shakespeare's *Lear*, not Tate's.]

Has not the Author here most strongly pointed out the Mixture of Grief and passion? But supposing he had not, who can be so unfeeling . . . not to know that these Transitions from Rage to Grief were necessary to support the Character? *Lear* is old and choleric, and of

Consequence, when his Rage is spent and his Powers fail him he must naturally . . . sink into Sorrow . . . [Here the author goes on to quote, again from the original text, various passages in which Lear makes reference to his welling tears.]

But now, . . . *for as farfetch'd a Fancy as ever you heard*; the Critick undertakes to demonstrate *that the Desire of Royalty is the Point distracts* Lear's *Judgment; and that* Shakespeare *has not put one Expression into his Mouth throughout the Madness, but what bears a visible Relation to this first Cause!* Now it unfortunately happens that there is not a single Word mention'd (except once) in the first and second Scene of his Madness that has the least Relation to Royalty. It is evidently the Usage of his Daughters that continually rankles in his Mind . . .

. . . [I]t does not follow that you or any Actor should drop the Majesty of the Character to *pick Straws, play with 'em, or use boyish Actions*: these are the Critick's Allegations. [The author goes on to defend Garrick's representation of Lear's madness by references to Cordelia's description of her father as crowned with weeds.] . . .

. . . Thus, Mr G-rr-ck, I have endeavour'd to vindicate you where I thought you justifiable, and shall now as freely censure where I think you erroneous. In the first Place, why will you do so great an Injury to *Shakespeare* as to perform *Tate's* execrable Alteration of him? Read and consider the two Plays seriously, and then make the Publick and the Memory of the Author some amends by giving us *Lear* in the *Original, Fool* and all. . . .

When Kent discovers to you that he was *Caius* you say (in the Nonsense of the Alteration)

'Caius! *Wer't thou my trusty* Caius?

Enough – Enough.'

and then you faint away . . . . This *Second* Fit has no Effect, and you might as well cut a Caper. You will say the alter'd Play has mark'd it so; to which I answer that it can be no Mitigation of your Fault to plead that *Mr Nahum Tate* has seduc'd you. Tho' you are not the Principal you are accessary to the Murder, and will be brought in Guilty. How can you keep your Countenance when you come to the *Spheres stopping their Course, the Sun making halt,* and *the Winds bearing on their rosy Wings* that Cordelia *is a Queen*? . . . □

Vickers, 3:261–9

This anonymous essay was not the first complaint about Tate's *Lear*: there had been some attacks on his adaptation right from the start and there were an increasing number by the late eighteenth century. In 1748, for example, in a note to a postscript to *Clarissa*, Samuel Richardson had expressed amazement that 'the altered *King Lear* of Mr Tate is constantly acted on the English stage, in preference to the original, though written by Shakespeare himself!' 'Whether this strange prefer-ence be owing to the false delicacy or affected tenderness of the players,' Richardson went on,

■ or to that of the audience, has not for many years been tried. And perhaps the former have not then courage to try the public taste upon it. And yet if it were *ever* to be tried, *now* seems to be the time, when an *actor* and a manager, [Garrick] in the *same person*, is in being, who deservedly engages the public favour in all that he undertakes, and who owes so much, and is sensibly grateful that he does, to that great master of the human passions.[19] □

But it was not until the beginning of the nineteenth century that a real reassessment of Shakespeare's *King Lear* took place, and it is to the Romantics, who orchestrated that reassessment, that we will now turn.

CHAPTER TWO

Romanticism

Introduction

■ . . . THE NINETEENTH century has for its august mother the French Revolution . . . It honours men of genius, and if need be salutes them when despised, proclaims them when ignored, avenges them when persecuted, re-enthrones them when dethroned: it venerates them, but it does not proceed from them. The nineteenth century has for family itself, and itself alone. It is the characteristic of its revolutionary nature to dispense with ancestors. □

Victor Hugo, *William Shakespeare* (1864)[1]

■ Genuine successors . . . of the ancients . . . have ever been as rare as their mechanical spiritless copyists are common. Seduced by the form, the great body of critics have been but too indulgent to these servile imitators. These were held up as correct modern classics, while the great truly living and popular poets, whose reputation was a part of their nation's glory, and to whose sublimity it was impossible to be altogether blind, were at best but tolerated as rude and wild natural geniuses. □

Augustus William Schlegel, *Course of Lectures on Dramatic Art and Literature* (1808)[2]

■ A great writer rarely obtains, in the generation succeeding his own, the homage which posterity will lavish upon him. Sometimes even, long spaces of time are necessary for the revolution commenced by a superior man to accomplish its course, and to bring the world to perceive its merits. □

M. Guizot, *Shakespeare and His Times* (1952)[3]

■ Who can read . . . our sweet Shakespeare, and dream of any congeniality between him and one that . . . appears to have been as mere a player as ever existed . . . : that any resemblance should be dreamed of between him and Shakespeare . . .

I am almost disposed to deny to Garrick the merit of being an admirer of Shakespeare. A true lover of his excellences he certainly was not – for would any true lover of them have admitted into his matchless scenes such ribald trash as Tate . . . [has] foisted into the acting [play] of Shakespeare? I believe it impossible that he could have had a proper reverence for Shakespeare . . . □

Charles Lamb, 'On the Tragedies of Shakespeare, considered with reference to their fitness for stage representation' (1811)[4]

As our opening quotations indicate, many writers of the early and mid-nineteenth century saw themselves, quite self-consciously, as writing in a time of revolution. 'The nineteenth century has for its august mother the French Revolution,' proclaims Victor Hugo; it is 'a birth of civilisation', (Hugo, p. 289) he goes on shortly afterwards to say. For Hugo, the historical French Revolution is only one manifestation of a deeper, more profound, and completely all encompassing transmutation of all that is important in human thought: 'The triple movement – literary, philosophical, and social – of the nineteenth century,' he maintains, 'is one single movement, is nothing but the current of the revolution in ideas. This current, after having swept away so many facts, flows on, broad and deep, through the minds of men' (Hugo, p. 291). Such a revolution, for the writers of the early nineteenth century, entailed a reaction against all that had gone before. Writer after writer returns, either explicitly or implicitly, to a sense of defying the past, and of starting out anew; writer after writer, moreover, expresses this project in terms of a rebellion against their immediate literary and cultural predecessors, as, in their different ways, do the authors of all of the four extracts quoted above. Literature, in short, became the ground upon which and through which a battle of ideas was to be fought. As Guizot puts it:

■ Literature does not escape from the revolutions of the human mind; it is compelled to follow it . . . – to consider the questions which it discusses under the new aspects . . . in which they are placed by the new state of thought and of society. □

(Guizot, p. 2)

And if literature was the battleground, Shakespeare was the great prize. For Romantic writers, the most immediate literary 'ancestors' with whom to 'dispense' were the Neo-Classicists, 'seduced by form', who were 'too indulgent to servile imitators' (such as – to take Schlegel more literally than he probably intended to be taken – Tate), and whose strictures on Shakespeare's lapses of judgement, taste, and form we have covered in Chapter One. Hugo, for example, begins the second part of *William Shakespeare* with a first (and somewhat partisan) chapter composed in its entirety of derogatory remarks on Shakespeare from the preceding two hundred years:

■ 'Shakespeare', says Forbes [Hugo begins], 'had neither the tragic talent nor the comic talent. His tragedy is artificial and his comedy is instinctive.' Dr Johnson confirms the verdict. 'His tragedy is the product of industry, and his comedy the product of instinct.' □

(Hugo, p. 147)

This is not entirely fair to Dr Johnson, but Hugo's list does serve to illustrate the degree to which Romantic writers saw themselves in conflict with the writers of their immediate past. For this listing of Shakespeare's detractors was a recurrent trope in writings about Shakespeare in the nineteenth century. Guizot also attacked those most prominent in furthering the view that Shakespeare was a poor poet and a poor dramatist: 'Dryden,' he says, 'did not understand Shakespeare, grammatically speaking; . . . [and] has proved, by re-casting [Shakespeare's] pieces, that poetically he comprehended him as little' (Guizot, p. 139). Schlegel, similarly, attacks Pope's edition of Shakespeare: 'all the scenes and passages which did not square with the littleness of [Pope's] own taste,' he complains, 'he wished to place to the account of interpolating players; and he was in the right road, had his opinion been taken, of giving us a miserable dole of a mangled Shakespeare' (Schlegel, p. 347). Schlegel wants to 'separate himself entirely' from past commentators upon Shakespeare; 'I have hardly ever found either truth or profundity in their remarks,' he goes on, 'and these critics seem to me to be but stammering interpreters of the general . . . admiration of [Shakespeare's] countrymen' (Schlegel, p. 346). 'To me,' he concludes, Shakespeare 'appears a profound artist, and not a blind and wildly luxuriant genius' (Schlegel, p. 358).

Rejecting the terms even of Shakespeare's previous admirers (most notably, here, the appeal to a 'natural', or primitive, force in some way at odds with the Neo-Classicist conception of proper culture and civilisation), the Romantics sought to contest their immediate literary forebears by rehabilitating Shakespeare as the greatest of all previous literary artists. And this revolution in the valuation of Shakespeare was concomitant with a revolution in the view of the role of the critic. Not all were quite as idealistic, or so infused with revolutionary fervour, as was Hugo when he stated that:

■ The writers . . . of the nineteenth century have the . . . good fortune of proceeding from a genesis, of arriving after an end of the world, of accompanying a reappearance of light, of being the organs of a new beginning. This imposes on them . . . the duties of intentional reformers and direct civilizers. They continue nothing; they form everything anew. . . . The function of thinkers in our days is complex; it no longer suffices to think – one must love; it no longer suffices to think and to love – one must act. To think, to love, and to act, no longer suffice – one must suffer. □

(Hugo, p. 294)

If Hugo was exceptional in the degree to which he embraces revolution in a directly political as well as an aesthetic sense (his style, piling clause upon clause, mirrors his sense of the momentous character of his moment in history) he was not exceptional in his emphatic conviction that the role of the 'thinker' in this new world is at once central and in need of definition. For Hugo, it is no longer enough merely to think: the thinker must know why he thinks, and to what purpose his thought is ultimately directed. Other writers shared Hugo's perception of the centrality of the thinker's role, as well as his perception that 'thinking', or literary criticism, should rest upon the firm foundation of a coherent, and well-examined, body of ideas. Thus Schlegel, for instance, emphasises the need for a 'general theory' which:

■ seeks to analyze that essential faculty of human nature – the sense of the beautiful, which at once calls the fine arts into existence, and accounts for the satisfaction which arises from the contemplation of them; and also points out the relation which subsists between this and all other sentient and cognizant faculties of man. □

(Schlegel, p. 17)

But like Hugo, Schlegel considers the construction of a coherent aesthetic theory to be a necessary, but not a sufficient, condition for the production of great criticism: 'to the man of thought and speculation,' he argues, the 'general theory' 'is of the highest importance, but by itself alone it is quite inadequate to guide and direct the essays and practices of art' (Schlegel, p. 17). The true critic requires not only an aesthetic theory, but also a particular turn of mind: 'no man can be a true critic', Schlegel maintains,

■ without universality of mind, without that flexibility which enables him, by renouncing all personal predilections . . . to adapt himself to the peculiarities of other ages . . . – to feel them, as it were, from their proper central point, and, what ennobles human nature, to . . . appreciate whatever is beautiful . . . under the external accessories which were necessary to its embodying, even though occasionally they may seem to disguise and distort it. There is no monopoly of poetry for particular ages and nations; and consequently that despotism in taste, which would seek to invest with universal authority the rules which at first, perhaps, were but arbitrarily advanced, is but a vain and empty pretension. □

(Schlegel, p. 17)

Romantic aesthetic theory, then, set out to replace the aesthetics it had inherited, an aesthetics 'despotic in taste', 'monopolistic' in its sense of the origin and nature of great poetry, and hence blindly unappreciative both of true beauty, and of the quality from which that beauty proceeds, and to which it aspires: the ennoblement of human nature.

As we have seen in Chapter One, objections to Neo-Classicism, and especially to the Neo-Classical attack on Shakespeare, had been mooted before. But it was not until the advent of Romanticism that attacks on Neo-Classicism could be conducted from a position which had something else to offer in exchange for the dogmatic attachment to rules of which it wished to dispose. It is perhaps intrinsic to the nature of Grand Theories that they will persist until a stronger theory emerges to contest them (purely negative critiques, which offer no positive alternatives, are often of limited potency). In contradistinction to the Neo-Classicist theory which it contested, Romantic aesthetic theory offered a body of ideas which was at once open to, and liberal about, the infinite variety of forms that great poetry can encompass in different ages and in different nations. It saw itself as embodying a new sense of sympathy for the thought of ages past, and as substituting for the Neo-Classical appeal to external literary precedent a conception of poetry revolving instead around the individual reader's experience of the literary work, an experience whose profundity depended on the reader's capacity to sympathise – or, in Hugo's phrase, to suffer – with the protagonists of the works that they contemplated.

This emphasis on contemplation, on suffering, and on the interiority of the aesthetic experience is underscored in Keats' account, in a letter to his friend Benjamin Robert Haydon, of his experience in reading *King Lear*. 'I sat down yesterday to read *King Lear* once again: the thing appeared to demand the prologue of a sonnet,' he writes. 'I wrote it, and began to read. (I know you would like to see it)':

■ On Sitting Down to Read *King Lear* Once Again.

O golden-tongued Romance with serene lute!
Fair plumed Syren! Queen! if far away!
Leave melodizing on this wintry day,
Shut up thine olden volume, and be mute.
Adieu! for once again the fierce dispute,

Betwixt Hell torment and impassioned clay,
Must I burn through; once more assay
The bitter sweet of this Shakespearian fruit.
Chief Poet! and ye clouds of Albion,
Begetters of our deep eternal theme,
When I am through the old oak forest gone
Let me not wander in a barren dream,
But when I am consumed with the Fire.
Give me new Phoenix-wings to fly at my desire.[5] □

For Keats, the reading of *King Lear* is a solitary and isolated experience. It is indeed significant that Keats experiences the text at home, and alone, rather than with others in a theatre, that he reads (indeed rereads) it rather than watching a performance of it. And for Keats, the aesthetic pleasure that he derives from reading the text is indivisible from the pain it causes him, a pain to which he voluntarily submits (for he has chosen to reread *King Lear*) but which he also, paradoxically, seems to consider it a kind of duty to undergo (he 'must' 'burn through' 'the fierce dispute/ Betwixt Hell torment and impassioned clay'): it is the duty of the thinker to suffer. Similar responses to *King Lear* emerge in the first of our lengthier extracts, which can also be read as exemplary of the distance between the criticism of *King Lear* that we covered in the last chapter, and the criticism of the play we are to cover in this.

From Charles Lamb, 'On the tragedies of Shakespeare considered with reference to their fitness for stage representation' (1811)

■ TAKING a turn the other day in the Abbey, I was struck with the affected attitude of a figure, which I do not remember to have seen before, and which upon examination proved to be a whole-length of the celebrated Mr. Garrick. Though I would not go so far . . . as to shut players altogether out of consecrated ground, yet I own I was not a little scandalized at the introduction of theatrical airs and gestures into a place set apart to remind us of the saddest realities. Going nearer, I found inscribed under this harlequin figure the following lines:

To paint fair Nature, by divine command,
Her magic pencil in his glowing hand,
A Shakespeare rose: then, to expand his fame
Wide o'er this breathing world, a Garrick came.
Though sunk in death the forms the Poet drew,
The Actor's genius bade them breathe anew;
Though, like the bard himself, in night they lay,
Immortal Garrick call'd them back to day:

And till Eternity with power sublime
Shall mark the mortal hour of hoary Time,
Shakespeare and Garrick like twin-stars shall shine,
And earth irradiate with a beam divine.

It would be an insult to my readers' understandings to attempt anything like a criticism on this farrago of false thoughts and nonsense.
But the reflection it led me into was a kind of wonder, how, from the
days of the actor here celebrated to our own, it should have been the
fashion to compliment every performer in his turn, that has had the
luck to please the town in any of the great characters of Shakespeare,
with the notion of possessing *a mind congenial with the poet's*: how
people should come thus unaccountably to confound the power of
originating poetical images and conceptions with the faculty of being
able to read or recite the same when put into words; or what connexion that absolute mastery over the heart and soul of man, which a
great dramatic poet possesses, has with those low tricks upon the eye
and ear, which a player by observing a few general effects, which
some common passion, as grief, anger, &c. usually has upon the
gestures and exterior, can so easily compass. To know the internal
workings and movements of a great mind . . . seems to demand a reach
of intellect of a vastly different extent from that which is employed
upon the bare imitation of the signs of these passions in the countenance or gesture, which . . . can after all but indicate some passion . . . ;
but of the motives and grounds of the passion, . . . of these the actor
can give no more idea by his face or gesture than the eye (without a
metaphor) can speak, or the muscles utter intelligible sounds. But
such is the instantaneous nature of the impressions which we take in
at the eye and ear at a playhouse, compared with the slow apprehension oftentimes of the understanding in reading, that we are apt not
only to sink the play-writer in the consideration which we pay to the
actor, but even to identify in our minds in a perverse manner, the actor
with the character which he represents. . . .

Never let me be so ungrateful as to forget the very high degree of
satisfaction which I received . . . from seeing for the first time a tragedy
of Shakespeare performed . . . . It seemed to embody and realize conceptions which had hitherto assumed no distinct shape. But dearly do
we pay all our life after for this juvenile pleasure, this sense of dis-
tinctness. When the novelty is past, we find to our cost that instead of
realizing an idea, we have only materialized and brought down a fine
vision to the standard of flesh and blood. We have let go a dream, in
quest of an unattainable substance. . . .

. . . [T]he plays of Shakespeare are less calculated for performance
on a stage, than those of almost any other dramatist whatever. Their

distinguished excellence is a reason that they should be so. There is so much in them, which comes not under the province of acting, with which eye, and tone, and gesture, have nothing to do.

The glory of the scenic art is to personate passion, and the turns of passion; and the more coarse and palpable the passion is, the more hold upon the eyes and ears of the spectators the performer obviously possesses. For this reason, scolding scenes . . . have always been the most popular upon our stage . . . because the spectators are here most palpably appealed to. . . . Talking is the direct object of the imitation here. But . . . in Shakespeare above all, how obvious it is, that the form of *speaking*, . . . is only a medium, and often a highly artificial one, for putting the reader or spectator into possession of that knowledge of the inner structure and workings of mind in a character, which he could otherwise never have arrived at *in that form of composition* by any gift short of intuition. . . .

. . . [T]he practice of stage representation reduces everything to a controversy of elocution. Every character . . . must play the orator. The . . . intimate . . . sweetness of nuptial colloquy between an Othello or a Posthumus with their married wives, all those delicacies which are so delightful in the reading, . . . by the inherent fault of stage representation, how are these things sullied and turned from their very nature by being exposed to a large assembly; when such speeches . . . come drawling out of the mouth of a hired actress, whose courtship, though nominally addressed to [her lover] is manifestly aimed at the spectators, who are to judge of her endearments and her returns of love. . . .

The truth is, the Characters of Shakespeare are so much the objects of meditation rather than of interest or curiosity as to their actions that while we are reading any of his great criminal characters . . . we think not so much of the crimes which they commit, as of the ambition, the aspiring spirit, the intellectual activity, which prompts them to overleap those moral fences. . . . [S]o little do the actions [of Shakespeare's criminal characters] . . . affect us, that while the impulses, the inner mind in all its perverted greatness, solely seems real and is exclusively attended to, the crime is comparatively nothing. But when we see these things represented, the acts which they do are comparatively everything, their impulses nothing. . . . [W]hen we no longer read it in a book, when we have given up that vantage-ground of abstraction which reading possesses over seeing, and come to see a man in his bodily shape before our eyes actually preparing to commit a murder . . . the painful anxiety about the act, the natural longing to prevent it while it yet seems unperpetrated, the too close pressing semblance of reality, give a pain and an uneasiness which totally destroy all the delight which the words in the book convey, where the deed doing never presses upon us with the painful sense of presence: it rather seems to belong to history – to something past and inevitable, if it has anything to do with time at all. The sublime images, the poetry alone, is that which is present to our minds in the reading.

So to see Lear acted – to see an old man tottering about the stage with a walking-stick, turned out of doors by his daughters in a rainy night, has nothing in it but what is painful and disgusting. We want to take him into shelter and relieve him. That is all the feeling which the acting of Lear ever produced in me. But the Lear of Shakespeare cannot be acted. The contemptible machinery by which they mimic the storm which he goes out in, is not more inadequate to represent the horrors of the real elements, than any actor can be to represent Lear. . . . The greatness of Lear is not in corporal dimension but in intellectual: the explosions of his passion are terrible as a volcano: they are storms turning up and disclosing to the bottom that sea, his mind, with all its vast riches. It is his mind which is laid bare. This case of flesh and blood seems too insignificant to be thought on: even as he himself neglects it. On the stage we see nothing but corporal infirmities and weakness, the impotence of rage; while we read it, we see not Lear, but we are Lear – we are in his mind, we are sustained by a grandeur which baffles the malice of daughters and storms; in the aberrations of his reason, we discover a mighty irregular power of reasoning, immethodized from the ordinary purposes of life, but exerting its powers, as the wind blows where it listeth, at will upon the corruptions and abuses of mankind. What have looks, or tones, to do with that sublime identification of his age with that of the *heavens themselves,* when in his reproaches to them for conniving at the injustice of his children, he reminds them that 'they themselves are old'. What gesture shall we appropriate to this? What has the voice or the eye to do with such things? But the play is beyond all art, as the tamperings with it show: it is too hard and stony; it must have love-scenes, and a happy ending. It is not enough that Cordelia is a daughter, she must shine as a lover too. Tate has put his hook in the nostrils of this Leviathan – for Garrick and his followers, the showmen of the scene, to draw the mighty beast about more easily. A happy ending! – as if the living martyrdom that Lear had gone through, – the flaying of his feelings alive, did not make a fair dismissal from the stage of life the only decorous thing for him. If he is to live and be happy after, if he could sustain this world's burden after, why all this pudder and preparation – why torment us with all this unnecessary sympathy? As if the childish pleasure of getting his gilt robes and sceptre again could tempt him to act over again his misused station – as if at his years, and with his experience, anything was left but to die.

Lear is essentially impossible to be represented on a stage. . . . □

(Lamb, pp. 81–96)

Lamb's essay really ought to be read in its entirety; it is difficult to do it justice in extraction, even when the extract is lengthy. In Lamb's attack on the acting of Shakespeare, and in particular in his attack on David Garrick, he speaks for his times in a number of ways. Most specifically, he voices a new sense of disapprobation with the version of *King Lear* still current on the English stage at the time of Lamb's encounter with the statue of Garrick in Westminster Abbey (that is, Tate's – see Chapter One). Lamb, in other words, is writing at the close of a period in which almost all representations of Shakespearean plays on the English stage were adaptations of the originals, and to some degree this must have motivated his profound disgust with the acting institution, and with Garrick in particular. Lamb complains that 'we are apt . . . to identify . . . the actor with the character which he represents'; for Lamb, it would seem, Garrick is identified with the character of Tate's Lear, and as such, occupies the initial focus of his attack. But Lamb's attack on Tate's desecration of what is for Lamb an almost sacred text is also spoken from the perspective of a more literate culture, in which the hegemonic literary form of the Renaissance, drama, has given way, first to poetry, and then (increasingly in the latter part of the nineteenth century) to the novel. Such supra-cultural literary movements would have profound consequences for the interpretations of *King Lear* offered by critics such as Bradley. And so too had they for the criticism of the Romantics. It is no coincidence, in other words, that the dominant, or hegemonic, form of literature in the Romantic period (at least in England) is poetry, and that Lamb's essay here proceeds along an argument which privileges reading over performance.

Lamb wants to read *King Lear* as we read poetry, (as indeed does Keats) and sees the encounter with the literary text as one which is private, singular, and individual (again, like Keats). Thus Lamb employs a separation in this essay between the body and the soul, the corporeal and the intellectual. Reading Shakespeare's text allows one to commune with the 'heart and soul of man', with the 'internal workings and movings of a great mind', whilst watching the play, or hearing it recited, appeals only to the 'eye and ear', and hence forbids you this communion. This is in part because reading is a slower, more contemplative, experience than is the 'quick apprehension' of a dramatic performance, but it is also because, for Lamb, it is only in reading that we cannot only encounter real passion, but examine 'the motives and the grounds' of those passions. Theatrical performances can only hope to give us 'bare imitations of the signs of these passions', for passion is an interior phenomenon, and an imitation is, by definition, and however good, not identical with the real thing. And in the very act of mimicking the signs of passion, the theatrical performance enacts the expression of passion at the expense of any understanding of passion's motivations, which, Lamb believes, it is the ultimate objective of great literature to communicate.

With hindsight, we can see that Lamb's emphasis on reading over performance renders him blind to some of the more 'performative' aspects of Shakespeare's plays. He would, for example, have been unable to perceive the ways in which Shakespeare can play, within his texts, with the circumstances of theatrical performance. That, for instance, in *Hamlet*, the scene in which Claudius and Polonius watch Hamlet watching Ophelia is already inscribed in a context in which the spectators of the drama are themselves enacting a surveillance of all of these characters would have passed Lamb by. But when we remember that Lamb's championing of the importance of motive over action is written when Tate's *Lear* is still extant on the stage, we can see why he insists so emphatically on the subordination of action to motivation. The offspring of the Rules of Neo-Classicism insofar as *King Lear* was concerned, was melodrama, in which action was privileged over motivation, to the extent of the eradication of all subtlety concerning a character's 'grounds for passion'. One of the things achieved by the revolution in the conception of artistry and great art afforded by Romantic aesthetic theory was to open up critical thinking about *King Lear* to a whole range of nuances in the text to which previous criticism had been both deaf and blind, and it is to a more detailed examination of the nature of that revolution that we now turn.

Part One: The Romantic Revolution

■ I will not reproach Shakespeare with having set aside all rules of the art, they are infinitely less important than those of taste, because the one prescribes what must be done, while the other only forbids what must be avoided. It is impossible to prescribe limits to the different combinations of a man of genius . . . . The rules of art are a calculation of probabilities upon the means of success; and if this success is obtained, it is of little importance to have submitted to them; but it is not the same with the rules of taste, to despise them is to relinquish all beauties . . . □

Madame de Staël, 'On Literature' (1800)[6]

The perception that an attachment to the 'Rules' placed grave limitations on the critic's capacity properly to appreciate Shakespeare began to be expressed, with increasing force, very early in the nineteenth century. The preceding extract from Madame de Staël's 'On Literature' stands on the verge of a new concept of aesthetics. On the one hand de Staël here lodges a critique against the Rules which is far more profound than it might at first seem, for in these sentences she shifts the ground upon which the appeal to Rules had previously, in general, been invoked. For the Neo-Classicists, the measure of artistic value lay ultimately in the degree to which a work of art conformed to the Rules: the Rules were, in other words, an end in themselves. But for de Staël, the Rules are only one of many means to a different end; they are, moreover, a relatively unimportant means, simply a 'calculation of probabilities'.

Madame de Staël's sense of possibility, and her openness to variety in her notion of what constitutes great art are characteristic of the new cultural liberalism of the early nineteenth century. But in her appeal to the category of 'taste', she betrays a lingering attachment to the aesthetics of an earlier age – to those of Pope, for example, whose edition of Shakespeare had proceeded upon the assumption that his own taste was sufficient grounds to delete passages which he found unpalatable, as well as to asterisk those of which he approved. Romantic aesthetic theory needed to do more than does de Staël here if it wished to overturn the aesthetics that preceded it: more in a negative sense, in the provision of coherent reasons to reject the 'Rules', as well as more in a positive sense, in the provision of new reasons to justify one's perception that a given work of literature is great. In the following pages we shall look first at the ways in which Romantic critics attacked their Neo-Classical predecessors, and then at the conception of tragedy which they formulated to replace it.

Two main features of the Romantic attack on Neo-Classicism are pertinent to our understanding of the criticism produced on *King Lear* in the period. One was the Romantic challenge to the notion of purity of genre. As we have seen in Chapter One, one of the objections that Neo-Classical writers had to the tragedies of Shakespeare was that they fail, in general, to keep levity and gravity 'properly' separate, interspersing in the course of their tragic action scenes of a primarily comic nature. For Guizot, such an objection denoted a failure to understand the true nature of Shakespearean drama, since comedy and tragedy only truly show themselves in the relief, as it were, of the opposite form. 'We can discern true comedy only when we meet with Shylock,' Guizot maintains, '– that is, with tragedy':

■ Shakspeare's works . . . cannot . . . be divided into these two styles, but must be separated into the fantastic and the real, the romance and the world. The first class contains most of his comedies; the second . . . his tragedies [in which] . . . the comic element is introduced whenever its character of reality gives it the right of admission . . . Thus we find the entire world, the whole of human realities, reproduced by Shakspeare in tragedy, which, in his eyes, was the universal theatre of life and truth. □

(Guizot, pp. 97–9)

Such a rejection of the claim that the mixing of modes is improper allowed writers to pay far more attention to aspects of *King Lear* which had hitherto been overlooked: most notably, of course, the Fool. Thus Hugo invokes the Fool as an example of the grotesque, which he sees as:

■ one of the supreme beauties of the drama. It is not a convenience simply, it is oftentimes a necessity. Sometimes it appears in homogeneous masses, in characters which are grotesque and nothing else . . . ; sometimes impregnated with terror . . . ; sometimes, too, with a veil of charm . . . . It creeps in everywhere, for just as the most commonplace minds rise oftentimes to sublime heights, so do the greatest frequently pay tribute to the trivial and the ridiculous. . . . Sometimes it injects laughter, sometimes horror into tragedy. . . . Sometimes it may, without producing a discordant note, as in the scene between King Lear and his fool, mingle its shrill voice with the most sublime, the most melancholy, the dreamiest music of the soul.[7] □

For Hugo here, the mixing of generic modes intrinsic to the grotesque is not merely allowable, nor simply opportune, but necessary, and utilised for a variety of effects: comic relief, sometimes, but also its opposite, the introduction of horror into tragedy. For Coleridge, comic relief was never the purpose of Shakespeare's mixing of modes, although, like Hugo, Coleridge reads the presence of the Fool in *King Lear* as a necessary mixing of modes which enhances and intensifies the tragedy with which it is contrasted:

■ [Shakespeare's] genius . . . taught him to use . . . characters [such as the Fool] with terrible effect, in aggravating the . . . agony of some of his most distressing scenes. This result is especially obvious in *King Lear*: the contrast of the Fool wonderfully heightens the colouring of some of the most painful situations, where the old monarch in the depth . . . of his despair, complains to the . . . elements of the ingratitude of his daughters. . . .

Just afterwards, the Fool interposes, to heighten and inflame the passion of the scene.

. . . [I]n no instance can it be justly alleged of [Shakespeare] . . . that he introduced his fool . . . merely [to excite] the laughter of his audiences. Shakespeare had a loftier . . . purpose, and . . . availed himself of resources, which, it would almost seem, he alone possessed.[8] □

And elsewhere, Coleridge reiterates the point: 'The Fool [is] . . . no forced condescension of Shakespeare's genius to the taste of his audiences', he maintains: 'Accordingly, he is *prepared* for – brought into living connection with the pathos of the play, with the sufferings'.[9] Coleridge sees the Fool's role as inseparable from the play's larger concerns (nothing, we can note, can be further from an understanding of the role of comedy in tragic texts as one of 'relief'): in a comment on Lear's expostulation 'O, let me not be mad, not mad,' (at 1.5.43) Coleridge writes:

■ The mind's own anticipation of madness.

   The deepest tragic notes are often struck by a half sense of an impending blow. The Fool's conclusion of this act by a grotesque prattling seems to indicate the dislocation of feeling that has begun and is to be continued. □

(Coleridge, vol I, p. 64)

If challenging the notion of the purity of genre allowed criticism to review the role of the Fool, much more was achieved by the second main strand of the Romantic attack on Neo-Classicism: the attack on the notion of the unities. 'The observation of the two unities of place and time is . . . a habit of which we can rid ourselves with difficulty,' pronounced Stendhal in 1823, 'but . . . these unities are in no way necessary to produce profound emotion and true dramatic effect'.[10] Stendhal constructs an imaginary dialogue between proponents of the opposing systems, exposing in the process the untenability of the Neo-Classical justification of the observance of these unities, which lay in their conviction that the dramatic illusion of reality is fractured by large movements between different times and places (since the spectator perceives too acutely the disjunction between real and represented time, and cannot be expected to believe that actors are in one country in one scene, and another in the next). 'It is evidently contrary to all plausibility that the spectator could imagine that a year, a month, or even a week has passed, since he . . . entered the theatre' Stendhal's 'Academician' (or Neo-Classicist) maintains, to which the Romantic replies:

■ THE ROMANTIC: And who has told you that the spectator cannot imagine that?
THE ACADEMICIAN: It is reason which tells me.
THE ROMANTIC: I beg your pardon; reason would not be able to teach you that. How would you manage to know that the spectator can imagine that twenty-four hours have passed, while in fact he has been seated only two hours . . . if experience did not teach you? How could you know that the hours which seem so long to a man who is bored seem to fly for one who is entertained, if experience did not teach you? In a word, it is experience alone which must decide between you and me. □
(Stendhal, p. 219)

Stendhal's emphasis on experience is shared by other Romantic writers in their discussion of the unities. Guizot, for instance, differed from

Stendhal in that he wanted to retain some notion of temporal and spatial unity, but he was in accord with Stendhal's rejection of the Neo-Classical explanation of their necessity, and with his belief in the flexibility of the human imagination.

And although Guizot wanted to retain, to some degree, the notion of the unities, he was also concerned to make it far more flexible than it had been before; for Guizot, therefore, a good dramatist can manipulate time and place so long as he ensures that:

■ the chain of the impressions has not been broken, and the position of the characters has not changed; . . . time has not acted upon them; [the lapse of time] counts for nothing in the feelings with which [the characters] inspire us; it finds them, and us, in the same disposition of soul . . .

(Guizot, pp. 158–9)

And in fact, Guizot uses *King Lear* to exemplify the ways in which Shakespeare can successfully transgress the unities of time and of place:

■ Between two events evidently separated by a [long] interval . . . Shakspeare interposes a scene which may belong . . . to either the first or the second epoch, and he makes us pass from one to the other without shocking us by its intimate connection with the scene which immediately precedes or follows it. Thus, in *King Lear*, between the time when Lear divides his kingdom among his daughters, and the moment when Goneril . . . determines to get rid of him – the scenes at Gloster's castle, and the commencement of Edmund's intrigue, are interposed. . . . [T]he poet knows that our imagination will traverse without effort both time and space with him, if he spares those moral improbabilities which could alone arrest its progress. □

(Guizot, pp. 167–8)

For Guizot, unity of time (and, to a lesser degree, of place) are primarily useful insofar as they can preclude disorientation with respect to our understanding of the interiority of the protagonist, and unnecessary only insofar as the dramatist can ensure, by other means, that the relation between reader, or spectator, and character, remains the same. In this concern with the interiority of the characters of a drama, and in their understanding of literature, and especially of tragedy, as a vehicle for the communing of human minds and souls, the Romantics served as the precursors of that criticism which concentrated almost exclusively on the central character in a drama, the primary exponent of which was Bradley, as we shall see later in this book. And in turning to the third unity, that of action, we can see the degree to which the experience of tragedy is increasingly focused upon the figure of the hero:

■ Unity of action [is] indispensable to unity of impression . . . But how . . . could [Shakespeare] maintain it in . . . that immense field which includes so many places, so many years, all conditions of society, and the development of so many positions? Shakspeare succeeded in maintaining it [by seizing] . . . upon its fundamental condition, which consists in placing the centre of interest where he finds the centre of action. The character which gives movement to the drama, is also the one upon which the moral agitation of the spectator is bestowed. □
(Guizot, p. 168)

For Guizot, then, all action in Shakespearean tragedy inheres in the tragic protagonist, and he utilises this notion of the centrality of the tragic protagonist to open up the action allowable, or required, in a tragedy.

But it was Augustus William Schlegel (from whom other critics, including Guizot, borrowed liberally), who produced the most extensive, most methodical, and most intelligent of Romantic critiques of their Neo-Classical predecessors. In his attack on Neo-Classicism, for instance, Schlegel notes that the very foundation of their theory of the unities lies in a misreading of the authority they most often invoked: Aristotle. As Schlegel points out, Aristotle says nothing at all about spatial Unity, mentions temporal Unity very little, and only addresses 'with any degree of fulness' unity of action (Schlegel, p. 237). And like Stendhal and Guizot, Schlegel attacks the theory of illusion governing the Neo-Classical insistence that the spectator can only believe in the drama given parity between real and represented time. 'This idea of illusion,' he states, often betrays

■ the . . . erroneous belief that represented action is reality. In that case the terrors of Tragedy would be a true torture to us. . . . No, . . . every . . . poetical illusion, is a waking dream, to which we voluntarily surrender ourselves. To produce it, the poet . . . must powerfully agitate the mind, and the probabilities of calculation do not in the least contribute towards it. This demand of literal deception, pushed to the limit, would make all poetic form impossible . . . What an unpoetical spectator were he who, instead of following the incidents with his sympathy, should . . . with watch . . . in hand, count out to the heroes of tragedy, the minutes which they still have to live and act! Is our soul then a piece of clock-work, that tells the hours and minutes with infallible accuracy? . . . Our body is subjected to external . . . time, because the organical operations are regulated by it; but our mind has its own ideal time, which is no other but the consciousness of the progressive development of our beings. In this measure of time the intervals of an indifferent activity pass for nothing, and two important moments, though they lie years apart, link themselves immediately to each other. . . . [O]ur imagination overleaps . . . the times which are supposed . . . intimated . . . it dwells solely on the decisive moments placed before it, by the compression of which the poet gives wings to the lazy course of days and hours. □

(Schlegel, pp. 246–7)

And he brings similar objections to bear on the unity of place:

■ The objection to the change of scene is founded on the same erroneous idea of illusion . . . But . . . Johnson . . . observes, that if our imagination [can transport] . . . us eighteen hundred years back to Alexandria, in order to figure to ourselves the story of Antony and Cleopatra . . . the next step, of transporting ourselves from Alexandria to Rome, is easier. The capability of our mind to fly in thought . . . through the immensity of time and space, is well known . . . ; and shall poetry, whose very purpose it is to add all manner of wings to our mind, and which has at command all the magic of genuine illusion, that is, of a lively and enrapturing fiction, be alone compelled to renounce this universal prerogative? □

(Schlegel, pp. 249–50)

Schlegel, then, can and does make a much stronger case than Guizot, implying as he does here that the unities of time and place are irrelevant to the tragedy of his age. But it is on unity of action that Schlegel is at his most interesting. For a start, he poses 'obvious' questions which had not been examined properly before: 'What is action?' he asks:

■ Most critics pass over this point, as if it were self-evident. In the higher, proper signification, action is an activity dependent on the will of man. Its unity will consist in the direction towards a single end; and to its completeness belongs all that lies between the first determination and the execution of the deed. □

(Schlegel, p. 240)

But such a conception of action, Schlegel maintains, is irrelevant to

■ the greater part of modern tragedies, at least if the action is to be sought in the principal characters. What comes to pass through them, and proceeds with them, has frequently no more connexion with a voluntary determination, than a ship's striking on a rock in a storm. □

(Schlegel, p. 240)

Moreover, plot complication, as Schlegel points out,

■ arises mostly out of the contradictory motives and views of the acting personages. If, therefore, we limit the notion of an action to the determination and the deed, then we shall, in most cases, have two or three actions in a single tragedy. Which now is the principal action? □
(Schlegel, p. 241)

For Schlegel, our understanding of what tragic action should encompass is mediated through far wider intellectual concerns, whose recognition is neither universal nor transcendent, but which instead emerges from the historical circumstances in which author and reader find themselves. Thus, he claims, in modern (as opposed to ancient) tragedy, we can observe

■ a new condition in the notion of action, namely, the reference to the idea of moral liberty, by which alone man is considered as the original author of his own resolutions. For, considered within the province of experience, the resolution, as the beginning of an action, is not a cause merely, but is also an effect of antecedent motives. It was in this reference to a higher idea, that we previously found the *unity* and *wholeness* of Tragedy in the sense of the ancients; namely, its absolute beginning in the assertion of Free-will, and the acknowledgement of Necessity as its absolute end. □

(Schlegel, pp. 241–2)

Schlegel, then, extends to the concept of action the same liberality with which he treats the unities of time and of place. The notion of siting the beginning of an action in the resolution to act is for him senseless, since that resolution itself emerges from previous motivation.

This attack on the strictness of the Neo-Classical understanding of tragic unity, and the revolutionary environment from which that attack emanated, enabled critics to read Shakespearean texts from a perspective far more sympathetic to some of their concerns than had been available to previous critical generations. One of its most direct consequences was that a more liberal understanding of tragic action permitted, for the first time, a sustained recognition of the double plotting of many of Shakespeare's dramas, and in particular, of *King Lear*, as these extracts, the first from Johann Gottfried Herder and the second from Hugo, will show:

From Johann Gottfried Herder, 'Shakespeare' (1773)

■ Whereas in Sophocles's drama the unity of a single action is domi-nant, Shakespeare aims at the entirety of an event. . . . Whereas

Sophocles makes a single tone predominate . . . , Shakespeare uses all the characters, estates, walks of life . . . to produce the concerted sound of his drama. . . . When I read him, it seems to me as if theatre, actors, scenery all vanish! Single leaves from the book of events, providence, the world, blowing in the storm of history. Individual impressions of nations, classes, souls . . . combine to form a whole theatrical image, a grand event whose totality only the poet can survey . . .

Step then before his stage, as before an ocean of events, where wave thunders upon wave. Scenes from nature come and go before our eyes; however disparate they seem, they are dynamically related; they create and destroy one another so that the intention of their creator, who seems to have put them together according to a crazy and disorderly plan, may be fulfilled – dark little symbols that form the silhouette of a divine theodicy. Lear, the rash, hot-headed old man, noble in his weakness as he stands before his map giving away crowns and tearing countries apart – the very first scene already bears within its seed the harvest of his fate in the dark future. Behold, soon we shall see the generous spendthrift, the hasty tyrant, the childish father even in his daughters' antechambers, pleading, praying, begging, cursing, raving, blessing – o Heavens, and presaging madness! Then he will soon go bareheaded in the thunder and lightning, cast down to the lowest of the low, in the company of a fool, in a crazy beggar's cave, almost calling down madness from above. And now see him as he is, in all the light-yoked majesty of the poor abandoned wretch; and now restored to himself, illumined by the last rays of hope only for them to be extinguished for ever! Imprisoned, dead in his arms the child and daughter who had comforted and forgiven him; dying over her body; and his faithful servant dying after the old king! O God, what vicissitudes of times, circumstances, tempests, climes, and ages! And all of it not merely a single story, a heroic political action, if you will, moving from a single beginning to a single end according to Aristotle's strictest rule; but draw nearer and feel too the human spirit which integrated every person and age and character, down to the smallest secondary thing, into the picture. Two old fathers and all their very different children. The son of the one, grateful in his misfortune towards his deceived father; the other hideously ungrateful towards his affectionate father, even in his abominable good fortune. One father against his daughters, his daughters against him, their husbands, suitors, and all their accomplices in fortune and misfortune! Blind Gloucester supported by his unrecognised son, and mad Lear at the feet of his rejected daughter! And now the moment at the cross-roads of fortune, when Gloucester dies beneath his tree, and the trumpet calls, all the incidental circumstances, motives, characters, and situations concentrated into the poetic work, all in a world of fiction, all developing into a whole, a whole made up of fathers, children, kings and fools, beggars and misery, but throughout which the soul of the great event breathes even in the most disparate scenes, in which places, times, circumstances, even, I would say, the pagan philosophy of fate and the stars which reigns throughout, all belong so essentially to the whole that I could change nothing, move nothing, nor transfer parts from other plays, or to other plays. And that is not a drama?[11] □

From Victor Hugo, *William Shakespeare* (1864)

■ ALL Shakespeare's plays, with the exception of *Macbeth* and *Romeo and Juliet* . . . offer to the observer one peculiarity which seems to have escaped . . . the most eminent . . . critics; one which is unnoticed by the Schlegels, . . . and of which it is impossible not to speak. It is the double action which traverses the drama and reflects it on a small scale. Beside the tempest in the Atlantic is the tempest in the tea-cup. Thus . . . in *King Lear*, side by side and simultaneously, Lear, driven to despair by his daughters Goneril and Regan and consoled by his daughter Cordelia, is repeated in Gloster, betrayed by his son Edmund and loved by his son Edgar. The idea bifurcated, the idea echoing itself, a lesser drama copying and elbowing the principal drama, the action attended by its moon – smaller action like it – unity cut in two; surely the fact is a strange one. . . .

These double actions are . . . the sign of the sixteenth century. . . . The Renascence was a subtle time, a time of reflection. The spirit of the sixteenth century was reflected in a mirror. . . .

Shakespeare, faithful to the spirit of his time, must needs . . . make the filial piety of Edgar a comment on the filial piety of Cordelia, and bring out in contrast, weighed down by the ingratitude of unnatural children, two wretched fathers, each bereaved of one of the two kinds of light – Lear mad, and Gloster blind. □

(Hugo, pp. 213–15)

Attacks on the Neo-Classical conception of the unities, then, and on its strictures against the mixing of modes, had allowed criticism to pay attention to aspects of *King Lear* such as the Fool's role, and the double plot. But these specific differences in approach were concomitant with a fundamental and general shift in the understanding of the nature of tragedy itself. Whereas the Neo-Classicists saw observance of specific rules as an end in itself, it being in the strict observance of these rules that the beauty and success of a tragedy lay, the Romantics held a very different notion of the qualities of tragedy. Their rejection of Neo-Classicism did not entail a rejection of the notion of proper form *per se* but the substitution of an utterly different conception of form: what Schlegel called 'organical form', which he explained thus:

■ most critics, . . . interpret [form] merely in a mechanical, and not in an organical sense. Form is mechanical when, through external force, it is imparted to any material merely as an accidental addition without reference to its quality; as, for example, when we give a particular shape to a soft mass that it may retain the same after its induration. Organical form, again, is innate; it unfolds itself from within, and acquires its determination contemporaneously with the perfect development of the germ. We everywhere discover such forms in nature throughout the whole range of living powers, from the crystallisation of salts and minerals to plants and flowers, and from these again to the human body. In the fine arts, as well as in the domain of nature – the supreme artist, all genuine forms are organical, that is, determined by the quality of the work. In a word, the form is nothing but a significant exterior, the speaking physiognomy of each thing, which, as long as it is not disfigured by any destructive accident, gives a true evidence of its hidden essence. □

(Schlegel, p. 340)

For the Romantics, the different elements of a tragedy were not akin, say, to the different elements that make up the function of a watch: form and content are intrinsic to each other in a way that was completely contrary to the understandings of the past. 'Organical form' is something much more than the transgression of rules; as Schlegel goes on to explain, the greatness of Shakespearean tragedies:

■ does not consist merely in the bold neglect of the Unities of Place and Time, and in the commixture of comic and tragic elements: that they were unwilling or unable to comply with the rules and with right reason, . . . may be considered as an evidence of merely negative properties. The ground of the resemblance [between the great drama of Spain and of England] lies far deeper, in the inmost substance of the fictions, and in the essential relations, through which every deviation of form becomes a true requisite, which, together with its validity, has also its significance. □

(Schlegel, p. 342)

Great drama, he goes on later to say

■ does not . . . separate seriousness and the action . . . from among the whole ingredients of life; it embraces at once the whole of the chequered drama of life with all its circumstances; and while it seems only to represent subjects brought accidentally together, it satisfies the unconscious requisitions of fancy, buries us in reflections on the inexpressible signification of the objects which we view blended by order, nearness and distance, light and colour, into one harmonious whole; and thus lends, as it were, a soul to the prospect before us. □

(Schlegel, p. 344)

This sense of the holistic unity of Shakespearean tragedy was also adopted by English critics, most notably by Coleridge. But others, even if they did not use Schlegel's terminology, also responded to a sense of the intrinsic unity of Shakespeare's plays, and expressed a similar conviction that individual elements of his drama were inherent in the whole. We can see the germs of Schlegel's 'organical form' in Herder's perception of the totality of Shakespearean drama, in his experience of Shakespearean tragedy as a representation of 'the world, blowing in the storm of history'. Schlegel's 'organical form' is also akin to Guizot's (less intellectually satisfying) 'unity of impression'. And William Hazlitt, although he did not adopt Schlegel's phraseology, responded, analogously, to the inherent unity which he saw in Shakespeare's drama.[12] 'The whole "coheres semblably together" in time, place, and circumstance', Hazlitt maintained,[13] 'a word, an epithet paints a whole scene, or throws us back whole years in the history of the person represented' (Hazlitt, p. 182). For Hazlitt, Shakespeare

■ brings together images the most alike, but placed at the greatest distance from each other; that is, found in circumstances of the greatest dissimilitude. From the remoteness of his combinations, and the celerity with which they are effected, they coalesce the more indissolubly together. The more the thoughts are strangers to each other, and the longer they have been kept asunder, the more intimate does their union become. □

(Hazlitt, p. 188)

Part Two: Longer Essays on *King Lear*

It is time now to leave the theoretical section of this chapter, and to move to our final section, in which are reprinted some longer extracts from the Romantics' writings on *King Lear*. I want to leave these longer extracts to stand, in the main, for themselves: the material included in the introduction to this chapter, and in the preceding section, should already provide an adequate framework in which to understand them. In addition to what I have already said, I should note also two further tendencies of Romantic criticism of Shakespeare, and in particular of their treatment of *King Lear*. First, Romantic critics tended to pay little attention to the politics of the play, and to read Shakespearean tragedy predominantly through the figure of its central protagonist; in this concentration, they laid the way for the almost exclusive concentration on character exemplified later in A.C. Bradley's *Shakespearean Tragedy*. A second Romantic legacy, apparent in several of the extracts reproduced here, was the idealisation of Cordelia.

From Schlegel, *Course of Lectures on Dramatic Art and Literature* (1808)

['Who can possibly enumerate the different combinations and situations by which our minds are here, as it were stormed by the poet?' asks Schlegel in the course of this extract on *King Lear*. Schlegel's conception of tragedy's embodiment of organical form enables him to pay attention to, amongst other things, the role of the Fool, connections between different characters (such as Lear and Edgar), and the levels of suffering around which the play revolves, Lear's own suffering being itself threefold: as king, as father, and as old man.]

■ As in *Macbeth* terror reaches its utmost height, in *King Lear* the science of compassion is exhausted. The principal characters here are not those who act, but those who suffer. We have . . . in this . . . a fall from the highest elevation into the deepest abyss of misery, where humanity is stripped of all external and internal advantages, and given up a prey to naked helplessness. The threefold dignity of a king, an old man, and a father, is dishonoured by the cruel ingratitude of his unnatural daughters; the old Lear, who out of a foolish tenderness has given away every thing, is driven out to the world a wandering beggar; the childish imbecility to which he was fast advancing changes into the wildest insanity, and when he is rescued from the disgraceful destitution to which he was abandoned, it is too late: the kind consolations of filial care and attention and of true friendship are now lost on him; his bodily and mental powers are destroyed beyond all hope of recovery, and all that now remains to him of life is the capability of loving and suffering beyond measure. What a picture we have in the meeting of Lear and Edgar in a tempestuous night and in a wretched hovel! The youthful Edgar has, by the wicked arts of his brother, and through his father's blindness, fallen, as the old Lear, from the rank to which his birth entitled him; and as the only means of escaping further persecution, is reduced to assume the guise of a beggar tormented by evil spirits. The King's fool, notwithstanding the voluntary degradation which is implied in his situation, is, after Kent, Lear's most faithful associate, his wisest counsellor. This goodhearted fool clothes reason with the liberty of his motley garb; the high born beggar acts the part of insanity; and both, were they even in reality what they seem, would still be enviable in comparison with the King, who feels that the violence of his grief threatens to overpower his reason. The meeting of Edgar with the blinded Gloster is equally heartrending; nothing can be more affecting than to see the ejected son become the father's guide, and the good angel, who under the disguise of insanity, saves him by an ingenious and pious fraud from the horror and despair of self-murder. But who can possibly enumerate all the different combinations and situations by which our minds are here as it were stormed by the poet? Respecting the structure of the whole I will only make one observation. The story of Lear and his daughters was left by Shakspeare exactly as he found it in a fabulous tradition, with all the features characteristical of the simplicity of old times. But in that tradition there is not the slightest trace of the story of Gloster and his sons, which was derived by Shakspeare from another source. The incorporation of the two stories has been censured as destructive of the unity of action. But whatever contributes to the intrigue or the *dénouement* must always possess unity. And with what ingenuity and skill are the two main parts of the composition dovetailed into one another! The pity felt by Gloster for the fate of Lear becomes the means which enables his son Edmund to effect his complete destruction, and affords the outcast Edgar an opportunity of being the saviour of his father. On the other hand, Edmund is active in the cause of Regan and Gonerill; and the criminal passion which they both entertain for him induces them to execute justice on each other and on themselves. The laws of the drama have therefore been sufficiently complied with; but . . . it is the very combination which constitutes the sublime beauty of the work. The two cases resembles [*sic*] each other in the main: an infatuated father is blind towards his well-disposed child, and the unnatural children, whom he prefers, requite him by the ruin of all his happiness. But all the circumstances are so different, that these stories, while they each make a correspondent impression on the heart, form a complete contrast for the imagination. Were Lear alone to suffer from his daughters, the impression would be limited to the powerful compassion felt by us for his private misfortune. But two such unheard of examples taking place at the same time have the appearance of a great commotion in the moral world: the picture becomes gigantic and fills us with such alarm as we should entertain at the idea that the heavenly bodies might one day fall from their appointed orbits . . . Lear is choleric, overbearing, and almost childish from age, when he drives out his youngest daughter because she will not join in the hypocritical exaggerations of her sisters. But he has a warm and affectionate heart, which is susceptible of the most fervent gratitude; and even rays of a high and kingly disposition burst forth from the eclipse of his understanding. Of Cordelia's heavenly beauty of soul, painted in so few words, I will not venture to speak. . . . Her death has been thought too cruel; and in England the piece is in acting so far altered that she remains victorious and happy. I must own, I cannot conceive what ideas of art and dramatic connexion those persons have who suppose that we can at pleasure tack a double conclusion to a tragedy; a melancholy one for hardhearted spectators, and a happy one for souls of a softer mould. After surviving so many sufferings, Lear can only die; and what more truly tragic end for him than to die from grief for the death of Cordelia? and if he is also to be saved and to pass the remainder of his days in happiness, the whole loses its signification. According to Shakspeare's plan the guilty, it is true, are all punished, for wickedness destroys itself; but the virtues that would bring help and succour are everywhere too late, or overmatched by the cunning activity of malice. The persons of this drama have only such a faint belief in Providence as heathens may be supposed to have; and the poet here wishes to show us that this belief requires a wider range than the dark pilgrimages on earth to be established in full extent. □

(Schlegel, pp. 411–3)

From Samuel Taylor Coleridge on *King Lear*, circa 1813[14]

[Coleridge's note on the opening lines of the play (1.1.1–6) is illustrative of the way in which the Romantic conception of tragic unity allowed the critic to pay attention to minor characters (such as Cornwall and Albany) and to spin almost infinite webs of meaning out of individual words and phrases. Coleridge's painstaking 'practical criticism' of the text (it was he who invented the term) allows him, for instance, to note the apparent contradiction at the very opening of *King Lear*, where the division of the kingdoms is referred to as a *fait accompli* even though it has not yet actually happened. And Romantic emphasis on motivation rather than on action enables Coleridge to treat the figure of Edmund with extraordinary perception and sympathy (one might compare, here, Lamb's remarks on Shakespeare's criminal characters in the essay printed at the end of the introduction to this chapter).]

■ It was [not] without forethought, and it is not without its due significance, that the triple division is stated here as already determined and in all its particulars, previously to the trial of professions, as the relative rewards of which the daughters were to be made to consider their several portions. The strange, yet by no means unnatural, mixture of selfishness, sensibility, and habit of feeling derived from and fostered by the particular rank and usages of the individual; the intense desire to be intensely beloved, selfish, and yet characteristic of the selfishness of a loving and kindly nature – a feeble selfishness, self-supportless and leaning for all pleasure on another's breast; the selfish craving after a sympathy with a prodigal disinterestedness, contradicted by its own ostentation and the mode and nature of its claims; the anxiety, the distrust, the jealousy, which more or less accompany all selfish affections, and are among the surest contra-distinctions of mere fondness from love, and which originate Lear's eager wish to enjoy his daughter's violent professions, while the inveterate habits of sovereignty convert the wish into claim and positive right, and the incompliance with it into crime and treason; – these facts, these passions, these moral verities, on which the whole tragedy is founded, are all prepared for, and will to the retrospect be found implied in, these first four or five lines of the play. They let us know that the trial is but a trick; and that the grossness of the old king's rage is in part the natural result of a silly trick suddenly and most un-expectedly baffled and disappointed.[15] This having been provided in the fewest words, in a natural reply to as natural [a] question, which yet answers a secondary purpose of attracting our attention to the dif-ference or diversity between the characters of Cornwall and Albany; the premises and data, as it were, having been thus afforded for our after-insight into the mind and mood of the person whose character, passions, and sufferings are the main *subject-matter* of the play; – from Lear, the *persona patiens* of his drama, Shakespeare passes without delay to the second in importance, to the main *agent* and prime mover – introduces Edmund to our acquaintance, and with the same felicity of judgement . . . prepares us for his character in the seemingly casual communication of its origin and occasion. From the first drawing up of the curtain he has stood before us in the united strength and beauty of earliest manhood. Our eyes have been questioning him. Gifted thus with high advantages of *person*, and further endowed by nature with a powerful intellect and a strong energetic will, even without any con-currence of circumstances and accident, pride will be the sin that most easily besets him. But he is the known and acknowledged son of the princely Gloster. Edmund, therefore, has both the germ of pride and the conditions best fitted to evolve and ripen it into a predominant feeling. Yet hitherto no reason appears why it should be other than the not unusual pride of person, talent, and birth, a pride auxiliary if not akin to many virtues, and the natural ally of honorable [impulses?]. But alas! in his own presence his own father takes shame to himself for the frank avowal that he is his father – has 'blushed so often to acknowledge him that he is now braz'd to it'. He hears his mother and the circumstances of his birth spoken of with a most degrading and licentious levity – described as a wanton by her own paramour, and the remembrance of the animal sting, the low criminal gratifications connected with her wantonness and prostituted beauty assigned as the reason why 'the whoreson must be acknowledged'. This, and the consciousness of its notoriety – the gnawing conviction that every shew of respect is an effort of courtesy which recalls while it represses a contrary feeling – this is the evertrickling flow of wormwood and gall into the wounds of pride, the corrosive virus which inoculates pride with a venom not its own, with envy, hatred, a lust of that power which in its blaze of radiance would hide the dark spots on his disk, [with] pangs of shame personally undeserved and therefore felt as wrongs, and a blind ferment of vindictive workings towards the occasions and causes, especially towards a brother whose stainless birth and lawful honors were the constant remembrancers of *his* debasement, and were ever in the way to prevent all chance of its being unknown or overlooked and forgotten. Add to this that with excellent judgement, and provident for the claims of the moral sense, for that which relatively to the drama is called poetic justice; and as the fittest means for reconciling the feelings of the spectators to the horrors of Gloster's after sufferings – at least, of rendering them somewhat less unendurable (for I will not disguise my conviction that in this one point the tragic has been urged beyond the outermost mark and *ne plus ultra* of the dramatic)[16] – Shakespeare has precluded all excuse and palliation of the guilt incurred by both the parents of the base-born Edmund by Gloster's confession that he was at the time a married man and already blest with a lawful heir of his fortunes. The mournful alienation of brotherly love occasioned by primogeniture in noble families, or rather by the unnecessary distinctions engrafted thereon, and this in children of the same stock, is still almost proverbial on the continent – especially, as I know from my own observation, in the south of Europe – and appears to have been scarcely less common in our own island before the Revolution of 1688, if we may judge from the characters and sentiments so frequent in our elder comedies. . . . Need it be said how heavy an aggravation the stain of bastardy must have been, were it only that the younger brother was liable to hear his own dishonor and his mother's infamy related by his father with an excusing shrug of the shoulders, and in a tone betwixt waggery and shame.

By the circumstances here enumerated as so many predisposing causes, Edmund's character might well be deem'd already sufficiently explained and prepared for. But in this tragedy the story or fable constrained Shakespeare to introduce wickedness in an outrageous form, in Regan and Goneril. He had read nature too heedfully not to know that courage, intellect, and strength of character were the most impressive forms of power, and that to power in itself, without reference to any moral end, an inevitable admiration and complacency appertains. . . . But in the display of such a character it was of the highest importance to prevent the guilt from passing into utter *monstrosity* – which again depends on the presence or absence of causes and temptations sufficient to account for the wickedness, without the necessity of recurring to a thorough fiendishness of nature for its origination. For such are the appointed relations of intellectual power to truth, and of truth to goodness, that it becomes both morally and poetic[ally] unsafe to present what is admirable – what our nature compels us to admire – in the mind, and what is most detestable in the heart, as coexisting in the same individual without any apparent connection, or any modification of the one by the other. . . . [I]n the present tragedy, in which he [was] compelled to present a Goneril and Regan, it was most carefully to be avoided; and, therefore, the one only conceivable addition to the inauspicious influences on the preformation of Edmund's character is given in the information that all the kindly counteractions to the mischievous feelings of shame that might have been derived from co-domestication with Edgar and their common father, had been cut off by an absence from home and a foreign education from boyhood to the present time, and the prospect of its continuance, as if to preclude all risk of his interference with the father's views for the elder and legitimate son:

He hath been out nine years, and away he shall again. . . . □

From William Hazlitt, *Characters of Shakespeare's Plays* (1817)[17]

[Hazlitt ranges very widely in this essay. Like Coleridge, he pays attention to embedded meaning in small fragments of the text; like Coleridge, he extends his sympathetic readings even to characters such as Edmund. He touches upon the Fool; he draws distinctions between different forms of madness in the play.]

■ We wish that we could pass this play over, and say nothing about it. All that we can say must fall far short of the subject; or even of what we ourselves conceive of it. To attempt to give a description of the play itself or of its effect upon the mind, is mere impertinence: yet we must say something. – It is then the best of all Shakespear's plays, for it is the one in which he was the most in earnest. He was here fairly caught in the web of his own imagination. The passion which he has taken as his subject is that which strikes its root deepest into the human heart; of which the bond is the hardest to be unloosed; and the cancelling and tearing to pieces of which gives the greatest revulsion to the frame. This depth of nature, this force of passion, this tug and war of the elements of our being, this firm faith in filial piety, and the giddy anarchy and whirling tumult of the thoughts at finding this prop failing it, the contrast between the fixed, immoveable basis of natural affection, and the rapid, irregular starts of imagination, suddenly wrenched from all its accustomed holds and resting-places in the soul, this is what Shakespear has given, and what nobody else but he could give. So we believe. – The mind of Lear, staggering between the weight of attachment and the hurried movements of passion, is like a tall ship driven about by the winds, buffeted by the furious waves, but that still rides above its anchor fixed in the bottom of the sea; or it is like the sharp rock circled by the eddying whirlpool that foams and beats against it, or like the solid promontory pushed from its basis by the force of an earthquake.

The character of Lear itself is very finely conceived for the purpose. It is the only ground on which such a story could be built with the greatest truth and effect. It is his rash haste, his violent impetuosity, his blindness to every thing but the dictates of his passions or affections, that produces all his misfortunes, that aggravates his impatience of them, that enforces our pity for him. The part which Cordelia bears in the scene is extremely beautiful: the story is almost told in the first words she utters. We see at once the precipice on which the poor old king stands from his own extravagant and credulous importunity, the indiscreet simplicity of her love (which, to be sure, has a little of her father's obstinacy in it) and the hollowness of her sisters' pretensions. Almost the first burst of that noble tide of passion, which runs through the play, is in the remonstrance of Kent to his royal master on the injustice of his sentence against his youngest daughter – "Be Kent unmannerly, when Lear is mad!" This manly plainness, which draws down on him the displeasure of the unadvised king, is worthy of the fidelity with which he adheres to his fallen fortunes. The true character of the two eldest daughters, Regan and Gonerill (they are so thoroughly hateful that we do not even like to repeat their names) breaks out in their answer to Cordelia who desires them to treat their father well – "Prescribe not us our duties" – their hatred of advice being in proportion to their determination to do wrong, and to their hypocritical pretension to do right. Their deliberate hypocrisy adds the last finishing to the odiousness of their characters. It is the absence of this detestable quality that is the only relief in the character of Edmund the Bastard, and that at times reconciles us to him. We are not tempted to exaggerate the guilt of his conduct, when he himself gives it up as a bad business, and writes himself down "plain villain". Nothing more can be said about it. His religious honesty in this respect is admirable. One speech of his is worth a million. . . . – The whole character, its careless, lighthearted villainy, contrasted with the sullen, rancorous malignity of Regan and Gonerill, its connection with the conduct of the underplot, in which Gloster's persecution of one of his sons and the ingratitude of another, form a counterpart to the mistakes and misfortunes of Lear, – his double amour with the two sisters, and the share which he has in bringing about the fatal catastrophe, are all managed with an uncommon degree of skill and power.

It has been said, and we think justly, that the third act of *Othello* and the three first acts of LEAR, are Shakespear's great master-pieces in the logic of passion: that they contain the highest examples not only of the force of individual passion, but of its dramatic vicissitudes and striking effects arising from the different circumstances and characters of the persons speaking. We see the ebb and flow of the feeling, its pauses and feverish starts, its impatience of opposition, its accumulating force when it has time to recollect itself, the manner in which it avails itself of every passing word or gesture, its haste to repel insinuation, the alternate contraction and dilatation of the soul, and all 'the dazzling fence of controversy' in this mortal combat with poisoned weapons, aimed at the heart, where each wound is fatal. . . . In . . . [*King Lear*] that which aggravates the sense of sympathy in the reader, and of uncontroulable anguish in the swoln heart of Lear, is the petrifying indifference, the cold, calculating, obdurate selfishness of his daughters. His keen passions seem whetted on their stony hearts. The contrast would be too painful, the shock too great, but for the intervention of the Fool, whose well-timed levity comes in to break the continuity of feeling when it can no longer be borne, and to bring into play again the fibres of the heart just as they are growing rigid from over-strained excitement. The imagination is glad to take refuge in the half-comic, half-serious comments of the Fool, just as the mind under the extreme anguish of a surgical operation vents itself in sallies of wit. The character was also a grotesque ornament of the barbarous times, in which alone the tragic groundwork of the story could be laid. In another point of view it is indispensable, inasmuch as while it is a diversion to the too great intensity of our disgust, it carries the pathos to the highest pitch of which it is capable, by showing the pitiable weakness of the old king's conduct and its irretrievable consequences in the most familiar point of view. Lear may well 'beat at the gate which let his folly in,' after, as the Fool says, 'he has made his daughters his mothers'. The character is dropped in the third act to make room for the entrance of Edgar as Mad Tom, which well accords with the increasing bustle and wildness of the incidents; and nothing can be more complete than the distinction between Lear's real and Edgar's assumed madness, while the resemblance in the cause of their distresses, from the severing of the nearest ties of natural affection, keeps up a unity of interest. Shakespear's mastery over his subject, if it was not art, was owing to a knowledge of the connecting links of the passions, and their effect upon the mind, still more wonderful than any systematic adherence to rules, and that anticipated and outdid all the efforts of the most refined art, not inspired and rendered instinctive by genius. . . .

Four things have struck us in reading LEAR:

1. That poetry is an interesting study, for this reason, that it relates to whatever is most interesting in human life. Whoever therefore has a contempt for poetry, has a contempt for himself and humanity.

2. That the language of poetry is superior to the language of painting; because the strongest of our recollections relate to feelings, not to faces.

3. That the greatest strength of genius is shewn in describing the strongest passions: for the power of the imagination, in works of invention, must be in proportion to the force of the natural impressions, which are the subject of them.

4. That the circumstance which balances the pleasure against the pain in tragedy is, that in proportion to the greatness of the evil, is our sense and desire of the opposite good excited; and that our sympathy with actual suffering is lost in the strong impulse given to our natural affections, and carried away with the swelling tide of passion, that gushes from and relieves the heart. □

From M. Guizot, *Shakespeare and His Times* (1852)

[Guizot's contention that *King Lear* revolves around the fact that five of its principal characters, Lear, Cordelia, Kent, Edgar and Gloucester, all experience misfortune derives from his search for a 'unity of impression' in the play, and underlies his ascription of the madness of Lear and the death of Gloucester to a similar cause: both, he argues, are direct, although contrasting, responses to their analogous situations. Like Hugo, he wishes to celebrate what he calls Shakespeare's 'emancipation from form'. At the beginning of his essay (not reproduced here), Guizot has compared Shakespeare's *Lear* with other versions of the stories that it tells: Lear's, that is, and Gloucester's.]

■ It is evident that the situation of King Lear and of the King of Paphlagonia, both persecuted by the children whom they preferred, and succoured by the one whom they rejected, struck Shakspeare as fitted to enter into the same subject, because they belonged to the same idea. Those who have blamed him for having thus injured the simplicity of his action, have given their opinion according to their own system, without taking the trouble to examine that of the author whom they criticised. Starting even from the rules which they are desirous to impose, we might answer that the love of the two women for Edmund, which serves to effect their punishment, and the intervention of Edgar at this part of the *dénouement*, are sufficient to acquit the play of the charge of duplicity of action; for, provided that all the threads at last unite in one knot which it is easy to seize, the simplicity of the progress of an action depends much less upon the number of the interests and personages concerned in it, than upon the natural and clearly visible play of the springs which set it in motion. But further, we must never forget, that unity, in Shakspeare's view, consists in one dominant idea, which, reproducing itself under various forms, incessantly produces, continues, and redoubles the same impression. Thus . . . in *King Lear*, he depicts him in conflict with misfortune, the action of which is modified according to the different characters of the individuals who experience it. The first spectacle which he brings under our notice is the misfortune of virtue, or of persecuted innocence, as exemplified in Cordelia, Kent, and Edgar. Then comes the misfortune of those who, by their passion or blindness, have rendered themselves the tools of justice, namely, Lear and Gloster; and upon these the effort of compassion is directed. As for the wicked personages, we do not witness their sufferings; the sight of their misfortune would be disturbed by the remembrance of their criminality; they can have no punishment but death.

Of the five personages subjected to the action of misfortune, Cordelia, a heavenly figure, hovers almost invisible and half-veiled over the composition, which she fills with her presence, although she is almost always absent from it. She suffers, but never complains, never defends herself: she acts, but her action is manifested only by its results; serene regarding her own fate, reserved and restrained even in her most legitimate Feelings, she passes and disappears like a denizen of a better world, who has traversed this world of ours without experiencing any mere earthly emotion.

Kent and Edgar each have a very decided physiognomy; the first of them is, like Cordelia, a victim to his duty; the second interests us at first only by his innocence. Having entered upon misfortune at the same time, so to speak, that he entered into life, and equally new to both conditions, Edgar gradually develops his faculties, learns their character at once, and discovers within himself, as need requires, the qualities with which he is gifted; in proportion as he advances, his duties, and his difficulties, and his importance increase; he grows up and becomes a man, but at the same time he learns how costly is this growth; and he finally discovers, when bearing it with nobleness and courage, the whole weight of that burden which he had hitherto borne almost with gaiety. Kent, on the contrary, a wise and firm old man, has known all, and foreseen all, from the very outset; as soon as he enters upon action, his march is determined and his object defined. He is not, like Edgar, urged by necessity, or met by chance; his will determines his conduct; nothing can change or disturb it; and the aspect of the misfortune to which he devotes himself, scarcely wrings from him an exclamation of grief or pain.

Lear and Gloster, in an analogous situation, receive from it an impression which corresponds to their different characters. Lear, impetuous and irritable, spoilt by power and by the habit and need of admiration, rebels both against his position and against his own conviction; he cannot believe in what he knows; his reason offers no resistance; and he becomes mad. Gloster, naturally weak, yields to his misery, and is equally incapable of resistance to his joy; he dies on recognising Edgar. If Cordelia were alive, Lear would still find strength to live; but he breaks down by the effort of his grief. . . . □

(Guizot, pp. 217–21)

From Victor Hugo, *William Shakespeare* (1864)

[Victor Hugo, like Coleridge, possesses a sense of the many levels upon which *King Lear* is constructed. In a paragraph not reproduced here, Hugo compares the play to the Giralda of Seville: both are, in his view, artistic artifices in which every part coheres in the whole, and in which form, in Schlegel's term, 'unfolds itself from within'. Hugo is perhaps most interesting in his treatment of Cordelia, and his remarks upon the way in which the play represents a kind of inverse maternity might fruitfully be juxtaposed with several late twentieth-century feminist treatments of the text, such as, for instance, Coppélia Kahn's (see Chapter Five).]

■ Lear is the occasion for Cordelia. Maternity of the daughter toward the father. Profound subject! A maternity venerable among all other maternities, so admirably translated by the legend of that Roman girl who in the depth of a prison nurses her old father. The young breast near the white beard: there is no holier sight! Such a filial breast is Cordelia!

Once this figure dreamed of and found, Shakespeare created his drama. Where should he put this consoling vision? In an obscure age. Shakespeare has taken the year of the world 3105, the time when Joash was king of Judah, Aganippus king of France, and Leir king of England. The whole earth was at that time mysterious. Picture to yourself that epoch. The temple of Jerusalem is still quite new; the gardens of Semiramis, constructed nine hundred years before, are beginning to crumble; . . . [Here follows a very long list of the people and events who have only just, or not yet, come into being at the time in which Hugo imagines *Lear* to be set.] The Picts and the Celts (the Scotch and the English) are tattooed. A redskin of the present day gives a vague idea of an Englishman then. It is this twilight that Shakespeare has chosen – a long, dreamy night in which the inventor is free to put anything he likes: this King Lear, and then a king of France, a duke of Burgundy, a duke of Cornwall, a duke of Albany, an earl of Kent, and an earl of Gloucester. What matters your history to him who has humanity? Besides, he has with him the legend, which is also a kind of science, and as true as history, perhaps, although from another point of view. Shakespeare . . . has every right to believe in King Lear and to create Cordelia. This site adopted, the place for the scene marked out, the foundation laid deep, he takes all in hand and builds his work – unheard-of edifice. He takes tyranny, of which at a later period he will make weakness – Lear; he takes treason – Edmund; he takes devotion – Kent; he takes Ingratitude, which begins with a caress, and he gives to this monster two heads – Goneril . . . and Regan . . .; he takes paternity; he takes royalty; he takes feudality; he takes ambition; he takes madness, which he divides, and he places face to face three madmen – the king's buffoon, madman by trade; Edgar of Gloucester, mad for prudence's sake; the king, mad through misery. It is at the summit of this tragic pile that he sets the bending form of Cordelia. . . .

The father is the pretext for the daughter. That admirable human creature, Lear, serves, as a support to this ineffable divine creation, Cordelia. All that chaos of crimes, vices, manias, and miseries, finds its justification in this shining vision of virtue. Shakespeare, bearing Cordelia in his brain, in creating this tragedy was like a god who, having an Aurora to establish, should make a world to put her in.

And what a figure is that father! What a caryatid! It is man stooping. He does nothing but shift his burdens for others that are heavier. The more the old man becomes enfeebled, the more his load augments. He lives under an over-burden. He bears at first power, then ingratitude, then isolation, then despair, then hunger and thirst, then madness, then all Nature. Clouds overcast him, forests heap their shadow upon him, the hurricane swoops down upon the nape of his neck, the tempest makes his mantle heavy as lead, the rain weighs upon his shoulders, he walks bent and haggard as if he had the two knees of Night upon his back. Dismayed and yet colossal, he flings to the winds and to the hail this epic cry: 'Why do ye hate me, tempests? Why do ye persecute me? *Ye are not my daughters*'.[18] And then all is over; the light is extinguished; Reason loses courage, and leaves him; Lear is in his dotage. This old man, being childish, requires a mother. His daughter appears, his only daughter, Cordelia. For the two others, Regan and Goneril, are no longer his daughters – save so far as to entitle them to the name of parricides.

Cordelia approaches – 'Sir, do you know me?' 'You are a spirit, I know', replies the old man, with the sublime clairvoyance of frenzy. From this moment the filial nursing begins. Cordelia applies herself to nursing this old despairing soul, dying of inanition in hatred. Cordelia nourishes Lear with love, and his courage revives: she nourishes him with respect, and the smile returns; she nourishes him with hope, and confidence is restored; she nourishes him with wisdom, and reason awakens. Lear, convalescent, rises again, and step by step returns again to life; the child becomes again an old man, the old man becomes a man again. And behold him happy, this wretched one! It is upon this expansion of happiness that the catastrophe is hurled down. Alas! there are traitors, there are perjurers, there are murderers. Cordelia dies. Nothing more heart-rending than this. The old man is stunned; he no longer understands anything; and, embracing her corpse, he expires. He dies upon his daughter's breast. He is saved from the supreme despair of remaining behind her among the living, a poor shadow, to feel the place in his heart empty, and to seek for his soul, carried away by that sweet being who is departed. O God! those whom Thou lovest Thou takest away.

To live after the flight of the angel; to be the father orphaned of his child; to be the eye that no longer has light; to be the deadened heart that knows no more joy; from time to time to stretch the hands into obscurity and try to reclasp a being who was there (where, then, can she be?); to feel himself forgotten in that departure; to have lost all reason for being here below; to be henceforth a man who goes to and fro before a sepulchre, not received, not admitted – this is indeed a gloomy destiny. Thou hast done well, poet, to kill this old man. □

(Hugo, pp. 189–93)

CHAPTER THREE

Realism

Introduction

WRITTEN IN 1838, the longer extract with which I start this chapter is, broadly speaking, anachronistic to it, since the bulk of the material covered in this section of the book was produced around the turn of the century. But much as academics would sometimes wish them to be, shifts in thinking are rarely, if ever, tied to an exactness of chronology, and the seeds of what is to come can generally be found in what went before. The extract that follows is also out of place for another reason, in that it concerns, once again, Tate's *Lear* (which by now, probably, we had hoped to forget) and thus might have been placed more appropriately at the beginning of the last chapter. It certainly would have been better placed there if a narrative of Tate's *Lear* was the only story this book was trying to tell. But there's more than one strand in the history of the reception of *King Lear*, and the reasons for my decision to reprint this extract at this point in the book will, I hope, shortly become evident.

From Charles Dickens, *The Restoration of Shakespeare's 'Lear' to the stage* (1838)

■ . . . The last of [Mr Macready's] . . . efforts to vindicate the higher objects and uses of the drama has proved the most brilliant and the most successful.[1] He has restored to the stage Shakespeare's true *Lear*, banished from it, by impudent ignorance, for upwards of a hundred and fifty years.

A person of the name of Boteler has the infamous repute of having recommended to a notorious poet-laureate, Mr Nahum Tate, the 'new modelling' of *Lear*. 'I found the whole,' quoth Mr. Tate, addressing the aforesaid Boteler in his dedication, 'to answer your account of it; a heap of jewels unstrung and unpolished, yet so dazzling in their disorder, that I soon perceived I had seized a treasure.' And accordingly to work set Nahum very busily indeed: strung the jewels and polished them with a vengeance; omitted the grandest things, the *Fool* among them; polished all that remained into commonplace; interlarded love-scenes; sent *Cordelia* into a comfortable cave with her lover, to dry her clothes and get warm, while her distracted and homeless old father was still left wandering without, amid all the pelting of the pitiless storm; and finally, rewarded the poor old man in his turn, and repaid him for all his suffering, by giving him back again his gilt robes and tinsel sceptre!

... Mr. Tate['s] ... disgusting version ... was adopted successively by Boheme, Quin, Booth, Barry, Garrick, Henderson, Kemble, Kean. Mr. Macready has now, to his lasting honour, restored the text of Shakespeare, and we shall be glad to hear of the actor foolhardy enough to attempt another restoration of the text of Mr. Tate! Mr. Macready's success has banished that disgrace from the stage for ever.

The *Fool* in the tragedy of *Lear* is one of the most wonderful creations of Shakespeare's genius. The picture of his quick and pregnant sarcasm, of his loving devotion, of his acute sensibility, of his despairing mirth, of his heartbroken silence – contrasted with the rigid sublimity of *Lear's* suffering, with the huge desolation of *Lear's* sorrow, with the vast and outraged image of *Lear's* madness – is the noblest thought that ever entered into the heart and mind of man. Nor is it a noble thought alone. Three crowded houses in Covent Garden Theatre have now proved by something better than even the deepest attention that it is for action, for representation; that it is necessary to an audience as tears are to an overcharged heart; and necessary to *Lear* himself as the recollections of his kingdom, or as the worn and faded garments of his power.... Shakespeare would have as soon consented to the banishment of *Lear* from the tragedy as to the banishment of his *Fool*. We may fancy him, while planning his immortal work, feeling suddenly, with an instinct of divinest genius, that its gigantic sorrows could never be presented on the stage without a suffering too frightful, a sublimity too remote, a grandeur too terrible – unless relieved by quiet pathos, and in some way brought home to the apprehensions of the audience by homely and familiar illustration. At such a moment that *Fool* rose to his mind, and not till then could he have contemplated his marvellous work in the greatness and beauty of its final completion.

The *Fool* in *Lear* is the solitary instance of such a character, in all the writings of Shakespeare, being identified with the pathos and passion of the scene. He is interwoven with *Lear*, he is the link that still associates him with *Cordelia's* love, and the presence of the regal estate he has surrendered. The rage of the wolf *Goneril* is first stirred by a report that her favourite gentleman had been struck by her father 'for chiding of his fool,' – and the first impatient questions we hear from the dethroned old man are: 'Where's my knave – my fool? Go you and call my fool hither.' – 'Where's my fool? Ho! I think the world's asleep.' – 'But where's my fool? I have not seen him these two days.' – 'Go you and call hither my fool,' – all which prepare us for that affecting answer stammered forth at last by the knight in attendance: 'Since my young lady's going into France, sir, the fool hath much pined away.' Mr. Macready's manner of turning off at this with an expression of half impatience, half illrepressed emotion – 'No more of that, *I have noted it well*' – was inexpressibly touching. We saw him, in the secret corner of his heart, still clinging to the memory of her who was used to be his best object, the argument of his praise, balm of his age, 'most best, most dearest'. And in the same noble and affecting spirit was his manner of fondling the *Fool* when he sees him first, and asks him with earnest care, 'How now, my pretty knave? *How dost thou?* Can there be a doubt, after this, that his love for the *Fool* is associated with *Cordelia*, who had been kind to the poor boy, and for the loss of whom he pines away? And are we not even then prepared for the sublime pathos of the close, when *Lear*, bending over the dead body of all he had left to love upon the earth, connects with her the memory of that other gentle, faithful, and loving being who had passed from his side – unites, in that moment of final agony, the two hearts that had been broken in his service, and esclaims, 'And my poor fool is hanged!'

Mr. Macready's *Lear*, remarkable before for a masterly completeness of conception, is heightened by this introduction of the *Fool* to a surprising degree. It accords exactly with the view he seeks to present of *Lear's* character. The passages we have named, for instance, had even received illustration in the first scene, where something beyond the turbulent greatness or royal impatience of *Lear* had been presented – something to redeem him from his treatment of *Cordelia*. The bewildered pause after giving his 'father's heart' away – the hurry yet hesitation of his manner as he orders *France* to be called – 'Who stirs? Call *Burgundy*' – had told us at once how much consideration he needed, how much pity, of how little of himself he was indeed the master, how crushing and irrepressible was the strength of his sharp impatience. We saw no material change in his style of playing the first great scene with *Goneril*, which fills the stage with true and appalling touches of nature. In that scene he ascends indeed with the heights of *Lear's* passion; through all its changes of agony, of anger, of impatience, of turbulent assertion, of despair, and mighty grief, till on his knees, with arms upraised and head thrown back, the tremendous Curse bursts from him amid heaving and reluctant throes of suffering and anguish. The great scene of the second act had also its great passages of power and beauty: his self-persuading utterance of '*hysterias passio*' – his anxious and fearful tenderness to *Regan* – the elevated grandeur of his appeal to the heavens – his terrible suppressed efforts, his pauses, his reluctant pangs of passion, in the speech 'I will not trouble thee, my child,' – and surpassing the whole, as we think, in deep simplicity as well as agony of pathos, that noble conception of shame as he hides his face on the arm of *Goneril* and says –

> I'll go with thee;
> Thy fifty yet doth double five and twenty,
> And thou art twice her love!

The *Fool's* presence then enabled him to give an effect, unattempted before, to those little words which close the scene, when, in the effort of bewildering passion with which he strives to burst through the phalanx of amazed horrors that have closed him round, he feels that his intellect is shaking, and suddenly exclaims, 'O *Fool*! I shall go mad!' This is better than hitting the forehead and ranting out a self-reproach.

But the presence of the *Fool* in the storm-scene! The reader must witness this to judge its power and observe the deep impression with which it affects the audience. Every resource that the art of the painter and the mechanist can afford is called in aid of this scene – every illustration is thrown on it of which the great actor of *Lear* is capable, but these are nothing to that simple presence of the *Fool*! He has changed his character there. So long as hope existed he had sought by his hectic merriment and sarcasms to win *Lear* back to love and reason, but that half of his work is now over, and all that remains for him is to soothe and lessen the certainty of the worst. *Kent* asks who is with *Lear* in the storm, and is answered –

> None but the *Fool* who labours to outjest
> His heartstruck injuries!'

When all his attempts have failed, either to soothe or to outjest these injuries, he sings, in the shivering cold, about the necessity of 'going to bed at noon'. He leaves the stage to die in his youth, and we hear of him no more till we hear the sublime touch of pathos over the dead body of the hanged *Cordelia*.

The finest passage of Mr. Macready's scenes upon the heath is his remembrance of the 'poor naked wretches,' wherein a new world seems indeed to have broken upon his mind. Other parts of these scenes wanted more of tumultuous extravagance, more of a preter-natural cast of wildness. We should always be made to feel something beyond physical distress predominant here. His colloquy with *Mad Tom*, however, was touching in the last degree, and so were the two last scenes, the recognition of *Cordelia* and the death, which elicited from the audience the truest and best of all tributes to their beauty and pathos. Mr. Macready's representation of the father at the end, broken down to his last despairing struggle, his heart swelling gradually upwards till it bursts in its closing sigh, completed the only perfect picture that we have had of *Lear* since the age of Betterton.[2] □

Charles Dickens' account of the reinstatement of Shakespeare's *King Lear* on the English stage is interesting for a number of reasons (not least because in his attack on Tate's *Lear* he appears to be suggesting that Tate was primarily at fault not in changing tragedy into melodrama, but in transforming it into romance: in his recapitulation of Tate's *Lear*, he seems here to be accusing Tate of turning *King Lear* into *The Tempest*[3]). For our immediate purposes, the significance of Dickens' account of the 'new' *King Lear* stems from his reading of the Fool. As we have seen in the preceding chapter, the Romantics had already paid attention to the role of the Fool in *Lear*. Unlike the generations who preceded them, who encountered the text either in Tate's version in the theatres, or in reading it under the influence of Neo-Classical aesthetic prescriptions (see Chapter One), the Romantics, in reading the text as poetry – as well as in reading it *per se* – perceived that the role of the Fool is intrinsic to the greater meaning of the play, and could not be cut without changing that meaning. Dickens, seeing the play performed for the first time with the Fool reinstated, obviously shares that perception.

Yet Dickens' reading of the Fool differs from the Romantics' in some very important ways. The Romantics tended to read the Fool as a formal device. They celebrated his centrality to the play, and sometimes idealised him: Schlegel, for instance, calls him 'the good-hearted fool', and refers to him as the voice of reason clothed in motley. But by and large, they saw his role as a formal one, reading his importance in terms of his embodiment of the juxtaposition of comedy with tragedy, and arguing that his presence, insofar as it is comic, intensifies the pathos of the tragedy. Dickens also sees the Fool's 'loving devotion', 'acute sensibility', 'despairing mirth' and 'heartbroken silence' as important in the contrast that they form to Lear's terrible suffering: they are, for Dickens, 'a relief by quiet pathos'. But at the same time, in his very invocation of these qualities, Dickens indicates that he sees the Fool as a character: not, in other words, as a primarily formal device. And this interest in character is communicated also, and paradoxically, in Dickens' emphasis on the way in which the revival of the Fool affects the 'view' that Macready 'seeks to present of Lear's character'. It is obvious that Dickens approves of this 'view'. But it is equally obvious that Dickens' approval issues out of a conception that part of the interest of the character of Lear lies in its susceptibility to differing interpretations.

It is not that Dickens' Romantic peers were uninterested in questions of character. But for them, character was a subordinate aspect of the play: 'characterization', says Schlegel, 'is merely one ingredient of the dramatic art, and not dramatic poetry itself. It would be improper in the extreme, if the poet were to draw our attention to superfluous traits of character, at a time when it ought to be his endeavour to produce other impressions'. Thus for Schlegel a critical concern with character is legitimate when brought to bear, say, on the central figure of a drama, but misguided when it focuses on minor figures, whose presence in the drama is intended by the dramatist to fulfil quite other functions. In certain circumstances, maintains Schlegel, 'the characteristical necessarily falls into the background':

■ many of [Shakespeare's] figures . . . are like secondary persons in a public procession, to whose physiognomy we seldom pay much attention; their only importance is derived from . . . the duty in which they are engaged. □

(Schlegel, pp. 363–4)

The Fool, of course, is not a 'minor' figure. But is he a 'character' in the way that Dickens here suggests that he is? It is perhaps in part because Dickens sees him as a character that he is so eager to negate the odd way in which Shakespeare, having made such extensive use of the Fool throughout the first three acts of the play, seems then to lose sight of him in the last two. Others have also had difficulties with this aspect of *King Lear*. Swinburne, for instance, shared Dickens' perception of the Fool's affection for Cordelia, but unlike Dickens rejected the comforting thought that the Fool's memory is recuperated in the play's closing lines, remarking in the course of a (very moving) examination of another of Shakespeare's 'lost' characters that:

■ at the very end [of *The Winter's Tale*] . . . it may be that we remember [the dead boy Mamillius] all the better because the father whose jealousy killed him and the mother for love of whom he died would seem to have forgotten the little brave sweet spirit with all its truth of love and tender sense of shame as perfectly and unpardonably as Shakespeare himself at the close of *King Lear* would seem to have forgotten one who never had forgotten Cordelia. □

Algernon Charles Swinburne, *A Study of Shakespeare*[4] (1880)

It is probably not coincidental that Dickens reads the Fool as a character. For the increasing concern with character in nineteenth-century interpretations of *King Lear* was coexistent with the emerging status of the novel as England's hegemonic literary form. One of the major foci of the nineteenth-century novel, in other words, is the interiority not only of its protagonists, but also of its minor characters: it is not, then, surprising that a concern with character should preoccupy Dickens in his experience of *King Lear* (and in particular, of this particular production of *King Lear*), nor that an interest in character should increasingly preoccupy critics who wrote on Shakespearean drama.[5] Nor, perhaps, given Dickens' personal commitment to social reform, should it surprise us that he singles out for especial praise the 'scenes upon the heath'. For Dickens, evidently, *King Lear* is not only a play about character, but also a play about the social world, a world in which 'houseless poverty' and 'unfed sides' lie just beyond the boundaries of your castle gate, and in which the divisions between rich and poor are very great indeed. For Dickens, as well as for Macready, it is in the 'remembrance of the "poor naked wretches"' that 'a new world seems indeed to have broken upon [Lear's] mind.'

Sustained attention to *King Lear*'s representation of the social world was not to become a major critical concern for more than a century and a half after Dickens wrote this review. But the turn of the nineteenth century did see a few readers of *King Lear* feeling, as had Dickens, that the play's interest in its protagonist is embedded in a framework of social critique. The two sections of this chapter will try to address both of these critical reactions to *King Lear*: the concern with character on the one hand, and some responses to the politics of the play on the other.

Part One: Character Criticism and the Redemption of King Lear: Jameson's *Characteristics of Women* and A.C. Bradley's *Shakespearean Tragedy*

Were he to walk the English earth at the beginning of the twentieth century, the ghost of Augustus William Schlegel might, one suspects, have felt a little disappointed at the current state of Shakespeare criticism. For in the wake of the publication of A.C. Bradley's *Shakespearean Tragedy* (1904), Schlegel's warning about the dangers of paying too much attention to issues of character was buried in an avalanche of critical interest in Shakespeare's characterisation, which extended to the most minor of Shakespeare's creations: even the Oswalds of his texts were to find themselves the subject of psychological scrutiny. 'Every Frenchman who has sucked in his Boileau with his mother's milk,' Schlegel had remarked, 'considers himself a born champion of the Dramatic unities' (Schlegel, p. 237); every English student who similarly imbibed of his or her Bradley, it seemed, automatically became a champion of the view that psychological complexity was, exclusively, what Shakespeare's plays were all about. Bradley's influence was, and is still, extraordinarily tenacious: his legacy persists, as any college English lecturer will attest, in the inordinate number of student essays which read Shakespearean tragedy exclusively through the lens of the 'fatal flaws'[6] of its principal characters.

Character criticism, of course, was not an invention of A.C. Bradley's. We have already seen how some of the seeds of Bradley's account of Shakespearean tragedy were sown by Guizot, and other critics writing at the time of the Romantics were equally intrigued by the characters of Shakespeare's plays. One of the most notable of these was Anna Jameson (otherwise known as 'Mrs Jameson'), whose *Shakespeare's Heroines* was first published in 1832 (and, significantly, reissued in 1905). It is actually somewhat unjust to invoke Anna Jameson in the same breath as A.C. Bradley, for her approach to Shakespeare's characters differs widely from Bradley's (as well as from her better-known Romantic peers) in the sense that it issues out of a profound concern with the social. Jameson was an early feminist, writing at a time when feminist voices were as ridiculed as they were rare, as is witnessed by the introduction to her volume, in which the putative female author 'Alda' tries, for thirty pages, to gain the attention of her (very patronising) male interlocutor 'Medon'. In the course of these pages 'Alda' has stated that her intention is not to hold forth on the virtues of women, but to illustrate, through her readings of Shakespeare's heroines, that 'the [present] condition of women in society . . . is false in itself, and injurious to them – that the [present] education of women . . . is founded in mistaken principles, and . . . increase[s] fearfully the . . . misery . . . in both sexes'.[7] Jameson, almost uniquely in her time (and for more than a century afterwards) thus reads her Shakespeare through an explicit examination of her own politics; countering Medon's claim that Shakespeare's women are dramatically inferior to his men, for example, 'Alda' remarks:

■ If [you] . . . mean that Shakspeare's women are inferior in power to his men, I grant it at once; for in Shakspeare the male and female characters bear . . . the same relation to each other that they do in . . . in society; they are not equal in prominence or in power; they are subordinate throughout. . . . [O]ur limited sphere of action, consequently of experience – the habits of self-control rendering the outward distinctions of character and passion less . . . strong – all this we see in Shakspeare as in nature . . . □

(Jameson, p. 12)

Jameson's grasp on the degree to which it is desirable for women to rebel against their lot has its limits (at one point she refers to having seen a painting by Artemisia Gentileschi,[8] which she 'looked at once, but once, and wished then, as I do now, for the privilege of burning it to ashes' (Jameson, p. 31, n.1). Her reading of Cordelia, extracts of which follow, does not, as twentieth-century feminist criticism would do, situate either the actions or the character of Cordelia within a context of gendered relations of power. Rather, it exhibits Jameson's beliefs that Shakespeare's characters 'combine history and real life [and] . . . are complete individuals,' representing, moreover, 'character in its essential truth, not modified by . . . customs, by fashion, by situation'. She also wants to read them as role models for how women ought to be were the world a politically more perfect one; in Cordelia she finds that role model *par excellence*:

From Anna Jameson, *Shakespeare's Heroines* (1832).

■ THERE is in the beauty of Cordelia's character an effect too sacred for words, and almost too deep for tears; within her heart is a fathomless well of purest affection, but its waters sleep in silence and obscurity, never failing in their depth and never overflowing in their fulness. Everything in her seems to lie beyond our view, and affects us in a manner which we feel rather than perceive. The character appears to have no surface, no salient points upon which the fancy can readily seize: there is little external development of intellect, less of passion, and still less of imagination. It is completely made out in the course of a few scenes, and we are surprised to find that in those few scenes there is matter for a life of reflection, and materials enough for twenty heroines. If 'Lear' be the grandest of Shakspeare's tragedies, Cordelia . . . , as a human being governed by the purest and holiest . . . motives, the most refined from all dross of selfishness and passion, approaches near to perfection; and, in her adaptation as a dramatic personage to a determinate plan of action, may be pronounced altogether perfect. The character, to speak of it critically as a poetical conception, is not, however, to be comprehended at once, or easily; and in the same manner Cordelia, as a woman, is one whom we must have loved before we could have known her, and known her long before we could have known her truly.

. . . General acknowledgment of her excellence [cannot] . . . satisfy those who have studied the character . . . Amid the . . . convulsions of . . . suffering, and pictures of moral and physical wretchedness . . . , the tender influence of Cordelia, like that of a celestial visitant, is felt and acknowledged without being quite understood. . . . [T]he impression it leaves is beautiful and deep, but vague. Speak of Cordelia to a critic . . . all agree in the beauty of the portrait . . . ; but when we come to details, I have heard more . . . opposite opinions relative to her than any other of Shakspeare's characters – a proof . . . that, from the simplicity with which the character is dramatically treated, and the small space it occupies, few are aware of its internal power or its wonderful depth of purpose.

It appears to me that the whole character rests upon the two sublimest principles of human action – the love of truth and the sense of duty; but these, when they stand alone . . . are apt to strike us as severe and cold. Shakspeare has, therefore, wreathed them round with the dearest attributes of our feminine nature, the power of feeling and inspiring affection. The first part of the play shows us how Cordelia is loved, the second part how she can love. To her father she is the object of a secret preference; . . . he . . . 'thought to set his rest on her kind nursery'. . . . The faithful . . . Kent is ready to brave death . . . in her defence; and . . . a further impression of her benign sweetness is conveyed . . . when we are told that 'since the Lady Cordelia went to France, her father's poor fool had much pined away'. . . . She takes up arms, 'not for ambition, but a dear father's right'. In her speech, after her defeat, we have a calm fortitude and elevation of soul, arising from the consciousness of duty, and lifting her above all consideration of self. . . . She thinks and fears only for her father . . . To complete the picture, her very voice is characteristic, 'ever soft, gentle, and low; an excellent thing in woman'.

. . . What is it, then, which lends to Cordelia that . . . truth of character which distinguishes her from every other human being? It is a natural reserve, a tardiness of disposition . . . ; a . . . veiled shyness thrown over all her emotions, her language and her manner, making the outward demonstration invariably fall short of what we know to be the feeling within. . . .

When [Lear] says to his daughters, 'I gave ye all!' we feel that he requires all in return, with a jealous, restless, exacting affection which defeats its own wishes. How many such are there in the world! How many to sympathize with [him] . . . when he shrinks . . . from Cordelia's . . . reply! . . . [This reply] is perfectly natural. . . . Is it not obvious that . . . [Cordelia] must be disgusted with [her sisters'] . . . 'plaited cunning'; and would retire from all competition with what she so disdains and abhors – even into the opposite extreme? . . . For the very expressions of Lear . . . are enough to strike dumb for ever a generous, delicate, but shy disposition, . . . by holding out a bribe for professions.

If Cordelia were not thus portrayed, this deliberate coolness would strike us as verging on harshness or obstinacy; but it is beautifully represented as . . . the necessary result of feelings habitually, if not naturally, repressed . . .

'*Tous les sentimens naturels ont leur pudeur*' was a *viva voce* observation of Madame de Staël, when disgusted by the sentimental affection of her imitators. This 'pudeur,' carried to an excess, appears to me the peculiar characteristic of Cordelia. . . .

. . . Just as our sense of human misery and wickedness . . . becomes nearly intolerable . . . then, like a redeeming angel, [Cordelia] descends to mingle in the scene . . . relieving the impressions of pain and terror by those of admiration and a tender pleasure. For the catastrophe, it is indeed terrible! . . . When Lear enters with Cordelia dead in his arms, compassion and awe so seize on all our faculties, that we are left only to silence and to tears. But if I might judge from my own sensations, the catastrophe of Lear is not so overwhelming as the catastrophe of Othello. We do not turn away with the same feeling of absolute un-mitigated despair. Cordelia is a saint ready prepared for heaven – our earth is not good enough for her; and Lear! O who, after sufferings and tortures such as his, would wish to see his life prolonged? What! replace a sceptre in that shaking hand? – a crown upon that old grey head, . . . O never, never ! . . . [Tate] has converted the seraph-like Cordelia into a puling love heroine, and sent her off with drums and colours flying – to be married to Edgar. Now anything more absurd, more discordant with all our previous impressions, and with the characters unfolded to us, can hardly be imagined. . . .

Cordelia reminds us of . . . one of the Madonnas in the old Italian pictures, . . . and as that heavenly form is connected with our human sympathies only by the expression of maternal tenderness or maternal sorrow, even so Cordelia would be almost too angelic, were she not linked to our earthly feelings, bound to our very hearts, by her filial love, her wrongs, her sufferings and her tears. □

(Jameson, pp. 203–18)

There were, then, signs of a move towards seeing character as central to the understanding of Shakespeare's tragedies well before Bradley produced his *Shakespearean Tragedy*. Indeed, as we shall see, Bradley was some-thing of a critical magpie. He pilfers from Jameson's account in his own discussion of Cordelia, and his theory of tragedy had its roots not only in Guizot's Romanticism, but also, amongst others, in Aristotle, and in Hegel.

According to Bradley, Shakespearean tragedy is characterised by its observance of certain key principles. 'It is pre-eminently', he says, 'the story of one person, the "hero" . . . [and its] story . . . leads up to, and includes, the *death* of the hero. . . . It is . . . essentially a tale of suffering and calamity conducting to death.'[9] This suffering is 'exceptional', 'un-expected, and contrasted with previous happiness or glory' (Bradley, p. 8); it involves a 'total reverse of fortune' the subject of which is always a person of high degree (Bradley, p. 9) whose 'fate affects the welfare of a whole nation or empire' (Bradley, p. 10). Now so far, this is a broadly Aristotelian conception of tragedy, including, for example, notions of *peripeteia* (reversal of fortune), and a conception of the tragic hero as being of high estate, removed, at least to a degree, from us ordinary mortals. Where Bradley moves away from Aristotle is in his conception of tragic action. 'The calamities of tragedy,' says Bradley,

■ do not simply happen, nor are they sent; they proceed mainly from actions, and those the actions of men.
　　We see a number of human beings placed in certain circumstances; and we see, arising from the co-operation of their characters in these circumstances, certain actions. These actions beget others . . . until this series of inter-connected deeds leads by an apparently inevitable sequence to a catastrophe. The effect of [this] . . . is to make us regard the sufferings . . . and the catastrophe . . . not only or chiefly as something which happens to the persons concerned, but equally as something which is caused by them. This at least may be said of the principal persons, and, among them, of the hero, who always contributes . . . to the disaster in which he perishes. □

(Bradley, pp. 11–12)

Now this still sounds very like Aristotle, who, like Bradley, insisted upon the centrality of the protagonist's action in bringing about the catastrophe: for Aristotle, the protagonist commits a tragic error – *hamartia* – which precipitates the tragic events. But in Bradley's adoption of this essentially Aristotelian idea, he transforms it into something quite different. For Bradley,

■ The 'story' or 'action' of a Shakespearean tragedy does not consist . . . solely of human . . . deeds; but these deeds are the predominant factor. And these deeds are, for the most part, actions in the full sense of the word; not things done "tween asleep and wake,' but acts or omissions thoroughly expressive of the doer – characteristic deeds. The centre of the tragedy, therefore, may be said . . . to lie in action issuing from character, or in character issuing in action. □

(Bradley, p. 12)

'The dictum that, with Shakespeare, "character is destiny"', Bradley goes on later, 'is the exaggeration of a vital truth' (Bradley, p. 13).
　　What Bradley does, then, is to transform Aristotle's 'tragic error', which need have nothing to do with character at all, into a 'tragic trait' which has nothing to do with anything else. In other words, Bradley both psychologises Aristotle, and also moralises him, for the doer, in Bradley's account, must to some degree be conscious of his deed. This is rather different from Aristotle's account, since an 'error' need not issue from personality, nor need it signify an ethical transgression (a mistake can be 'just' a mistake, however dire its consequences may be).[10] And the degree to which Bradley departs from Aristotle becomes clearer as

Bradley explains what, in his view, constitutes conflict in Shakespearean tragedy. 'Who are the combatants in this conflict?' he asks (Bradley, p. 16):

■ No doubt most of the characters in . . . *King Lear* . . . can be arranged in opposed groups; and no doubt there is a conflict; and yet it seems misleading to describe this conflict as one *between these groups* . . . .

    The truth is, that the type of tragedy in which the hero opposes to a hostile force an undivided soul, is not the Shakespearean type. The souls of those who contend with the hero may be thus undivided; they generally are; but, as a rule, the hero . . . is . . . torn by an inward struggle. . . . □

(Bradley, pp. 17–18)

Once again, Bradley is not original here; although he denies it, the germs of this account lie, it seems to me, partly in Hegel, who had remarked in *The Philosophy of Fine Art* (1836–1838) that:

■ . . . in modern tragedy . . . [men act] in the interest of the inner experience of their . . . emotion, or the peculiar qualities of their personality . . . [T]he conflict . . . essentially abides within the *character* itself, to which the individuals concerned in their passion give effect . . . for the simple reasons that they are the kind of men they are. . . .

    In modern tragedy we meet characters . . . [who] are essentially under the sway of two opposed passions, which make them fluctuate from one resolve or kind of deed to another. . .

    [Sometimes] the change in spiritual condition of the entire man itself appears as a consequence of . . . its own kind of self-detachment, so that only that is developed . . . which essentially . . . lay in the character. As an example, we find in Shakespeare's *Lear* that the original folly of the old man is intensified to the point of blindness much in the same way that Gloucester's spiritual blindness is converted into actual physical blindness, in which for the first time his eyes are opened to the true distinction in the love he entertains for his two sons. . . . It is . . . Shakespeare who . . . supplies us with the finest examples of essentially stable and consequential characters, who go to their doom precisely in virtue of this tenacious hold upon themselves and their ends. . . . [C]arried onward by the formal necessity of their personality, they suffer themselves to be involved in their acts by the coil of external circumstances, or they plunge blindly therein and maintain themselves there by sheer force of will, even where all that they do is merely done because they are impelled to assert themselves against others, or because they have simply come to the particular point they have reached. The rise of insurgent passion, one essentially consonant with a certain type of character, . . . this . . . process of a great soul, with all the intimate traits of its evolution, this picture of its self-destructive conflict with circumstances, human and objective conditions and results, is the main content of some of Shakespeare's most interesting tragedies.[11] □

Bradley adopts what Hegel calls 'this tenacious hold upon themselves and their ends' in his description of the main aspects of Shakespeare's tragic heroes, in almost all of whom, he maintains,

■ we observe a marked one-sidedness, a predisposition in some particular direction; a fatal tendency to identify the whole being with one interest, object, passion, or habit of mind. This . . . is, for Shakespeare, the fundamental tragic trait. □

(Bradley, p. 22)

This view of Shakespearean tragedy as centred in the individual inhabited other critics that Bradley was reading when he wrote *Shakespearean Tragedy*: Gervinus, for instance, had remarked earlier that 'fate in Shakespeare is nothing else than man's own nature'.[12] But Gervinus had excepted *King Lear* from this observation, arguing that in the play Shakespeare 'takes a much wider subject: . . . whole ages and races are, as it were, represented' (Gervinus, p. 616). To some degree, Bradley pilfers this observation as well: *Lear*'s vastness, Bradley remarks, brings with it a feeling that 'we are witnessing something universal – a conflict not so much of particular persons as of the powers of good and evil in the world' (Bradley, pp. 262–3). But Gervinus' specific exception of *King Lear* from the claim that Shakespearean tragedy issues from individual character points to the fact that he reads the play as a social tragedy. This is precisely what Bradley does not want to do. In fact, Bradley's commitment to seeing Shakespearean tragedy solely in terms of character is such that he wants to 'put aside . . . ideas of justice and merit, and speak simply of good and evil' (Bradley, p. 33).

Bradley's conception of Shakespearean tragedy as centred in a 'struggle in the hero's soul', however, leads him into difficulties with *King Lear*. For as Schlegel had remarked *King Lear* does not revolve around action, but around suffering: Lear acts at the beginning of the drama, but is thereafter merely the passive object of the actions of others. This led Bradley to make some odd claims about the play (most notably, that Goneril, Regan, and Edmund are its 'leading characters' (Bradley, p. 53)), and to argue that the play owned certain 'structural weaknesses' in dramatic terms, being too huge for the stage (Bradley, p. 247), and owning a double action which 'overstretches' the reader's attention (Bradley, p. 255). But Bradley's two biggest (and interconnected) problems with the play were firstly, its ending, and secondly the universality of the destruction that *King Lear* portrays. Bradley cannot bring himself to say that Shakespeare was wrong in killing off Lear and Cordelia, but he does argue that when we experience the play 'simply as a drama' our 'feelings call for [a] "happy ending"' (Bradley, p. 254). And Bradley's recognition of the magnitude of the destruction represented in the play, coupled with his insistence on seeing tragic causality in terms only of character means that he finds it disturbing in the extreme that the play apparently offers us no coherent account of any reason for this waste; no answer to the question 'Who rules the world?' (Bradley, p. 271). Instead, as Bradley himself points out, the play returns time and again to conflicting statements about the governance of cruel deities and uncaring stars. This Bradley cannot bear: he cannot abide the suggestion that *King Lear* is the record of a time when contempt and loathing . . . had overmastered the poet's soul, and in despair he pronounced man's life to be simply hateful and hideous' (Bradley, p. 275). Instead, he argues, the 'keynote' of *King Lear* 'is . . . one in which pity and terror . . . are so blended with a sense of law and beauty that we feel at last, not depression and much less despair, but a consciousness of greatness in pain, and of solemnity in the mystery we cannot fathom' (Bradley, p. 279). Thus Bradley's reading of *King Lear* becomes an exercise in self-consolation, as he seeks to defend the play from Swinburne's charge (see below) that it is essentially nihilistic.

From A.C. Bradley, *Shakespearian Tragedy* (1904)

■ The position of the hero in this tragedy is in one important respect peculiar . . . When the conclusion arrives, the old King has for a long while been passive. We have long regarded him . . . almost wholly as a sufferer, hardly at all as an agent. His sufferings too have been so cruel, and our indignation against those who inflicted them has been so intense, that recollection of the wrong he did to Cordelia, to Kent, and to his realm, has been well-nigh effaced. Lastly, for nearly four Acts he has inspired in us, together with this pity, much admiration and affection. The force of his passion has made us feel that his nature was great; and his frankness and generosity, his heroic efforts to be patient, the depth of his shame and repentance, and the ecstasy of his reunion with Cordelia, have melted our very hearts. Naturally, therefore, at the close we are in some danger of forgetting that the storm which has overwhelmed him was liberated by his own deed.

Yet it is essential that Lear's contribution to the action of the drama should be remembered . . . because otherwise his fate would appear to us at best pathetic, at worst shocking, but certainly not tragic. . . . At the very beginning, it is true, we are inclined to feel merely pity. . . . The first lines tell us that Lear's mind is beginning to fail with age.

Formerly he had perceived how different were the characters of Albany and Cornwall, but now he seems either to have lost this perception or to be unwisely ignoring it. The rashness of his division of the kingdom troubles us, and we cannot but see with concern that its motive is mainly selfish. The absurdity of the pretence of making the division depend on protestations of love from his daughters, his complete blindness to the hypocrisy which is patent to us at a glance, his piteous delight in these protestations, the openness of his expressions of preference for his youngest daughter – all make us smile, but all pain us. But pity begins to give way to another feeling when we witness the precipitance, the despotism, the uncontrolled anger of his injustice to Cordelia and Kent, and the 'hideous rashness' of his persistence in dividing the kingdom after the rejection of his one dutiful child. We feel now the presence of force as well as weakness, but we feel also the presence of the tragic [hubris]. Lear, we see, is generous and unsuspicious, of an open and free nature . . . [but] is also choleric by temperament. . . . And a long life of absolute power . . . has produced in him [a] blindness to human limitations, and [a] presumptuous self-will. . . . Our consciousness that the decay of old age contributes to this condition deepens our pity . . ., but certainly does not lead us to regard the old King as irresponsible, and so to sever the tragic *nexus* which binds together his error and his calamities.

The magnitude of this first error is generally fully recognised by the reader owing to his sympathy with Cordelia . . . . But this is not so, I think, with the repetition of this error in the quarrel with Goneril. Here the daughter excites so much detestation, and the father so much sympathy, that we often fail to receive the due impression of his violence. There is not here, of course, the injustice of his rejection of Cordelia, but there is precisely the same [hubris]. This had been shown most strikingly in the first scene when, immediately upon the apparently cold words of Cordelia, 'So young, my lord, and true,' there comes this dreadful answer: [Here Bradley quotes Lear's curse of Cordelia at 1.1.105–120.] Now the dramatic effect of this passage is exactly, and doubtless intentionally, repeated in the curse pronounced against Goneril . . . Up to the moment of its utterance Goneril has done no more than to require him . . . [to reduce] his train of knights. Certainly her manner . . . in making this demand [is] . . . hateful, and probably her accusations against the knights are false; and we should expect from any father in Lear's position passionate distress and indignation. But surely the famous words which form Lear's immediate reply were meant to be nothing short of frightful: [Here Bradley quotes Lear's curse of Goneril at 1.4.272–1.4.287.] The question is not whether Goneril deserves these appalling imprecations, but what they tell us about Lear. They show that, although he has already recognised his injustice towards Cordelia, is secretly blaming himself, and is endeavouring to do better, the disposition from which his first error sprang is still unchanged. And it is precisely the disposition to give rise, in evil surroundings, to calamities dreadful but at the same time tragic because due in some measure to the person who endures them.

The perception of this connection . . . makes it impossible for us permanently to regard the world displayed in this tragedy as subject to a mere arbitrary or malicious power. It makes us feel that this world is so far at least a rational and a moral order, that there holds in it the law . . . of strict connection between act and consequence . . .

But there is another aspect of Lear's story, the influence of which modifies, in a way . . . peculiar to this tragedy, the impressions called pessimistic and even this impression of law. There is nothing more noble and beautiful in literature than Shakespeare's exposition of the effect of suffering in reviving the greatness and eliciting the sweetness of Lear's nature. The occasional recurrence, during his madness, of autocratic impatience or of desire for revenge serves only to heighten this effect, and the moments when his insanity becomes merely infinitely piteous do not weaken it. The old King who in pleading with his daughters feels so intensely his own humiliation and their horrible ingratitude, and who yet . . . constrains himself to practise a self-control and patience so many years disused; who out of old affection for his Fool, and in repentance for his injustice to the Fool's beloved mistress, tolerates incessant and cutting reminders of his own folly and wrong . . . ; who comes in his affliction to think of others first, and to seek, in tender solicitude for his poor boy, the shelter he scorns for his own bare head; who learns to feel and to pray for the miserable and houseless poor, to discern the falseness of flattery and the brutality of authority . . . ; whose sight is so purged by scalding tears that it sees at last how power and place and all things in the world are vanity except love; . . . – there is no figure, surely, in the world of poetry at once so grand, so pathetic, and so beautiful as his. Well, but Lear owes the whole of this to those sufferings which made us doubt whether life were not simply evil, and men like the flies which wanton boys torture for their sport. Should we not be at least as near the truth if we called this poem *The Redemption of King Lear*, and declared that the business of 'the gods' with him was neither to torment him, nor to teach him a 'noble anger,' but to lead him to attain through apparently hopeless failure the very end and aim of life? . . .

If to the reader, as to the bystanders, [the final] scene brings . . . unbroken pain, it is not so with Lear himself. His shattered mind passes from the first transports of hope and despair, as he bends over Cordelia's body and holds the feather to her lips, into an absolute forgetfulness of the cause of these transports. This continues so long after he can converse with Kent; becomes an almost complete vacancy; and is disturbed only to yield, as his eyes suddenly fall again on his child's corpse, to an agony which at once breaks his heart. And, finally, although he is killed by an agony of pain, the agony in which he actually dies is not one of pain but of ecstasy. Suddenly . . . he exclaims

> Do you see this? Look on her, look, her lips,
> Look there, look there!

These are the last words of Lear. He is sure, at last, that she lives: and what had he said when he was still in doubt?

> She lives! if it be so
> It is a chance which does redeem all sorrows
> That ever I have felt!

To us, perhaps, the knowledge that he is deceived may bring a culmination of pain: but if it brings *only* that, I believe we are false to Shakespeare, and it seems almost beyond question that any actor is false to the text who does not attempt to express, in Lear's last accents and gestures and look, an unbearable *joy*. □

(Bradley, pp. 280–91)

A.C. Bradley thus reads *King Lear* as a play about the progress of Lear's soul to a new kind of moral perception, and rewards Lear for his accession to this new moral knowledge by insisting that he dies happy. Cordelia's death, too, according to Bradley, is recuperable from the charge that it denotes Shakespeare's nihilism. Jameson, we have seen, accounts for Cordelia's death by seeing her as 'a saint ready prepared for heaven', too good for this earth. Bradley's phrasing is a bit happier (unlike Jameson, he doesn't make Cordelia sound like an oven-ready duck), but his point is the same: her nature, he argues, transcends any grief about her fate. What we feel about Cordelia, he claims, is 'that what happens to such a being does not matter; all that matters is that she is'. 'The more unmotivated, unmerited, senseless, monstrous, her fate,' he goes on:

■ the more do we feel that it does not concern her. The extremity of the disproportion between prosperity and goodness first shocks us, and then flashes on us the conviction that our whole attitude in . . . expecting that goodness should be prosperous is wrong; that, if only we could see things as they are, we should see that the outward [Cordelia's death] is nothing and the inward [Cordelia's soul] is all. □

(Bradley, pp. 325–6)

And if in Cordelia's death is the triumph of the moral good, in the deaths of Goneril, Regan and Edmund we see punishment of evil: *King Lear* shows us that 'the world in which evil appears seems to be at heart unfriendly to it' (Bradley, p. 304).

For Bradley, then, one of the morals that *King Lear* teaches us is the cliché that 'crime doesn't pay'. We saw in Chapter One how similar concerns with the communication of 'poetical justice' had resulted in the displacement of the original *King Lear* by Tate's version of the tale, and we noted in passing that Dickens' criticism of Tate's adaptation seems to berate him for turning *King Lear* into *The Tempest*. In this context, it is remarkable that in the conclusion of Bradley's discussion of *King Lear* he explicitly, and at some lengths, invokes Shakespeare's last play: 'like *The Tempest* Bradley concludes, *King Lear* 'seems to preach to us from end to end, "Thou must be patient," "Bear free and patient thoughts"' (Bradley, p. 330). In retrospect, we might say that to give the Neo-Classicists their due, they at least concluded that they had to adapt the play in order to find in it the crassly simplistic morals that their hearts desired, and to believe that King Lear is in the end saved from the consequences of his own actions and from the cruelty of others. It was Bradley's dubious distinction to inaugurate a tradition of reading *King Lear* (to which we will return in Chapter Four) which managed to find these things in the play itself.

Part Two: Social Criticism: Swinburne, Tolstoy and Orwell

Bradley's desire to defend *King Lear* from the imputation of nihilism was directed most explicitly at Swinburne, whose *A Study of Shakespeare* (1880) Bradley quotes at length. Indeed, one of Bradley's central claims (that we might rename the play *The Redemption of King Lear*) is itself an implicit counter to Swinburne's observation that 'requital [and] redemption are words without a meaning' in the world that *King Lear* portrays (Swinburne, p. 172). But in representing Swinburne's reading of *King Lear* as one in which only a conception of Shakespeare's nihilism is at issue, Bradley passes over in silence the context in which Swinburne's meditations on the play's darkness are lodged. Bradley's discussion of the play is conservative in the extreme: as R.A. Foakes has remarked, it 'elided [Lear's] terrible tyranny, sanctioned him as a figure representative of good, and implicitly lent approval to the kind of hierarchical society he stands for'.[13] Swinburne's ascription of nihilism, on the other hand, is embedded in a view of the play which accentuates its moments of social critique.

Swinburne was not the only voice in his time who read Shakespeare as a political writer, but he was one of few. Denton Snyder, writing in

1887, argued that the play 'reveals to us the disease of absolute authority, showing how such an authority wrecks society on the one hand, and, on the other, wrecks the monarch who exercises it'.[14] Gervinus (whose *Shakespeare Commentaries* was translated into English in 1863) remarked on the way in which the play presses outward beyond the bounds of the individuals it represents to depict 'the tragic end of a whole generation of a bloody race' (Gervinus, p. 641); he also saw the double action of the play as an indictment not only of the particular families concerned in the drama, but of families *per se*; paid some limited attention to the way in which Lear fails as a father; and drew some analogies between Lear as a father and Lear as a King, between 'the ruler both at home and abroad' (Gervinus, p. 622). And finally, George Brandes, (whose *William Shakespeare* was translated in 1898), claimed that:

■ it can scarcely have been . . . in the daytime, that [Shakespeare] conceived *King Lear*: No; it must have been on . . . one of those nights when a man, sitting at his desk at home, thinks of the wretches who are wandering in houseless poverty through the darkness, the blustering wind, and the soaking rain – when the rushing of the storm over the housetops and its howling in the chimneys sound in his ears like shrieks of agony, the wail of all the misery of earth.

For in *King Lear* . . . we feel that what we in our day know by the awkward name of the social problem, in other words, the problem of extreme wretchedness and want, existed already for Shakespeare. . . .[15] □

Brandes concludes his examination of the play by pointing to the 'titanic' nature of the tragedy:

■ The loss of a Cordelia – that is the great catastrophe. We all lose, or live under the dread of losing, our Cordelia. The loss of the dearest and the best, of that which alone makes life worth living – that is the tragedy of life. Hence the question: Is this the end of the world? Yes, it is. Each of us has only his world, and lives with the threat of its destruction hanging over him. And in the year 1606 Shakespeare was in no mood to write other than dramas on the doom of worlds.

For the end of all things seems to have come when we see the ruin of the moral world – when he who is . . . noble . . . like Lear is rewarded with ingratitude and hate; when he who is honest . . . like Kent is punished with dishonour; when he who is merciful like Gloucester . . . has the loss of his eyes for his reward; when he who is . . . faithful like Edgar must wander about in the semblance of a maniac, . . . when, finally, she who is the living emblem of womanly dignity and of filial tenderness towards an old father who has become as it were her child – when she meets her death before his eyes at the hands of assassins! What avails it that the guilty slaughter and poison each other afterwards? None the less is this the titanic tragedy of human life; there rings forth from it a chorus of passionate, jeering, wildly yearning, and desperately wailing voices.

Sitting by his fire at night, Shakespeare heard them in the roar of the storm against the window-pane, in the howling of the wind in the chimneys – heard all these terrible voices contrapuntally inwoven one with another as in a fugue, and heard in them the torture-shriek of suffering humanity. □

(Brandes, p. 141)

So Swinburne was not the only voice in the wilderness; although for Bradley he was the loudest. In the account against which Bradley is writing, an extract from which we now reprint, Swinburne pursues a comparison first made by Shelley between King Lear and Aeschylean drama.[16] Like Brandes, Swinburne sees the tragedy of Lear as 'titanic' in its conception; like Brandes, he sees in the play a protest against the social misery to which it occasionally, but significantly, alludes. But Swinburne is almost alone in his perception that to idealise Cordelia, as all critics from the Romantics on, had done, was to do her no favours.

From Algernon Charles Swinburne, *A Study of Shakespeare* (1880)

■ [*King Lear*] is by far the most Æschylean of [Shakespeare's] works; the most elemental and primæval, the most oceanic and Titanic in conception. . . .

But in one main point it differs radically from the . . . spirit of Æschylus. Its fatalism is of a darker and harder nature. . . . To [Aeschylus' protagonists the world was] . . . bitter . . . yet in the not utterly infinite . . . distance we see beyond them the promise of the morning on which mystery and justice shall be made one; when righteousness and omnipotence at last shall kiss each other. But on the horizon of Shakespeare's tragic fatalism we see no such twilight of atonement, such pledge of reconciliation as this. Requital, redemption, amends, equity, explanation, pity and mercy, are words without a meaning here.

As flies to wanton boys are we to the gods;
They kill us for their sport.

Here is no need of the Eumenides, children of Night everlasting; for here is very Night herself.

The words just cited are not casual or episodical; they strike the keynote of the whole poem, lay the keystone of the whole arch of thought. There is no contest of conflicting forces, no judgment so much as by casting of lots: far less is there any light of heavenly harmony or of heavenly wisdom . . . We have heard much and often from theologians of the light of revelation: and some such thing indeed we find in Æschylus: but the darkness of revelation is here.

For in this the most terrible work of human genius it is with the very springs and sources of nature that her student has set himself to deal. The veil of the temple of our humanity is rent in twain. Nature herself, we might say, is revealed – and revealed as unnatural. In face of such a world as this a man might be forgiven who should pray that chaos might come again. Nowhere else in Shakespeare's work or in the universe of jarring lives are the lines of character and event so broadly drawn or so sharply cut. Only the supreme self-command of this one poet could so mould and handle such types as to prevent their passing from the abnormal into the monstrous: yet even as much as this, at least in all cases but one, it surely has accomplished. In Regan alone would it be, I think, impossible to find a touch or trace of anything less vile than it was devilish. Even Goneril has her one splendid hour, her fireflaught of hellish glory; when she treads under foot the half-hearted goodness, the wordy and windy though sincere abhorrence, which is all that the mild and impotent revolt of Albany can bring to bear against her imperious and dauntless devilhood; when she flaunts before the eyes of her 'milk-livered' and 'moral fool' the coming banners of France about the 'plumed helm' of his slayer.

On the other side, Kent is the exception which answers to Regan on this. Cordelia[17] . . . has one passing touch of intolerance for what her sister was afterwards to brand as indiscretion and dotage in their father, which redeems her from the charge of perfection. . . . [S]he is not too inhumanly divine for the sense of divine irritation. Godlike though [she is], [her] very godhead is human and feminine; and only therefore credible, and only therefore adorable. . . . Regan [and] Goneril . . . have power to stir and embitter the sweetness of their blood. But for the contrast and even the contact of antagonists as abominable as these, the gold of [Cordelia's] spirit would be too refined, the lily of [her] holiness too radiant, the violet of [her] virtue too sweet. As it is, Shakespeare has gone down perforce among the blackest and the basest things of nature to find anything so equally exceptional in evil as properly to counterbalance and make bearable the excellence and extremity of [her] goodness. No otherwise could [this] angel have escaped the blame implied in the very attribute and epithet of blameless. But where the possible depth of human hell is so foul and unfathomable as it appears in the spirits which serve as foils to [Cordelia], we may endure that in [her] the inner height of heaven should be no less immaculate and immeasurable.

It should be a truism . . . to enlarge upon the evidence given in *King Lear* of a sympathy with the mass of social misery more wide and deep and direct and bitter and tender than Shakespeare has shown elsewhere. But as even to this day and even in respectable quarters the murmur is not quite duly extinct which would charge on Shakespeare a certain share of divine indifference to suffering, of godlike satisfaction and a less than compassionate content, it is not yet perhaps utterly superfluous to insist on the utter . . . falsity of their creed who . . . would rank him to his credit or discredit among such poets as . . . may be classed rather with Goethe than with Shelley and with Gautier than with Hugo.[18] A poet of revolution he is not, as none of his country in that generation could have been: but as surely as the author of *Julius Caesar* has approved himself in the best and highest sense of the word at least potentially a republican, so surely has the author of *King Lear* avowed himself in the only good and rational sense of the words a spiritual if not a political democrat and socialist . . . □

(Swinburne, pp. 170–6)

For Bradley, the keynote of *King Lear* is 'a consciousness of greatness in pain, and of solemnity in the mystery we cannot fathom' (Bradley, p. 279), for Swinburne it is the perception that the gods enjoy the suffering of mankind; for Bradley the play enjoins us to be patient of that suffering, for Swinburne, it shows us a world in which 'a man might be forgiven who should pray that chaos might come again'. Finally, and most comprehensively, for Bradley, Shakespeare is a conservative writer, who values hierarchy and seeks to preserve the status quo, whereas for Swinburne, Shakespeare is 'a spiritual if not a political democrat and socialist'.

Swinburne claims here that spiritual socialism is as far as an author writing in early seventeenth-century England can go. But a few years later, Swinburne was to intensify this claim. In 1909 he asserted that Lear voices a 'fiery protest against the social iniquities and the legal atrocities of civilized mankind'.[19] The play, he argued, is 'a cry on behalf of the outcasts of the world – the social sufferer, clean or unclean, innocent or criminal, thrall or free', and is also a call for a justice which would end 'the actual relations between the judge and the cutpurse, the beadle and the prostitute, the beggar and the king', a call, in short, not for 'political reform, but social revolution, absolute and radical' (Swinburne, *Three Plays*, pp. 17–19).

Why did Swinburne feel it necessary to intensify his claims concerning Shakespeare's social consciousness? Part of the answer to this question may lie in the publication of Leo Tolstoy's attack on Shakespeare, translated into English in 1907. Swinburne takes at least one explicit swipe at Tolstoy in this essay when he asks,

■ could anything [so radical as *King Lear*] be whispered . . . from . . . a Russian . . . theatre at the dawn of the twentieth [century]? When a Tolstoi . . . can do this . . . it will be allowed that his country is not more than three centuries behind England in civilization and freedom. □

(Swinburne, *Three Plays*, p. 19)

And Swinburne may also have had Tolstoy in mind when he described those who would attack Shakespeare's political judgement as

■ such dirty and dwarfish creatures of simian intellect and facetious idiocy as mistake it for a sign of wit instead of dullness, and of distinction instead of degradation, to deny the sun in heaven and affirm the fragrance of a sewer. □

(Swinburne, *Three Plays*, p. 13)

Tolstoy certainly had Swinburne (amongst many others) in mind when he composed his 'Shakespeare and the Drama'. This pamphlet, which we quoted briefly in the introduction to this volume, opens with a series of laudatory quotations about Shakespeare's genius from critics through the centuries (just as Romantic writers often began their volumes with lists of quotations from Shakespeare's attackers). And it then proceeds to lodge a sustained attack on Shakespeare, conducted principally through a reading of *King Lear*, which can only be described as a diatribe. Tolstoy begins this attack by recapitulating, at extraordinary length (19 pages in my edition of the text) the plot of the play. He maintains that he has 'endeavoured to make [his rendering of the play] as impartial as possible',[20] but as Orwell was later to point out this is untrue; 'It is obvious', Orwell remarks:

■ that when you are summarising *King Lear* for the benefit of someone who has not read it, you are not really being impartial if you introduce an important speech (Lear's speech when Cordelia is dead in his arms) in this manner: 'Again begin Lear's awful ravings, at which one feels ashamed, as at unsuccessful jokes'.[21] □

'On the whole,' Orwell concludes, 'it is difficult to feel that Tolstoy's criticisms are uttered in good faith' (Orwell, p. 106) The following (greatly condensed) extract from Tolstoy's account of the play will indicate just how disingenuous Tolstoy really was in claiming his account to be 'impartial':

From Leo Tolstoy, 'Shakespeare and the Drama' (1907)

■ Not to mention the pompous, characterless language of King Lear, . . .

the reader . . . cannot conceive that a king, however old and stupid he may be, could believe the words of the vicious daughters with whom he had passed his whole life, and not believe his favourite daughter. . . .

In the second scene . . . Kent, still unrecognized by Lear, without any reason, begins to abuse Oswald, . . . Kent, whom nobody recognizes, although both the King, . . . Cornwall, [and] . . . Gloucester . . . ought to know him well, continues to brawl. . . .

The third scene takes place on a heath. Edgar . . . hides in a wood and tells the public what kinds of lunatics exist there – beggars who go about naked, thrust wooden . . . pins into their flesh, scream with wild voices and enforce charity, and says that he wishes to simulate such a lunatic in order to save himself from persecution. Having communicated this to the public he retires. . . .

Lear says that for some reason during this storm all criminals shall be found out and convicted. . . . [T]he Fool pronounces a prophecy in no wise related to the situation and they all depart. . . .

Edgar comes out of the hovel, and, although all have known him, no one recognizes him – as no one recognizes Kent. . . . In the middle of this scene enters Gloucester (who also does not recognize either Kent or his son Edgar) . . . Edgar says: 'Frateretto calls me, and tells me Nero is an angler in the lake of darkness'. The Fool says: 'tell me whether a madman be a gentleman or a yeoman?' Lear, having lost his mind, says that the madman is a king. The Fool says no, the madman is the yeoman who has allowed his son to become a gentleman. Lear screams: 'To have a thousand with red burning spits/ Come hizzing in upon 'em' while Edgar shrieks that the foul fiend bites his back. At this the Fool remarks that one cannot believe 'in the tameness of a wolf'. . . . Lear . . . cries that he sees a mouse, which he wishes to entice by a piece of cheese. Then he suddenly demands the password from Edgar, and Edgar immediately answers him with the words 'Sweet marjoram'. Lear says 'Pass', and the blind Gloucester, who has not recognized either his son or Kent, recognizes the King's voice. . . . □

(Tolstoy, pp. 219–37)

Some of Tolstoy's objections to *King Lear* can be deduced from the tone and content of his summary of the play but Tolstoy goes on to explain, at some length, what he dislikes in *King Lear*. He finds the characters of the play to be poorly motivated and therefore unbelievable: 'their strife,' he maintains, 'does not flow from the natural course of events nor from their own characters, but is . . . arbitrarily established by the author, and therefore cannot produce on the reader that illusion which represents the essential condition of art' (Tolstoy, p. 238). He finds it unrealistic that Lear and Gloucester both jump so easily to the wrong conclusions about their offspring, and is irritated by the double plot itself: 'the fact that

Lear's relations with his daughters are the same as those of Gloucester with his sons,' Tolstoy complains, 'makes one feel yet more strongly that in both cases the relations are quite arbitrary and do not flow from the characters or the natural course of events' (Tolstoy, p. 238). Equally artificial are the repeated failures of the characters to see through the disguises of Kent and Edmund (Tolstoy pp. 238–9). Tolstoy also objects to the play's anachronistic representation of the past, to its setting of its action in ancient history, whilst representing its personages as, essentially, men and women of the seventeenth century; and he hates the way the characters talk: Shakespeare, he claims, is

■ lacking in the most important . . . means of portraying characters: individuality of language, that is, the style of speech of every person being natural to his character. . . . All his characters speak, not their own, but always one and the same Shakespearian pretentious and unnatural language, in which not only they could not speak, but in which no living man ever has spoken or does speak. □

(Tolstoy, pp. 240–1)

Comparing the play to *The True Chronicle History of King Leir*, Tolstoy concludes that 'the whole of this old drama is incomparably and in every respect superior to Shakespeare's adaptation' (Tolstoy, p. 245).

What motivated Tolstoy's antipathy to Shakespeare, and to *King Lear* in particular? To this question, George Orwell offered a lengthy and interesting answer, but as we shall see, Orwell's explanation was certainly an *ad hominem* one, and, in its own way, as unfair to Tolstoy as Tolstoy had been to Shakespeare. For Tolstoy's diatribe did not issue only out of anxieties concerning his own personality (as Orwell was to suggest), but also, first, out of a conception that drama should be 'realist'; and second, from a profound disgust with the criticism of the Romantics, and with the Shakespeare that the Romantics constructed. Insofar as Tolstoy's preconceptions of drama were concerned, they were these:

■ A . . . drama . . . must . . . excite in the spectator . . . the illusion that whatever the person represented is . . . experiencing, is . . . experienced by himself. . . . However eloquent or profound they may be, speeches, when put into the mouths of dramatic characters, if they be superfluous to the position and character, destroy the chief condition of dramatic art – the illusion owing to which the . . . spectator lives in the feelings of the persons represented. □

(Tolstoy, p. 252)

In some limited sense, then, we have come full circle here. As the Neo-Classicists insisted that a dramatist observe the unities of time and place in order not to break the spectator's illusion of reality, so Tolstoy makes a similar claim for the representation of interiority: that its success depends on the degree to which it instils in the spectators the illusion that they themselves experience the tribulations of the person represented. And for Tolstoy, a precondition of this illusion is the 'sincerity' of the author since it is the author's feelings with which the spectator ought ultimately to become 'infected'. Shakespeare, he thought, had no sincerity at all (Tolstoy, p. 259).

Tolstoy's second point of departure, as we have said, was his disgust with Romantic criticism, and with the Shakespeare that the Romantics offered us. The origin of this disgust for Tolstoy was itself twofold. First, he saw in the Romantics, and especially the German Romantics, an anti-religious bent which replaced any valorisation of Christian sentiment in art with what Tolstoy calls 'a theory of objective art' (Tolstoy, p. 268). For Tolstoy, on the contrary, drama should embody a 'religious essence', which he defines as 'the expression of a definite view of life corresponding to the highest religious understanding of a given time, which, serving as a motive for composition of the drama, penetrates, unknown to the author, through the whole of his work' (Tolstoy, p. 268). And if his Christianity motivated one aspect of his attack on the Romantics, and on *King Lear*, a kind of socialism motivated another. For Tolstoy's second objection to the Romantics lay, as he saw it, in their elitism. 'The word romantic,' Anna Jameson had remarked seventy odd years earlier, 'is a convenient "exploding word", and its general application signifies nothing more than "see how much finer I am than other people"' (Jameson, p. 17). Tolstoy broadly shares this conception of the Romantics, and believed (with some justification) that through the Romantic valorisation of a certain conception of high art, art had become alienated from the masses.[22]

Thus, reading *King Lear* through the Romantic account of the text, Tolstoy sees in it a text which valorises nobility and hierarchy, exhibits a profound lack of sympathy with the poverty-stricken masses who populate the land, and is machiavellian in its politics and sense of morality. It is difficult to excerpt Tolstoy's argument here, because his strategy is to intersperse his text with lengthy quotations from Shakespeare's admirers (Gervinus and Brandes), which Tolstoy then follows up with, as it were, his own punchline. But the following paragraphs offer some sense of Tolstoy's argument:

■ 'Activity is good, inactivity is evil', says Shakespeare according to Gervinus. . . . In other words, [Shakespeare] prefers death and murder through ambition to abstinence and wisdom.

According to Gervinus, Shakespeare believes that humanity need not set up ideals, but that only healthy activity and the golden mean is necessary in everything. Indeed, Shakespeare is so penetrated by this conviction, that, according to Gervinus's assertion, he allows himself to deny even Christian morality. . . . Shakespeare taught, says Gervinus, that one *may be too good*. . . .

Gervinus . . . expresses the whole of Shakespeare's moral theory by saying that Shakespeare does not write for those classes for whom definite religious principles and laws are suitable (that is, for 999 out of 1,000 men) but for the educated . . . [Here Tolstoy quotes Gervinus at length.]

. . . [O]ne should understand that according to [Shakespeare's] teaching it is stupid and harmful for the individual to overthrow the limits of established religious and state forms . . . [Again quotes Gervinus at length.] Property, the family, the State, are sacred; but aspiration towards the recognition of the equality of men is insanity. Its realisation would bring humanity to the greatest calamities. . . . [Quotes Brandes.] In other words, Shakespeare finally clearly saw that the moral of the aim is the only true and possible one; so that, according to Brandes, Shakespeare's fundamental principle, for which he extols him, is that *the end justifies the means*.

Action at all costs, the absence of all ideals, moderation in everything, the conservation of the forms of life once established, and the end justifies the means. If you add to this a chauvinist English patriotism . . . according to which the English throne is something sacred, Englishmen always vanquish the French . . . and so forth – such is the view of life of the wisest teacher of life according to his greatest admirers. And he who will attentively read Shakespeare's works cannot fail to recognize that the description of this Shakespearian view of life by his admirers is quite correct. □

(Tolstoy, pp. 255–9)

We started this chapter with one text anachronistic to it, and now end it with another. Orwell's 'Lear, Tolstoy and the Fool' was written in 1947, but for obvious reasons it seemed more appropriate to place it here. The main argument of Orwell's essay concerns the renunciation of power, and he uses this argument to lodge an attack on Christianity, and Christian readings of the play, at the same time that he deploys it against Tolstoy.

From George Orwell, 'Lear, Tolstoy and the Fool' (1947)

■ . . . This, then, is the substance of Tolstoy's pamphlet. One's first feeling is that in describing Shakespeare as a bad writer he is saying something demonstrably untrue. But . . . [i]n reality there is no kind of evidence . . . by which one can show that . . . any . . . writer is 'good'.

. . . Ultimately there is no test of literary merit except survival, which is itself an index to majority opinion. Artistic theories such as Tolstoy's are quite worthless. . . . Properly speaking one cannot answer Tolstoy's attack. The interesting question is: why did he make it? . . .

. . . [W]hy did Tolstoy . . . pick out *King Lear* as his especial target? . . . [F]or the purpose of a hostile analysis Tolstoy would probably choose the play he disliked most. Is it not possible that he bore an especial enmity towards this particular play because he was aware . . . of the resemblance between Lear's story and his own? But it is better to approach this clue from the opposite direction that is, by examining *Lear* itself, and the qualities in it that Tolstoy fails to mention.

. . . Tolstoy is not simply trying to rob others of a pleasure he does not share. He is doing that, but his quarrel with Shakespeare goes further. It is the quarrel between the religious and the humanist attitudes towards life. Here one comes back to the central theme of *King Lear*, which Tolstoy does not mention, although he sets forth the plot in some detail.

Lear is one of the minority of Shakespeare's plays that are unmistakably *about* something. . . . About a dozen of his plays . . . revolve around a single subject which in some cases can be reduced to a single word. *Macbeth* is about ambition, *Othello* is about jealousy, and *Timon of Athens* is about money. The subject of *Lear* is renunciation, and it is only by being wilfully blind that one can fail to understand what Shakespeare is saying.

Lear renounces his throne but expects everyone to continue treating him as a king. He does not see that if he surrenders power, other people will take advantage of his weakness: also that those who flatter him the most grossly . . . are exactly the ones who will turn against him. The moment he finds that he can no longer make people obey him as he did before, he falls into a rage which Tolstoy describes as 'strange and unnatural', but which in fact is perfectly in character. In his madness and despair, he passes through two moods which again are natural enough in his circumstances, though in one of them it is probable that he is being used partly as a mouthpiece for Shakespeare's own opinions. One is the mood of disgust in which Lear repents, as it were, for having been a king, and grasps for the first time the rottenness of formal justice and vulgar morality. The other is a mood of impotent fury in which he wreaks imaginary revenges upon those who have wronged him. Only at the end does he realize, as a sane man, that power, revenge and victory are not worthwhile . . . But by the time he makes this discovery it is too late, for his death and Cordelia's are already decided on. That is the story, and, allowing for some clumsiness in the telling, it is a very good story.

But is it not also curiously similar to the history of Tolstoy himself?

There is a general resemblance which one can hardly avoid seeing, because the most impressive event in Tolstoy's life, as in Lear's, was a huge and gratuitous act of renunciation. In his old age, he renounced his estate, his title and his copyrights, and made an attempt . . . to escape from his privileged position and live the life of a peasant. But the deeper resemblance lies in the fact that Tolstoy, like Lear, acted on mistaken motives and failed to get the results he had hoped for. According to Tolstoy, the aim of every human being is happiness, and happiness can only be attained by doing the will of God. But doing the will of God means casting off all earthly pleasures and ambitions, and living only for others. Ultimately, therefore, Tolstoy renounced the world under the expectation that this would make him happier. But if there is one thing certain about his later years, it is that he was *not* happy. On the contrary, he was driven almost to the edge of madness by the behaviour of the people about him, who persecuted him precisely *because* of his renunciation. Like Lear, Tolstoy was not humble and not a good judge of character. He was inclined at moments to revert to the attitudes of an aristocrat, in spite of his peasant's blouse, and he even had two children whom he had believed in and who ultimately turned against him though, of course, in a less sensational manner than Regan and Goneril. His exaggerated revulsion from sexuality was also distinctly similar to Lear's. Tolstoy's remark that marriage is 'slavery, satiety, repulsion' and means putting up with the proximity of 'ugliness, dirtiness, smell, sores', is matched by Lear's well-known outburst: 'But to the girdle do the gods inherit'. . . . And . . . even the ending of [Tolstoy's] life – the sudden unplanned flight across country, accompanied only by a faithful daughter, the death in a cottage in a strange village seems to have in it a sort of phantom reminiscence of Lear.

Of course, one cannot assume that Tolstoy was aware of this resemblance . . . But . . . [r]enouncing power, giving away your lands, was a subject on which he had reason to feel deeply. Probably, therefore, he would be . . . disturbed by the moral . . . [of *King Lear*]. But what exactly is the moral of *Lear*? Evidently there are two morals, one explicit, the other implied in the story.

Shakespeare starts by assuming that to make yourself powerless is to invite an attack. This does not mean that *everyone* will turn against you (Kent and the Fool stand by Lear from first to last), but in all probability *someone* will. If you throw away your weapons, some less scrupulous person will pick them up. If you turn the other cheek, you will get a harder blow on it than you got on the first one. This does not always happen, but it is to be expected, and you ought not to complain if it does happen. The second blow is, so to speak, part of the act of turning the other cheek. First of all, therefore, there is the vulgar, commonsense moral drawn by the Fool: 'Don't relinquish power, don't give away your lands.' But there is also another moral. Shakespeare never utters it in so many words, and it does not very much matter whether he was fully aware of it. It is contained in the story, which, after all, he made up, or altered to suit his purposes. It is: 'Give away your lands if you want to, but don't expect to gain happiness by doing so. Probably you won't gain happiness. If you live for others, you must live for others, and not as a roundabout way of getting an advantage for yourself.'

. . . Of course, Lear is not a sermon in favour of altruism. It merely points out the results of practising self-denial for selfish reasons. Shakespeare had a considerable streak of worldliness in him, and if he had been forced to take sides in his own play, his sympathies would probably have lain with the Fool. But at least he could see the whole issue and treat it at the level of tragedy. Vice is punished, but virtue is not rewarded. The morality of Shakespeare's later tragedies is not religious in the ordinary sense, and certainly is not Christian. . . . All of [them] . . . start out with the humanist assumption that life, although full of sorrow, is worth living, and that Man is a noble animal – a belief which Tolstoy in his old age did not share.

Tolstoy was not a saint, but he tried very hard to make himself into a saint . . . If only, Tolstoy says in effect, we would stop breeding, fighting, struggling and enjoying . . . then the whole painful process would be over and the Kingdom of Heaven would arrive. But a normal human being does not want the Kingdom of Heaven: he wants life on earth. . . . Most people get a fair amount of fun out of their lives, but on balance life is suffering, and only the very young or the very foolish imagine otherwise. Ultimately it is the Christian attitude which is self-interested and hedonistic, since the aim is always to get away from the painful struggle of earthly life and find eternal peace in some kind of Heaven. . . . The humanist attitude is that the struggle must continue and that death is the price of life. 'Men must endure their going hence, even as their coming hither: Ripeness is all' which is an un-Christian sentiment. Often there is a seeming truce between the humanist and the religious believer, but in fact their attitudes cannot be reconciled: one must choose between this world and the next. And the enormous majority of human beings, if they understood the issue, would choose this world. . . .

[Shakespeare] was not a saint . . . , he was a human being, and in some ways not a very good one. . . . [He] was capable of flattering the powerful in the most servile way. He is also noticeably cautious, not to say cowardly, in his manner of uttering unpopular opinions. . . . Throughout his plays the acute social critics, the people who are not taken in by accepted fallacies, are buffoons, villains, lunatics or persons who are shamming insanity or are in a state of violent hysteria. *Lear* is a play in which this tendency is particularly well marked. It contains a great deal of veiled social criticism – a point Tolstoy misses – but it is all uttered either by the Fool, by Edgar when he is pretending to be mad, or by Lear during his bouts of madness. In his sane moments Lear hardly ever makes an intelligent remark. And yet the very fact that Shakespeare had to use these subterfuges shows how widely his thoughts ranged. He could not restrain himself from commenting on almost everything, although he put on a series of masks in order to do so. . . .

. . . Tolstoy renounced wealth, fame and privilege; he abjured violence in all its forms and was ready to suffer for doing so; but it is not easy to believe that he abjured the principle of coercion, or at least the desire to coerce others. There are families in which the father will say to his child, 'You'll get a thick ear if you do that again', while the mother, her eyes brimming over with tears, will take the child in her arms and murmur lovingly, 'Now, darling, is it kind to Mummy to do that?' And who would maintain that the second method is less tyrannous than the first? The distinction that really matters is not between violence and non-violence, but between having and not having the appetite for power. . . . Creeds like pacifism and anarchism, which seem on the surface to imply a complete renunciation of power, rather encourage this habit of mind. For if you have embraced a creed which appears to be free from the ordinary dirtiness of politics – a creed from which you yourself cannot expect to draw any material advantage – surely that proves that you are in the right? And the more you are in the right, the more natural that everyone else should be bullied into thinking likewise. . . .

But . . . the most striking thing is how little difference it all makes. . . . Like every other writer, Shakespeare will be forgotten sooner or later, but it is unlikely that a heavier indictment will ever be brought against him. Tolstoy was perhaps the most admired literary man of his age, and he was certainly not its least able pamphleteer. He turned all his powers of denunciation against Shakespeare, like all the guns of a battleship roaring simultaneously. And with what result? Forty years later Shakespeare is still there completely unaffected, and of the attempt to demolish him nothing remains except the yellowing pages of a pamphlet which hardly anyone has read, and which would be forgotten altogether if Tolstoy had not also been the author of *War and Peace* and *Anna Karenina*. □

(Orwell, pp. 105–19)

I do not want to say a great deal about the subject of renunciation here, because it will be one of the main topics of the following chapter, and in that we will be able to flesh out in more detail other critics whose interpretation of *King Lear* Orwell is, in this essay, implicitly attacking. So I end here by pointing out that if both Bradley and Orwell saw renunciation as the principal theme of *King Lear*, they also interpreted the play as saying very different things about the act of renunciation. For Bradley the text declares: 'Let us renounce the world, hate it, and lose it gladly. The only real thing is the soul, with its courage, patience, devotion. And nothing outward can touch that' (Bradley, p. 327). For Orwell it tells us: 'Give away your lands if you want to, but don't expect to gain happiness by doing so. Probably you won't gain happiness. If you live for others, you must live for others, and not as a roundabout way of getting an advantage for yourself' (Orwell, p. 114).

CHAPTER FOUR

From Christianity to Chaos

Introduction

■ SHOULD WE not [call] this poem *The Redemption of King Lear*, and [declare] that the business of 'the gods' with [Lear] was . . . to lead him to attain . . . the very end and aim of life? □
A.C. Bradley, *Shakespearean Tragedy* (1904)[1]

■ Love is the last reality but one in Lear's story: love and God. □
G. Wilson Knight, *The Wheel of Fire* (1930)[2]

■ The play is not . . . pessimistic and pagan: it is rather an attempt to provide an answer to the undermining of traditional ideas by the new philosophy that called all in doubt. □
Kenneth Muir, editor, The New Arden Edition of *King Lear* (1953)[3]

■ [What emerge] from the play are . . . fundamentally Christian values . . . For what takes place in *King Lear* we can find no other word than renewal. □
L.C. Knights, *Some Shakespearean Themes* (1959)[4]

■ [T]he way the gods [delegate justice] . . . is by 'plaguing' us, and by inventing . . . instruments of torture; they are also facetious and full of mean jeering tricks. I think this pious acceptance of the gods does a great deal to recall the old picture of them as criminal lunatics. □
William Empson, 'Fool in *Lear*' (1951)[5]

■ Those critics who find [Christian allegory] in the play . . . are interested in the kind of 'poetic' statements which the play seems to make, in contradistinction from what actually happens. □
Barbara Everett, 'The New *King Lear*' (1960)[6]

■ King Lear makes a tragic mockery of all eschatologies: of the heaven promised on earth, and the heaven promised after death; . . . of both Christian and secular theodicies; . . . of the gods and natural goodness, of man made in the 'image and likeness'. In *King Lear* . . . orders of established values disintegrate. All that remains at the end of this gigantic pantomime is the earth, empty and bleeding. □

Jan Kott, *Shakespeare Our Contemporary* (1965)[7]

That Kenneth Muir's New Arden edition of *King Lear*, published in 1953, so firmly endorsed a reading of the play which saw it as offering a solution to the uncertainties that beset early modern England at the beginning of the seventeenth century is an indication of the degree to which explicitly or implicitly Christian readings of the play dominated its reception in the first half of this century. Critic after critic read *King Lear* as a text in which we could find evidence of Shakespeare's religious beliefs; Orwell was in a small minority in his contention that 'from the evidence of Shakespeare's writings it would be difficult to prove that he had any' (Orwell, p. 116). It was not until the early 1960s that this view of the play began seriously, or at least effectively, to be challenged, with the publication of Barbara Everett's 'The New *King Lear*' and Jan Kott's *Shakespeare Our Contemporary* (in 1960 and 1965 respectively), and with two important stage productions of the play: Herbert Blau's for the San Francisco Workshop, and Peter Brook's for Paul Scofield in London. We will look, in this chapter, at two Christian readings of *King Lear*, and at the challenge to that interpretation which occurred in the early 1960s, and we will also take a kind of detour through a couple of readings of the play which form, as it were, a kind of middle ground between these two opposing poles.

Part One: Christian Readings of *King Lear*, and a Note on New Criticism

Criticism of *King Lear* during the first half of the twentieth century bore a vexed relation to the work of A.C. Bradley. On the one hand critics conceived of themselves as writing in reaction to Bradley, and they did provide a much-needed corrective to the tendency of Bradleian and post-Bradleian criticism to view literary characters as more or less identical to real human beings; Wilson Knight, for instance, rejects the term 'character' altogether, 'since it is so constantly entwined with a false . . . criticism' (Wilson Knight, p. 9). One of the most explicit formulations of this reaction to Bradley was provided by L.C. Knights in his essay 'How Many Children had Lady Macbeth?' (1946), whose very title is an attack on Bradley and his followers.[8] To concentrate exclusively on the characters of a text, Knights complains, 'obscures' what is far more important in it, 'the system of values that gives emotional coherence to the whole';[9] and blinds us to the 'sight of the whole dramatic pattern' of the play (Knights, *Explorations*, p. 16). In order to achieve that more comprehensive vision, Knights maintains, we must turn our attention to other aspects of the play, which the 'mass of Shakespeare criticism' ignores, and must recognise that '"character" is merely an abstraction from the total response in the mind of the reader . . . , brought into being by . . . words' (Knights, *Explorations*, p. 4). 'How should we read Shakespeare?' Knights asks, and he answers his own question thus:

■ We start with so many lines of verse on a printed page which we read as we should read any other poem. We have to elucidate the meaning . . . and to unravel ambiguities; we have to estimate the kind and quality of the imagery and determine the precise degree of evocation of particular figures; we have to allow full weight to each word . . .

. . . A play of Shakespeare's is a precise particular experience, a poem – and precision and particularity are exactly what is lacking in the greater part of Shakespeare criticism, criticism that deals . . . in terms of abstractions that have nothing to do with the unique arrangement of words that constitutes these plays. □

(Knights, *Explorations*, pp. 16–17)

For the New Critics (of whom Knights and Wilson Knight are two) a play should be read with especial attention to its specifically *poetic* qualities: its structure and its form, its imagery and figurative language – the arrangement, in short, of the words on the page. And from Knights' description of the work of the critic, we can begin to anticipate some of the aspects of the text that might interest them.

There is, in other words, a broad analogy to be made between the method of New Criticism and its content. Insisting on the primacy of the words on the page, New Criticism, at its most extreme, rejected any contextualisation of the action of a play in historical change. It held that there is 'meaning' in a text which can be 'elucidated', and that ambiguities or paradoxes could be 'unraveled'. In its attempt to come to grips with the 'pattern' of a text (or, in T. S. Eliot's phrase, 'to pounce upon [its] secret',[10]) New Criticism often tended to examine the presence in it of dichotomies, such as Nature and Culture, or Appearance and Reality. And they conceived of these dichotomies as absolute, not relative: when L. C. Knights warns against the danger of 'obscur[ing]' 'the system of values that gives emotional coherence to the whole' his use of the definite article suggests that there can be only one such system at work in a text, and that the system of values that it embraces is, again, absolute and not relative. There was no place in New Criticism for, say, the (Marxist) claim that tragedy might emerge from a historical moment in which competing ideologies struggle unsuccessfully for supremacy, no sense, in other words, that a tragedy might dramatise not paradox (which can be resolved) but contradiction (which can't). Similarly, just as the text was assumed by the New Critics to be fundamentally coherent (the work of the critic being to seek out and define that coherence), so too was the mind of the author: the contention (of later psychoanalytic critics, for instance) that not merely the protagonists of a drama, but also its author, might own an unconscious, was something quite foreign to the majority of New Critics.

'We should not look for perfect verisimilitude to life', said Wilson Knight, 'but rather see each play as an expanded metaphor . . . [whose] persons, ultimately, are not human at all, but purely symbols of a poetic vision'.[11] As an instance of a kind of condensation of the attention to the words on the page which characterised New Criticism, we can look briefly at Caroline Spurgeon's account of *Shakespeare's Imagery*. Like Wilson Knight, Spurgeon sees the coherence of *King Lear* as lying in its extended meditation on a single theme: 'the intensity of . . . emotion in *King Lear* and the sharpness of its focus,' Spurgeon remarks, 'are revealed by the fact that . . . there runs throughout only one over-powering . . . continuous image. So compelling is this that even . . . subsidiary images are . . . used to augment and emphasise it'.[12] This 'continuous image', she explains, is that of the body in pain:

From Caroline Spurgeon, *Shakespeare's Imagery* (1935)

■ In the play we are conscious all through of the atmosphere of buffeting, strain and strife, and, at moments, of bodily tension to the point of agony. So naturally does this flow from the circumstances of the drama and the mental sufferings of Lear, that we scarcely realise how greatly this sensation in us is increased by the general 'floating' image, kept constantly before us, chiefly by means of the verbs used, but also in metaphor, of a human body in anguished movement, tugged, wrenched, beaten, pierced, stung, scourged, dislocated, flayed, gashed, scalded, tortured and finally broken on the rack.

One can scarcely open . . . the play without being struck by these images and verbs, for every kind of bodily movement, generally involving pain, is used to express mental and abstract, as well as physical facts. . . . Lear . . . pictures himself as a man *wrenched* and tortured by an 'engine', beating at the gate (his head) that let his folly in. Goneril has power to *shake* his manhood; he complains that she has *struck* him with her tongue; . . . his heart, he says, *will break into a hundred thousand flaws*. Albany wonders how far Goneril's eyes may *pierce*. . . . Kent longs *to tread* Oswald into mortar, and . . . evokes images of rats *biting* cords . . . while the fool adds the picture of a man being dragged along by *holding on* when a great wheel *runs down hill*, and *letting go* only in time to save his *neck being broken*.

. . . This use of verbs and images of bodily and generally anguished motion is almost continuous, and it is reinforced by similar words used in direct description, as in the treatment of Gloucester; he is *bound* to a chair, *plucked* by the beard, his hairs are *ravished* from his chin, he is *tied to a stake*, . . . and with his eyes blinded and bleeding, he is *thrust out* of the gates to *smell his way* to Dover. . . .

The sense of bodily torture continues to the end. Gloucester catches the recurrent theme of the tragedy, and crystallises it for ever in the terrible picture of men being torn limb from limb by the gods in sport, to whom they are but as 'flies to wanton boys'. . . . [A]t the close, when Kent breathes the only valediction possible over his dead master's body, it is still the same metaphor which rises to his lips:

> . . . he hates him
> That would upon the rack of this tough world
> Stretch him out longer. ☐

(Spurgeon, pp. 338–43)

Actually, the New Shakespearean Critics' contention that in paying such attention to the imagery of Shakespeare's plays they were doing something entirely different from what Bradley had done was not entirely true: Bradley also noted the plays' imagery and language, as in this (much condensed) passage where he remarks that 'a very striking characteristic of *King Lear* . . . [is its] incessant references to the lower animals and man's likeness to them':

■ The dog, the horse, . . . the sheep, the hog, . . . the wolf, . . . the owl, . . . the water-newt, the worm – I am sure I cannot have completed the list . . . Goneril is a kite: her ingratitude has a serpent's tooth: she has struck her father most serpent-like upon the very heart: she has tied sharp-toothed unkindness like a vulture on her father's breast . . . She and Regan are doghearted: they are tigers, not daughters: . . . the flesh of each is covered with the fell of a beast. Oswald . . . ☐

Bradley, *Shakespearean Tragedy*, p. 267

Spurgeon, in fact, acknowledged Bradley's influence, incorporating his list of animal references into her own claim about the *King Lear*'s obsessive return to images of 'horror and bodily pain' (Spurgeon, p. 342).

So in some ways, it can be said that the New Critics were indebted to the very person whom they believed they were trying to supersede. And if this was partially true even at the level of method, it was far more apparent at the level of content. As we have seen in the previous chapter, Bradley proposed a reading of *King Lear* which, as the New Critical readings of the play were to do, sought to bestow upon it a movement towards reconciliation in the soul of the hero, and which came very close to the imputation to it of a Christian system of values. Bradley himself did not go quite that far. But the New Critics did, and it is to their readings of the text that we now turn.

Our first extract comes from G. Wilson Knight's *The Wheel of Fire*. Wilson Knight's reading of *King Lear* acknowledged the pagan resonance of many of the explicit references in the text to 'the gods'. But he argued that the text charts a rejection of this paganism in favour of the acceptance of a much more Christian conception of God, a movement structurally reflected in three of the play's protagonists, Edmund, Lear, and Cordelia, who respectively 'correspond to three periods in man's evolution: the primitive, the civilized and the ideal' (Wilson Knight, p. 200) and to three temporal stages, the past, the present, and the future. Thus for Wilson Knight, *King Lear* is a 'purgatorial' text, wherein takes place the expiation of sins, in order to enable a purification through adversity in which those who suffer, awaking finally to 'a new consciousness of love', manage to 'find themselves more truly,' and in so doing, recognise 'the gods' mysterious beneficence'.

From G. Wilson Knight, 'The *Lear* Universe' (1930)

■ ... No Shakespearian work shows so wide a range of sympathetic creation: [in *King Lear*] we seem to be confronted ... with mankind. ... *King Lear* is a tragic vision of humanity, in its complexity, its interplay of purpose, its travailing evolution. The play is a microcosm of the human race ... [Its] technique [lends] the persons and their acts some element of mystery and some suggestion of infinite purposes working themselves out before us. ... [making] of its persons vague symbols of universal forces. ... *King Lear* is a work of philosophic vision. ... Mankind's relation to the universe is its theme, and Edgar's trumpet is as the universal judgement summoning vicious man to account. ... Therefore the clear demarcation of half the persons into fairly 'good', and half into fairly 'bad', is an inevitable effect of a balanced, universalized vision of mankind's activity on earth. ... [T]his play is Purgatory. Its philosophy is continually purgatorial.

... The play works out before us the problems of human suffering and human imperfection; the relation of humanity to nature on the one hand and its aspiration toward perfection on the other. I shall note (i) the naturalism of the Lear universe ... ; (ii) its 'gods'; (iii) its insistent questioning of justice, human and divine; (iv) the stoic acceptance by many persons of their purgatorial pain; and (v) the flaming course of the Lear-theme itself growing out of this dun world, and touching at its full height a transcendent, apocalyptic beauty. . . .

This world is rooted in nature. . . . We hear of the wolf, the owl, . . . of sheep, . . . dogs . . . , horses, rats and such like. Now there are two main directions for this animal and natural suggestion running through the play. First, two of the persons undergo a direct return to nature in their purgatorial progress; second, the actions of humanity tend to assume contrast with the natural world in point of ethics. . . .

Lear [like Edgar] . . . , falls back on nature. From the first there is a primitive, animal power about him . . . There is a pagan ferocity in Lear. . . . He prays to 'nature, dear goddess' to convey sterility into Goneril's womb (1.4.299). . . . Lear revolts from man, tries to become a thing of elemental, instinctive life . . . . Hence the relevance of animals, and animal-symbolism, to madness. For madness is the breaking of that which differentiates man from beast. . . .

Thoughts of nature are also related to human vice. The evil of mankind is often here regarded as essentially a defacing of 'nature', since this is now 'human nature', and human nature is moral. Thus Gloucester thinks Edmund is a 'loyal and natural boy' (2.1.86). . . . Goneril and Regan are 'most savage and unnatural', says Edmund . . . (3.3.7). It is man's nature to be loving: yet he behaves, too often, like the beasts. His inhumanity is therefore compared to animals. . . . Goneril is a 'detested kite' (1.4.286); she and her sister are 'she-foxes' (3.6.25); . . . She and Regan are 'tigers, not daughters' (4.2.40); they are 'dog-hearted' (4.3.47); their 'sharp-tooth'd unkindness' is fixed in Lear's heart like a 'vulture' (2.4.137). Such phrases . . . show how firmly based on thoughts of nature is the philosophy of King Lear. . . . Edmund is the 'natural' son of Gloucester. . . . [H]e is animal-like, both in grace of body and absence of sympathy. . . . Therefore 'nature' is his goddess . . .

In King Lear the religion, too, is naturalistic. We can distinguish three modes of religion stressed here by the poet. First, the constant references to the 'gods'; second the thoughts about ethical 'justice'; and, third, the moral or spiritual development illustrated by the persons before us. The 'gods' so often apostrophized are, however, slightly vitalized: one feels them to be figments of the human mind rather than omnipotent ruling powers . . . [T]his questioning as to the reality and nature of the directing powers . . . is one of the primary motives through the play. . . . The 'gods' are mentioned in various contexts where humanity speaks . . . its fears or hopes concerning divinity: they are no more than this.

. . . After seeing Lear in madness, Gloucester's sense of the King's sufferings brings home to him his despair's wrongfulness, and he asks forgiveness of the 'ever-gentle gods' (4.6.222). The 'gods' are to Gloucester kind, generous beings: and their kindness and generosity are made known to him through his, and others', sufferings. He becomes, strangely, aware of 'the bounty and the benison of heaven' (4.6.230). . . . Numerous other references to 'the gods' occur. Kent prays that 'the gods' may reward Gloucester's kindness to Lear (3.6.6); ironical enough in view of what happens to him. Cordelia prays to 'you kind gods' (4.7.14); Edgar challenges Edmund as 'false to thy gods' (5.3.136); and tells him that 'the gods are just'. These phrases do not, as a whole, form a convincing declaration of divine reality: some show at the most an insistent need in humanity to cry for justification to something beyond its horizon, others are almost perfunctory. Even Edmund can say, half-mockingly: 'Now, gods, stand up for bastards!' (1.2.22). These gods are, in fact, man-made. They are natural figments of the human mind, not in any other sense transcendent: *King Lear* is, as a whole, pre-eminently naturalistic. . . .

Lear himself shows . . . an excessive naturalism in point of religion. . . . He thinks purely in terms of the natural order. In these speeches his religion is pagan . . ., nearer primitive magic than religion. . . . His early primitivism gives place, however, to something more definite in the thought of 'the great gods who keep this dreadful pother o'er our heads', whose 'enemies' are wicked men (3.2.49). Thoughts of morality are being added to his first pagan selfishness. He questions the justice of 'the heavens' towards naked poverty (3.4.28). He thinks of fiends in his madness [3.6.17]. Of women, he says: 'But to the girdle do the gods inherit,/ Beneath is all the fiends' (4.6.129). These are transition thoughts from his early passionate paganism. The return to nature which he endures in the play's progress paradoxically builds in him a less naturalistic theology. At the end, he can speak to Cordelia those blazing lines:

> You do me wrong to take me out o' the grave:
> Thou art a soul in bliss; but I am bound
> Upon a wheel of fire, that mine own tears
> Do scald like molten lead. (4.7.45)

Now 'the gods themselves' throw incense on human sacrifices (5.3.20). He and Cordelia will be as 'God's spies' (5.3.17) – here not 'the gods', but 'God's'. Slowly, painfully, emergent from the *Lear* naturalism we see a religion born of disillusionment, suffering, and sympathy: a purely spontaneous, natural growth of the human spirit, developing from nature magic to 'God'.

The emergent religion here – the stoic acceptance, the purification through sympathy, the groping after 'the gods' – all these are twined with the conception of justice. The old Hebrew problem is restated: *King Lear* is analogous to the *Book of Job*. Is justice a universal principle?

. . . [Lear's] thoughts of naturalistic psychology hold a profound suggestion: they are a road to recognition of the universal injustice. For when earthly justice is thus seen to be absolutely non-existent and, in fact, impossible, the concept of 'justice' is drained of meaning. How then can we impose it on the universal scheme? . . .

This question of human justice is clearly part of the wider question: that of universal justice. . . . In the *Lear* universe we see humanity working at cross-purposes . . . . They are crude justicers: Lear, unjust himself, first cries for human justice, then curses it. But he also cries for heavenly justice: so, too, others here cry out for heavenly justice. Their own rough ideas of equity force them to impose on the universal scheme a similar judicial mode. We . . . are not surprised that 'the gods' show little sign of a corresponding sense. According to human standards things happen here unjustly. The heavens do not send down to take Lear's part; his curses on Goneril and Regan have no effect. . . . [I]t is all a purely natural process: there is no celestial avatar, to right misguided humanity . . . . Wrongdoers are . . . punished: but there is no sense of divine action. It is Edgar's trumpet, symbol of natural judgement, that summons Edmund to account at the end, sounding through the *Lear* mist from which right and wrong at this moment emerge distinct. Right wins, surely as the sun rises: but it is a natural, a human process. Mankind work out their own 'justice', crime breaks the implicit laws of human nature, and brings suffering alike on good and bad. But not all the good persons suffer, whereas all the bad meet their end swiftly. This is the natural justice of *King Lear*. . . . But, from an objective view of the *Lear* universe, other facts regarding the universal justice emerge, and we begin to have sight of some vague purpose working itself out in terms of nature and of man. . . .

. . . Gloucester moves beyond self-interest, through suffering, to the nobility and grandeur of his prayer [Here Wilson Knight quotes Gloucester's speech at 5.6.35: 'O you mighty gods!/ This world I do renounce, . . .'] He is to 'bear free and patient thoughts'. . . . Edgar . . . is, as it were, the high-priest of this play's stoicism, of endurance which forbids a facile exit in self-murder. He understands his father's purgatorial destiny, and thus helps to direct it. . . . Now Gloucester speaks gently of 'the bounty and the benison of heaven' (4.6.230).

Strange paradox. It is strange, and very beautiful, to watch this burning purgatory, these souls so palely lit by suffering, aureoled and splendid in their grief. Each by suffering finds himself more truly, more surely knows the centre on which human fate revolves, more clearly sees the gods' mysterious beneficence. Gloucester is blind – but he knows now that he 'stumbled when he saw'. We watch humanity pained and relieving pain, and finding peace. Gloucester's purgatory was contingent on his first lending aid to Lear and raising the hate of the adverse party: thus an act of goodness buys the inestimable gift of purgatorial agony. But suicide cheats the high gods of their purpose. Once again, when Gloucester longs for death, Edgar answers:

What, in ill thoughts again? Men must endure
Their going hence, even as their coming hither.
Ripeness is all.   (5.2.9)

That is, men must await ('endure') the destined hour of death, directing it no more than they direct the hour of birth: they must await till the harvest of their pain is ripe. Ripeness is all – so Gloucester is matured by suffering, and his death, when it comes, is sweet . . .

With Lear himself, too, ripeness is all. In . . . his reunion with Cordelia, he wakes to music, like a mortal soul waking to immortality, to find his daughter bright as 'a soul in bliss'; now both find the richness of love more rich for the interval of agony, misunderstanding, intolerance. . . . Now love returns, enthroned: 'misery' has again worked its 'miracle'. All woman's motherly love is caught up in Cordelia's speech [Here Wilson Knight quotes Cordelia's speech to Lear at 4.7.31: 'Was this a face/ To be opposed against the warring winds? . . .'] Lear is waked into love: now he is humble, he knows he is 'a foolish fond old man' (4.7.60). He will drink poison if Cordelia wishes it. His purgatory has been this: cruelly every defence of anger and pride that barriers his consciousness from his deepest and truest emotion – his love for Cordelia . . . – has been broken down. In those middle storm scenes we were aware of his hatred and thoughts of vengeance, together with a new-born sympathy addressed to suffering humanity throughout the world. Then the whirling ecstasies of lunacy: now the healing balm of uttermost humility and love. He humbles himself, not to Cordelia, but to the love now royally enthroned in his heart erstwhile usurped . . . His purgatory is almost complete; but . . . a greater sacrifice than from Gloucester is demanded. He and Cordelia are now prisoners. . . . Lear, at this last moment, touches exquisite apprehensions. Now simple things will please. Formerly a king, intolerant, fierce, violent, whom any opposition roused to fury, now an old man ready to be pleased with simplest things: they will 'talk of court news'; the gods themselves throw incense on such sacrifices; Lear and Cordelia will 'take upon's the mystery of things/As if we were God's spies' (5.3.16). God's spies, in truth: since Lear now sees only with eyes of love. Love is the last reality but one in Lear's story: love and God. Not the last. There are still the vague, inscrutable 'gods' of the Lear mist. . . . There remains death. Death and 'the gods' – if indeed those gods exist. Uttermost tragedy . . . has its way at the end. Love and 'God' exist herein, transcendent for a while, in golden scenes where Cordelia is bright with an angel brightness. But they do not last, cannot free Lear finally from the fiery wheel of mortal life: [Quotes Lear's 'wheel of fire' speech at 4.7.46] . . .

[T]he white presence of Cordelia, with restorative kiss, and the remediate virtues of earth's simples, the kindly nurse of anguish, sleep, and the strains of music, are all interwoven in the awakening of Lear from the wheel of fire to a new consciousness of love. Nature, human love, music – all blend in this transcendent scene: the agony of this play works up to so beautiful a moment, heavenly sweet, that one forgets the bleak world, the rough and cruel naturalism which gave it birth. . . . The naturalism of *King Lear* pales before this blinding shaft of transcendent light. This is the justification of the agony, the sufferance, the gloom. . . . From the travail of nature the immortal thing is born; time has given birth to that which is timeless. . . .

. . . So, too, in the ravenous slaughter of wood or ocean, love rules creation. That universal pulse is strong within the naturalism of *King Lear*, beats equally in the hearts of Goneril and Cordelia. And what of Edmund? . . . He recognizes love at last, its mystery, its power, its divinity. He knows himself to die aureoled in its unresisted splendour. Now he speaks quickly:

> I pant for life: some good I mean to do,
> Despite of mine own nature. Quickly send,
> Be brief in it, to the castle; for my writ
> Is on the life of Lear and on Cordelia:
> Nay, send in time. (5.3.245)

Again the *Lear* universe travails and brings forth its miracle. □
(Wilson Knight, pp. 177–206)

Like Wilson Knight, L. C. Knights also reads the play from a New Critical, and Christian, perspective, although his reading is not so sentimental as Wilson Knight's, nor expressive of the same disturbing sexuality. Despite his New Critical allegiances Knights does more in this essay than look merely at 'the words of the page'. For one aspect of his reading of *King Lear* is generated from (and/or supported by) his situation of the play in the context of Shakespeare's entire *oeuvre*, as the first and last sentences of the excerpt reprinted below will indicate. Knights also begins by setting *King Lear* in the context of an examination of the concept of Nature which is partially historicist in its approach. In the first part of his examination of the play (not reproduced here) Knights argues that the sixteenth-century conception of Nature (Knights always capitalises the word):

■ [took] for granted that Nature was often cruel . . . but [believed that] the whole disposition of things, independent of man's will, served a providential plan. Nature in this sense, though subject to disorder, was essentially ordered, and it was ordered for the good of man. □

(Knights, p. 75)

Shakespeare, Knights believes, was writing at a historical moment in which such 'established assumptions about Nature' were being eroded, so that 'to some minds Nature was ceasing to appear as a divinely ordained order and was beginning to appear as an amoral collection of forces'. And this erosion, Knights maintains, 'had a share in the undermining of the older conception of human nature and the traditional sanctions of morality' (Knights, p. 77). Knights, however, invokes this argument not in order to maintain (as would most post-1960 critics of the play) that Shakespeare shares this conception of an amoral world, but rather, as had Kenneth Muir, to account for the appearance of such a view within the play: 'If the "libertine" assumption – man is a natural force in a world of natural forces – is incorporated in *King Lear*', Knights maintains,

■ that is because it appeared to envisage nothing but the bare facts of existence; and for Shakespeare's . . . purpose . . . it was necessary to get at the bare facts. The positives that emerge from the play are indeed fundamentally Christian values, but they are reached by an act of profound individual exploration: the play does not take them for granted; it takes nothing for granted but Nature and natural energies and passions. □

(Knights, p. 79)

From L.C. Knights, *King Lear* (1959)

■ The fact that *King Lear* was written so soon after *Othello* (1604) is a reminder of how misleading the phrase 'Shakespearean Tragedy' can be. Each play is 'a new beginning' . . . for although there is development there is no repetition. . . . Thus *Othello* . . . comes closer than any of the other tragedies to . . . 'revelation of character', and its focus is on individual and, we might say, domestic qualities. *Lear*, on the other hand, is a universal allegory . . . and its dramatic technique is determined by the need to present certain permanent aspects of the human situation. . . . In the scenes on the heath, for example, we . . . are caught up in a great and almost impersonal poem in which we hear certain voices which echo . . . each other; all that they say is part of the tormented consciousness of Lear; and the consciousness of Lear is part of the consciousness of human kind. There is the same density of effect throughout. One character echoes another: . . . Gloucester learns to 'see better' . . . in his blindness, and Lear reaches his final insights, the recognition of his supreme need, through madness. . . . The poetry of *Lear* is not only vivid, close packed, and wide ranging, involving in the immediate action a world of experience, it has a peculiar resonance that should leave us in no doubt of Shakespeare's intention. It is what we hear when . . . Lear . . . exclaims, 'Who is it that can tell me whom I am?' and the Fool replies 'Lear's shadow' (1.4.238).

. . .

Lear's expression of revulsion and disgust, when, 'a ruin'd piece of nature', he confronts the blind Gloucester, is, I suppose, one of the profoundest expressions of pessimism in all literature. If it is not the final word in the play, it is certainly not because Shakespeare has shrunk from any of the issues. Pessimism is sometimes regarded as a tough and realistic attitude. Shakespeare's total view of human life in this play has a toughness and actuality that make most pessimism look like sentimentality. It is because the play has brought us to this vision of horror – seen without disguise or palliation – that the way is open for the final insights. In the successive stripping away of the layers of appearance, what remains to discover is the most fundamental reality of all. In the play it takes the form of the love and forgiveness of Cordelia. But that love has to be earned . . . by the full admission of a need, the achievement of honesty and humility, the painful shedding of all that is recognized as incompatible with the highest good, by, in short, making oneself able to receive whatever it may be. Now if there is one truth that the play brings home with superb force it is that neither man's reasons nor his powers of perception function in isolation from the rest of his personality . . . *How* Lear feels . . . is as important as *what* he feels, for the final 'seeing' is inseparable from what he has come to be. . . . Lear's vision of life can only be apprehended in close conjunction with the attitudes with which he confronts experience.

. . . Lear's dominant attitude is obviously self-will; his sentences fall naturally into the imperative mood, his commands are threats, and his threats are curses. . . . In all this, as Shakespeare takes care to tell us through the Fool, there is something conspicuously infantile – the craving not only for immediate gratification of his desires but for complete endorsement of the self, just as it is, the assumption of a power ludicrously beyond the possibility of performance, the resort to tantrums and tears of rage when that power proves inadequate. In these ways Lear proves his kinship with the common run of mankind long before he is prepared to admit it at a different level. Above all there is an immense capacity for self-pity. . . .

It is . . . through the storm . . . that reality breaks into a mind wilfully closed against it. The question of 'true need' has already been given some prominence (2.4.266–73); posed in this setting only the truth will serve.

> How dost, my boy? Art cold?
> I am cold myself. Where is this straw, my fellow?
> The art of our necessities is strange,
> And can make vile things precious. Come, your hovel.
> (3.2.68–71)

. . . [I]t is worth recalling here that earlier question in which Lear's self-revelation came to a head – 'Which of you shall we say doth love us most?' Then the question was asked in a tone that implied the expectation of a gratifying answer: the leisurely and expansive rhythm evokes the movement of settling with complacence into prepared comfort. Now the broken rhythm marks the confrontation of what is new and disturbing. Then the demand was for exclusive possession, for that 'all' which Cordelia could not pretend to give. Now what is in question is need that must be recognized as common to all. . . . Now comes the famous prayer on behalf of 'houseless poverty'. . . . This is pity, not self-pity; and condemnation of others momentarily gives way to self-condemnation: 'O! I have ta'en too little care of this'. It is also, we may say, a genuine prayer, and as such it is answered: it is *after* this that Lear endures the physic of his vision of unaccommodated man.

The nature of that vision . . . includes the suffering of the poor . . . the indifference of Nature and all the disreputable impulses . . . in the heart of man . . . . From now on the question put to Lear, which is indeed the question posed by the whole play, is how to cope with the world so revealed, with the self so revealed. . . . [Mad, and thus] no longer subjected to interference from the self hitherto offered to the world as Lear . . . he is free to express attitudes previously concealed from himself. . . . In this region where honesty is as it were compelled . . . impulses issue with the uninhibited frankness of the symbolic actions of dreams. At the centre of the whirlpool lies the obsession with guilt and punishment. What constitutes the torture – Lear's 'wheel of fire' – is that each successive attitude, bearing the stamp of its utter inadequacy, can only breed recoil and a fresh plunge into madness. Denial of involvement . . . bears a confession of guilt. Fantasies of aggression promptly transform themselves into situations where Lear himself is the victim. Most significant of all is the extended attempt to 'have the law on' the offenders. But the mock trial of Goneril and Regan (3.6.2056) is not only an obliquely ironic comment on human justice that will be made more explicit later, it offers a direct rebuff to Lear's habitual appeal to a merely legalistic code. . . .

If none of the familiar postures of the self will serve, for the correlative of each attitude is illusion, what is there to which Lear's mind can hold? Nothing, it seems, except the recognition of his own share in a depravity felt as universal. [But even after he has begun to recognise his shame] the nadir of Lear's vision is still to come.

. . .

Cordelia, though rarely appearing in the play, is very much a positive presence. Her tenderness is rooted in the same strength that enabled her to reject Lear's misconceived demands. Her love is of a kind that, confronted with a real demand, does not bargain or make conditions; it is freely given, and it represents an absolute of human experience that can stand against the full shock of disillusion. When Lear, dressed in 'fresh garments' and to the accompaniment of music (the symbolism is important) is brought into her presence, there follows one of the most tender and moving scenes in the whole of Shakespeare. But it is much more than moving. Since each line engages us to the whole extent of our powers the briefest reminders set vibrating all the chords of the past experience. It is even whilst we respond to the swift sure play of feeling – with a sense as of the actual bodily presence of the protagonists – that we are made to live again the central scenes. . . . Hence as recognition dawns in Lear, as consciousness first renews his suffering, then admits it has no terms for a world not known before, we are aware that this still moment is surrounded by nothing less than the whole action of the play; and if questions that have been asked now await their answer, the painful knowledge that has been won will reject anything that swerves a hair's breadth from absolute integrity. . . .

King Lear, however, is more than a purgatorial experience culminating in reconciliation: . . . [T]he absence of demonstrable answers, [to the questions that it raises] form an essential part of [its] meaning . . .

In the last act . . . the way is apparently cleared for an ending far different from that represented by the stark stage-direction: 'Enter Lear, with Cordelia dead in his arms'. The scene of Lear's final anguish is so painful that criticism hesitates to fumble with it: where no one can remain unaffected the critic's business is to supply something other than his own emotions. . . . [T]here are at least two reasons why no other ending would have been imaginatively right, and for a proper understanding they are of the greatest importance. We do not only look at a masterpiece, we enter into it and live with it. Our suffering, then, and our acceptance of suffering, not simply our sympathy with what we see on the stage, form an intrinsic part of what the play is; for as with Lear and Gloucester our capacity to see is dependent upon our capacity to feel. Now what our seeing has been directed towards is nothing less than *what man is*. The imaginative discovery that is the play's essence has thus involved the sharpest possible juxtaposition of rival conceptions of 'Nature'. In the Edmund–Goneril–Regan group the philosophy of natural impulse and egotism has been revealed as self-consuming, its claim to represent strength as a self-bred delusion. What Lear touches in Cordelia, on the other hand, is, we are made to feel, the reality, and the values revealed so surely there are established in the face of the worst that can be known of man or Nature. To keep nothing in reserve, to slur over no possible cruelty or misfortune, was the only way of ensuring that the positive values discovered and established in the play should keep their triumphant hold on our imagination, should assert that unconditional rightness which, in any full and responsive reading of *King Lear*, we are bound to attribute to them.

Perhaps a final question remains. It has been argued here that at the centre of the action is the complete endorsement of a particular quality of being. We may call it love so long as we remember that it is not simply an emotion, and that, although deeply personal, it has also the impersonality that comes from a self-forgetful concentration – this kind of impersonality – not a negation of personal consciousness but its heightening and fulfilment – that is most insisted on in Edgar's strange phrase, 'Ripeness is all' (5.2.11). In this sense . . . love is that without which life is a meaningless chaos of competing egotisms; it is the condition of intellectual clarity, the energizing centre from which personality may grow unhampered by the need for self-assertion or evasive subterfuge; it is the sole ground of a genuinely self-affirming life and energy. But . . . how does this apply to Lear when he prattles to Cordelia about gilded butterflies, or when, thinking his dead daughter is alive, his heart breaks at last? For answer, we must consider once more the play's marvellous technique, the particular way in which it enlivens and controls our sympathies and perceptions. King Lear is indeed, for most of the play, 'the centre of consciousness': what he sees we are forced to see. But the question, ultimately, is not what Lear sees but what Shakespeare sees, and what we, as audience, are prompted to see with him. At the end, however poignantly we may feel – Lear's suffering is one of the permanent possibilities, and we know it – we are still concerned with nothing less than the inclusive vision of the whole; and it is that which justifies us in asserting that the mind, the imagination, so revealed is directed towards affirmation in spite of everything. Other readings of the play are possible, and have been made. But those who think it is 'pessimistic', that it is no more than a deeply moving contemplation of man's helplessness, should consider a remarkable and obvious fact: that the tragedies written after *King Lear* everywhere proclaim an intellectual and imaginative energy that, in the firmness of its grasp, the assurance of its sense of life, shows no sign of perplexity, fear, or strain. For what takes place in *King Lear* we can find no other word than renewal. □

(Knights, pp. 79–101)

Part Two: Two Essays on Renunciation

The New Critical view of *King Lear* dominated discussion of the text until the early 1960s, almost all critics understanding the play as an essentially redemptive drama, and most seeing in it the endorsement of implicitly or explicitly Christian values. But George Orwell (see Chapter Three) was not quite alone in reading the play not for what it says about redemption, Christian or otherwise, but for what it says about renunciation. In the excerpt that follows, Sigmund Freud understands the emotional impact of *King Lear* to derive not merely from the King's renunciation of his crown, but from his renunciation of life itself. Like others before him, Freud remarks on the similarity to a fairy tale of the play's opening scene, but whereas for others, this likeness constituted an explanation of some of the play's problems, for Freud, the similarity only opens up a wider problem: why should this theme of choosing between three objects (be they caskets, as in *The Merchant of Venice*, or sisters, as in *King Lear*) recur so frequently? And why should the chooser invariably choose the third object? Freud answers this question by claiming that what the third object represents is death, or 'the Goddess of Death'. But why should the chooser choose death?, he then asks. In later years, most notably in *Beyond the Pleasure Principle*, Freud was to argue that all of us are driven towards the moment of our own annihilation, seeking that death which we simultaneously fear. Here, he makes a lesser claim: that in order to make palatable the truth that we must die, we effect a substitution between death and love, and render as choice what is in fact inexorable, in order to 'make friends with the necessity of dying'.

From Sigmund Freud, 'The Theme of the Three Caskets' (1913)[13]

■ Two scenes from Shakespeare . . . have lately given me occasion for . . . solving a small problem.

The first of these scenes is the suitors' choice between the three caskets in *The Merchant of Venice*. . . . Portia [must] . . . take as her husband only [he] . . . who chooses the right casket from among . . . three . . . caskets . . . of gold, silver and lead. . . . Two suitors have . . . departed unsuccessful: they have chosen gold and silver. Bassanio . . . decides in favour of lead; thereby he wins the bride. . . . Each of the suitors gives reasons for his choice in a speech in which he praises the metal he prefers. . . . The most difficult task thus falls to . . . the . . . third suitor; what he finds to say in glorification of lead . . . is little and has a forced ring. If in psycho-analytic practice we were confronted with such a speech, we should suspect that there were concealed motives behind the unsatisfying reasons produced.

Shakespeare did not . . . invent this oracle of the choice of a casket. . . . [W]e have here an ancient theme, which requires to be interpreted, accounted for and traced back to its origin. . . . [Freud here argues that to attempt to explain the theme by reference to its earlier manifestations is to look at the matter the wrong way round:] myths were [not] . . . read in the heavens and brought down to earth; . . . they were projected on to the heavens after having arisen elsewhere under purely human conditions . . .

. . . In the [older versions of the theme] . . . the subject is a girl choosing between three suitors; in . . . *The Merchant of Venice* the subject is apparently the same, but at the same time something appears in it that is in the nature of an inversion of the theme: a man chooses between three – caskets. If what we were concerned with were a dream, it would occur to us at once that caskets are also women, symbols of what is essential in woman, and therefore of a woman herself – like coffers, boxes, cases, baskets, and so on. If we boldly assume that there are symbolic substitutions of the same kind in myths as well, then the casket scene in *The Merchant of Venice* really becomes the inversion we suspected . . . [N]ow we see that the theme is a human one, *a man's choice between three women.*

This same content, however, is to be found in . . . one of [Shakespeare's] most powerfully moving dramas . . . [Freud recounts the action of *King Lear* 1.1] . . . Is not this once more . . . a choice between three women, of whom the youngest is the best, the most excellent one?

There will at once occur to us other scenes from myths, fairy tales and literature, with the same situation as their content. [Freud mentions here the stories of Paris, Cinderella, and Psyche.]

. . . In all the stories the three women, of whom the third is the most excellent one, must surely be regarded as in some way alike if they are represented as sisters. (We must not be led astray by the fact that Lear's choice is between three *daughters*; this may [only] mean . . . that he has to be represented as an old man. An old man cannot . . . choose between three women in any other way. Thus they become his daughters.)

But who are these three sisters and why must the choice fall on the third? . . . We have once already made use of an application of psycho-analytic technique, when we explained the three caskets symbolically as three women. If we . . . proceed in the same way, we shall be setting foot on a path which will lead us first to something unexpected and incomprehensible, but which will perhaps, by a devious route, bring us to a goal.

It must strike us that this excellent third woman has . . . certain peculiar qualities besides her beauty. . . . Cordelia makes herself unrecognizable, inconspicuous like lead, she remains dumb, she 'loves and is silent'. . . . In Bassanio's short speech while he is choosing the casket, he says of lead . . . : 'Thy paleness moves me more than eloquence.' That is to say: 'Thy plainness moves me more than the blatant nature of the other two.' Gold and silver are 'loud'; lead is dumb – in fact like Cordelia, who 'loves and is silent'.

. . . If we decide to regard the peculiarities of our 'third one' as concentrated in her 'dumbness', then psycho-analysis will tell us that in dreams dumbness is a common representation of death.

[Freud here relates a dream in which dumbness signified the death of the dreamer's friend, and argues that the paleness of lead also signifies death. He goes on to elaborate the way in which dumbness appears as a substitution for death in two of Grimm's fairy tales.] . . . These indications would lead us to conclude that the third one of the sisters . . . is a dead woman. But she may be something else as well – namely, Death itself, the Goddess of Death. Thanks to a displacement that is far from infrequent, the qualities that a deity imparts to men are ascribed to the deity himself. Such a displacement will surprise us least of all in relation to the Goddess of Death, since in modern . . . representations . . . Death itself is nothing other than a dead man.

But if the third of the sisters is the Goddess of Death, the sisters are known to us. They are the Fates, the Moerae, . . . the third of whom is called Atropos, the inexorable. . . .

But now it is time to return to the theme which we are trying to interpret . . . On our supposition the third of the sisters is the Goddess of Death, Death itself. But . . . in *King Lear* she is the one loyal daughter. We may ask whether there can be a more complete contradiction. Perhaps . . . there is a still more complete one lying close at hand. Indeed, there certainly is; since, whenever our theme occurs, the choice between the women is free, and yet it falls on death. For . . . no one chooses death, and it is only by a fatality that one falls a victim to it.

However, contradictions of a certain kind – replacements by the precise opposite – offer no serious difficulty to the work of analytic interpretation. . . . [T]here are motive forces in mental life which bring about replacement by the opposite in the form of what is known as reaction-formation; and it is precisely in the revelation of such hidden forces as these that we look for the reward of this enquiry. The Moerae were created as a result of a discovery that warned man that he too is a part of nature and therefore subject to the immutable law of death. Something in man was bound to struggle against this subjection, for it is only with extreme unwillingness that he gives up his claim to an exceptional position. Man . . . makes use of his imaginative activity . . .

to satisfy the wishes that reality does not satisfy. So his imagination rebelled against the recognition of the truth embodied in the myth of the Moerae, and constructed instead the myth derived from it, in which the Goddess of Death was replaced by the Goddess of Love and by what was equivalent to her in human shape. The third of the sisters was no longer Death; she was the fairest, best, most desirable and most lovable of women . . . [Here Freud explains that this substitution has a history in Classical Greek associations between the Goddesses of Love and Death.]

The same consideration answers the question how the feature of a choice came into the myth of the three sisters. Here again there has been a wishful reversal. Choice stands in the place of necessity, of destiny. In this way man overcomes death, which he has recognized intellectually. No greater triumph of wish-fulfilment is conceivable. A choice is made where in reality there is obedience to a compulsion; and what is chosen is not a figure of terror, but the . . . most desirable of women.

On closer inspection we observe . . . that [traces of] the original myth . . . show through and betray its presence. The free choice between the three sisters is . . . no free choice, for it must necessarily fall on the third if every kind of evil is not to come about, as it does in *King Lear*. The . . . best of women, who has taken the place of the Death-goddess, has kept certain characteristics that border on the uncanny, so that from them we have been able to guess at what lies beneath.

. . . We may now turn our interest to the way in which the dramatist has made use of the theme. We get an impression that a reduction of the theme to the original myth is being carried out in his work, so that we once more have a sense of the moving significance which had been weakened by the distortion. It is by means of this reduction of the distortion, this partial return to the original, that the dramatist achieves his more profound effect upon us.

To avoid misunderstandings, I should like to say that it is not my purpose to deny that King Lear's dramatic story is intended to inculcate two wise lessons: that one should not give up one's possessions and rights during one's lifetime, and that one must guard against accepting flattery at its face value. These and similar warnings are undoubtedly brought out by the play; but it seems to me quite impossible to explain the overpowering effect of *King Lear* from the impression that such a train of thought would produce. . . .

Lear is an old man. It is for this reason, as we have already said, that the three sisters appear as his daughters. The relationship of a father to his children, which might be a fruitful source of many dramatic situations, is not turned to further account in the play. But Lear is not only an old man: he is a dying man. In this way the extraordinary premise of the division of his inheritance loses all its strangeness. But the doomed man is not willing to renounce the love of women; he insists on hearing how much he is loved. Let us now recall the moving final scene, one of the culminating points of tragedy in modern drama. Lear carries Cordelia's dead body on to the stage. Cordelia is Death. If we reverse the situation it becomes intelligible and familiar to us. She is the Death-goddess who, like the Valkyrie in German mythology, carries away the dead hero from the battlefield. Eternal wisdom, clothed in the primaeval myth, bids the old man renounce love, choose death and make friends with the necessity of dying.

The dramatist brings us nearer to the ancient theme by representing the man who makes the choice between the three sisters as aged and dying. The regressive revision which he has thus applied to the myth, distorted as it was by wishful transformation, allows us enough glimpses of its original meaning to enable us perhaps to reach as well a superficial allegorical interpretation of the three female figures in the theme. We might argue that what is represented here are the three inevitable relations that a man has with a woman – the woman who bears him, the woman who is his mate and the woman who destroys him; or that they are the three forms taken by the figure of the mother in the course of a man's life – the mother herself, the beloved one who is chosen after her pattern, and lastly the Mother Earth who receives him once more. But it is in vain that an old man yearns for the love of woman as he had it first from his mother; the third of the Fates alone, the silent Goddess of Death, will take him into her arms. □

Like Freud, with whose interpretation of the text he agrees, William Empson also understands the main theme of *King Lear* to be that of renunciation. Empson is in some senses a critical oddity: sometimes classified as a New Critic, his work is nevertheless very different from that of his New Critical peers. Like the New Critics, Empson's attention is directed in the first instance to 'the words on the page', and it is from this attention that Empson produces his often dazzling readings of texts. But unlike the New Critics, whose readings were generally politically conservative ones, Empson is often radical in what he brings to texts and in what he finds in them. He hated Christianity, for instance, and the ethical codes he thought Christianity stood for (in his *Milton's God* Empson refers to the Christian god as the 'torture-monster'). And in more directly political terms Empson speaks from a position far more liberal than most of his peers, often (unlike them) alert to the ways in which a text may speak about repression and exploitation.

In his 'Fool in *Lear*' Empson takes as his point of departure Orwell's assertion that renunciation is the subject of *King Lear*, and that the play teaches that one cannot gain happiness for oneself from renunciation, but must live for others and not for the self. Empson agrees with this interpretation, which he sees anticipated in Freud. But Empson argues that in the play, 'the idea of renunciation is examined in the light of the complex idea of folly' and that properly to understand the text, we must give 'full weight to *fool*' a term used in the play forty-seven times (Empson, p. 125). According to Empson, words such as 'fool' are highly complex, expressing a range of diverse concepts (in this case, knave, imbecile and clown amongst others). And in Shakespeare, he argues, the 'use of fool is not a metaphor from the clown' but rather a 'generalised memory' of the way in which the term had earlier been used by the sixteenth-century humanist, Desiderius Erasmus, for whom, according to Empson, the term denoted 'an ordinary, simple man, who is held to be somehow right about life though more pretentious figures fail to see it'.[14]

One of Empson's concerns, then, is to render the idea of folly universal in the play, and to counter the prevailing, sentimental, view of the role of the Fool. I suspect that Empson may have read Dickens' account of the Fool (see Chapter Three); his essay bears comparison to Dickens in some respects, and Empson, moreover, notes that Dickens shared Erasmus' perspective on Fools (Empson, p. 110). And another of Empson's aims is, as we've mentioned, to connect this idea of folly to the play's meditation on renunciation. For Empson, Lear's problem is that he makes a confused and inadequate attempt at renunciation. Empson thinks that part of Lear's motivation for renunciation is religious: '*crawl towards death*', he says,

■ is the language of mystical piety in the mouth of so masterful a character, and the suggestion is that he will occupy himself with his prayers. The purpose of saying it in this rather misleading way is to announce a renunciation without any appearance of boasting about his highmindedness, which would be unsuited to the occasion. □

(Empson, pp. 126–7)

To an early modern audience, Empson maintains, conscious of the risk of civil war consequent on the division of the kingdoms, 'Lear would . . . already seem a very wrongheaded man but one acting from other-worldly motives' (Empson, p. 127), and it is this religious motivation to which we must look for an explanation of the extremity of Lear's shifts in mood:

■ Like many overbearing extroverts, [Lear] has periodical fits of trying to counteract his faults by vehement acts in the opposite direction; there is a saintly side of his character as well as the explosive one . . . if you start with the idea that Lear abdicates for religious reasons you are ready for both sides of his nature. □

(Empson, p. 128)

But whereas Wilson Knight had argued that the play charts a progression through paganism to Christianity, Empson sees the various references to god and the gods as of a part (Empson, p. 128). All gods, Christian or otherwise, are for Empson mean and cruel and petty. Thus for him the play offers no consolatory movement towards redemption or renewal: arguing explicitly against Bradley, and implicitly against New Critical readings of the play in the last part of his essay, Empson claims that the play offers us no such comforting vision of the ultimate establishment in the text of an ethics of caring Christianity, and rather maintains to the end a picture of the gods as a 'teasing riddle', whose motivations are obscure, and who are unable and unwilling to intervene in a world in which humanity's good intentions can only ever result in universal annihilation.

Empson's essay is difficult to excerpt, not so much because it is both long and rich, as because Empson's style is both allusive and breathtakingly rapid, moving between different ideas in very quick succession, and often leaving implicit the substantive connections between those ideas. So I have chosen here to extract shorter sections of the essay rather than to attempt to reproduce the main lines of his argument.

From William Empson, 'Fool in *Lear*' (1951)

■ . . . [Act 1 Scene 3] begins with the words: '*Gon.*: Did my father strike my gentleman for chiding of his fool?' so it is the Fool who causes the beginning of the storm against Lear, rather than his shadowy train of deboshed knights. She calls Lear a fool in her indignation: 'old fools are babes again'. We then see Lear calling for his Fool and his daughter simultaneously, and being treated with insolence. The Fool has been pining away at the loss of Cordelia; his first entry comes when Lear has begun to make himself ridiculous by encouraging a scuffle between the rival servants; he begins immediately to tease Lear for the folly of his behaviour, and to claim that only he can tell Lear the full truth. Kent has the usual line intended to warn the audience that this clown is meant to be taken seriously: 'This is not altogether fool, my lord.' The clown seizes the opportunity to say that 'lords and great men . . . will not let me have all fool to myself, they'll be snatching'. This folly that they insist on getting seems to be wickedness, the Biblical fool; no doubt they are foolish too, but it is because they are wicked that Lear was foolish to give up his power over them. . . .

Lear greets him affectionately as 'my pretty knave' and threatens him with the whip before he has spoken ten lines; there are six references to the whip during this short period of their comparative happiness together, and at least two of them are threats. The position of Lear's Fool is clearly meant to be a miserable one; we are to believe him when he says 'I would rather be anything than a fool, and yet I would not be thee, nuncle'.

Goneril then comes in and announces that she will cut down the knights:

Not only, sir, this your all-licensed fool
But others of your insolent retinue
Do hourly carp and quarrel.

She still seems more annoyed by the fool than by the knights. Lear makes his first great speech about ingratitude and appeals to the 'dear goddess' Nature to put unnatural and startling punishments on her . . . No doubt you can say that Lear, unlike Edmund, assumes that Nature is good and will punish wickedness, so that there are two views of Nature in the play; but one might also accuse Lear of believing that Nature is an amoral magical force which will obey his royal caprices.

. . . Lear returns to the stage after storming out, and the answer to his prayer is to learn that half his knights are already dismissed. He threatens to pluck out his eyes if they weep, because he wants to be angry and revengeful. When you know the story it gives him an obscure connection with Gloucester, but even so largely one of contrast; I think the chief idea is that even now, he is deliberately blinding himself to the realities of the process of renunciation. He sets out to go to Regan, and it is Goneril who makes the clown go with him, by the words 'You, sir, more knave than fool, after your master'. Outside the palace, Lear for the first time is seen to laugh at a joke by the clown [which] . . . seems meant to call Lear a fool. Till the blow had fallen he was trying to resist this suspicion, and the clown was particularly unwelcome, but now he has admitted his folly and the clown seems on his side. The determination of Bradley to bring out the best in the good characters sometimes makes his judgements rather brutal, oddly enough; I do not think we need say it was very magnanimous of Lear not to whip the clown. But no doubt he might have been expected to do it, so the clown has succeeded in making him appear tolerably human. Incidentally the clown says that Lear's asses have gone to get his horses ready, so that even the invisible knights are included in the universal accusation of folly. He then brings in the whip again:

FOOL: If thou wert my fool, nuncle, I'd have thee beaten for being old before thy time.
LEAR: How's that?
FOOL: Thou shouldst not have been old till thou hadst been wise.

> LEAR: Oh, let me not be mad, not mad, sweet heavens! Keep me in temper; I would not be mad!

There are two ways of looking at this. Bradley it appears would say that the teasing of the clown is intolerably irritating, and that Lear means 'if this nagging goes on I shall go off my head'. But Lear makes his feelings much plainer than that, and on the other hand he often does not listen to people; here he is giving the clown hardly any attention. During the jokes he has made two ejaculations about his own kindness and Goneril's ingratitude, and said 'I will forget my nature'; 'let me not be mad' simply follows his own line of thought. All the same, I think the presence of the clown has suggested the idea. Lear considers the clown as mad, and the whip was used on actual mad-men too; I think this first outburst of the horror of madness was put into his mind by seeing a lunatic before him. . . . The horses are ready, and the scene ends with an irrelevant bit of bawdy nonsense from the clown; which Bradley wanted to throw out as spurious, and indeed on his view it is completely out of place; but it is very much wanted if you are to treat the Fool as a real one.

The second act begins with the plots of the wicked, and then Kent attacks Oswald before Gloucester's castle. He complains that Oswald smiles at his speeches (which are very wild talk) as if he were a fool, and Cornwall asks if he is mad. Next Edgar in soliloquy explains that he will disguise himself as a mad beggar. Lear and the Fool then find Kent in the stocks, and realise that Regan will be no help; Lear again expresses fear of rising madness, and the Fool calls Kent a fool . . . It seems as well to point out these hints that Kent is in some peculiar sense another fool, because that completes the set of them for the mad scenes. . . . [A]nyone who comes near the charmed circle, whatever he does, is made a fool of some kind.

I am not clear how far we should suppose, as is commonly done, that the Fool is labouring to distract Lear from his anger and thus save him from going mad. He boasts of staying with Lear, but he has been sent with him, and would probably be afraid to go off alone. When we last see him he is again ordered to follow Lear, this time by Kent: 'Come, help to bear thy master. Thou must not stay behind.' This does not suggest that Kent took his faithfulness for granted. . . . The audience would not regard self-sacrifice as typical of clowns, and so far there has been nothing to suggest it. To be sure, the line just before his first entry: 'Since my young lady's going into France, sir, the Fool hath much pined away' is meant to put him clearly on the side of the good characters. But he may pine because he is frightened and actually ill-used, not because he loves her so much; what he expresses as soon as he appears is a keen sense of danger. I do not mean to deny that the

Fool is affectionate towards Lear and Cordelia, his only protectors (why shouldn't he be?), only that he is supposed to be a highminded and self-sacrificing character; also I think that the malice which is part of his role comes out plainly enough in his jokes to Lear.

After Gloucester has made clear that Regan will be no help we do get an impression, for the first time, that the Fool is sympathising with the real anxiety of Lear, which is fear of madness:

> LEAR: Oh me, my heart, my rising heart; but down!
> FOOL: Cry to it, nuncle, as the cockney did to the eels, when she put 'em up i' the paste alive; she knapped 'em o' the coxcombs with a stick, and cried 'down wantons, down!' 'Twas her brother that, in pure kindness to his horse, buttered his hay.

Even here, I think the chief impression is not of any depth of sympathy but that the Fool understands about madness because he is mad himself. George Orwell's view of him is that he stands merely for the cynical side of Shakespeare, a man who had no intention of renouncing anything, or at any rate that he stands for worldly common sense. Both the simpletons mentioned are in effect cruel, and the brother may well be a knave, as greasing hay was more usually done by deceitful ostlers; the worldly second anecdote makes one suspect a bawdy meaning in the first. Anyhow the Fool satirizes Lear's habit of giving orders all the time, even to his diseases, after he has renounced the power to get his orders obeyed. The text does not tell us the effect on Lear, because Regan enters at once; no doubt the important effect is on the audience – it broadens the suffering of Lear into a whole world of coarse wickedness and folly, and at the end of the great scene with Regan that follows we first hear the rumbling of the universal storm.

(Empson, pp. 129–33)

. . .

. . . Well may Gloucester achieve patience and Lear plunge with increasing violence into the mysteries of folly. A record-breaking display of evil is let loose by the process, and this forces us to hold in balance the ascetic and humanist views of the world; but the balance is held even, and the gods remain a teasing riddle.

[The gods] are in any case peculiar objects, because they are offered neither as the mythology of a definite historical period nor as a belief of the playwright. The view that they represent merely Nature, behind whom is the good God, does not seem to me a very obvious one for the audience. . . . What we gather directly about the gods is that they are confused; apparently they can suffer as well as cause suffering, but in any case they can fool and cause fooling. . . . The foolish Lear can compare the storm and the heavens to himself, and the stock metaphor from the clown and the lunatic can be extended to include the cosmos. Such is the impression from a literal reading, I think, and critics have either evaded it or hailed it as being anti-Christian. But, if you take it as simply a result of working out the key metaphor as far as it would go, you need not expect it to have a clear-cut theological conclusion; the problem for the dramatist was rather to keep such a thing at bay. The effect of the false renunciation is that Lear has made a fool of himself on the most cosmic and appalling scale possible; he has got on the wrong side of the next world as well as on the wrong side of this one. I do not think one need extract any more theology from the gods.

A rather interesting distinction, I think, needs to be drawn here. If you assume that a key word, or better no doubt a whole pattern of related key words, is the proper thing to follow in considering a poetic drama, you get a noticeably different result in this play from the result of the Victorian assumption that the characters ought to be followed separately. Maybe both are different from the result of a simple visit to the play, but the play could be produced to suit either assumption. What the key-word or 'pattern' approach brings you to, I submit, is a fundamental horror, an idea that the gods are such silly and malicious jokers that they will soon destroy the world. The question whether Shakespeare meant this or not is still quite a live controversy, and usually thought to be independent of any question of critical technique. It is most often raised about the words of Gloucester, 'As flies to wanton boys are we to the gods; they kill us for their sport', and I have noticed critics on both sides showing impatience with those who are so blind as to disagree with them . . . [A]s part of the pattern of clown-imagery in the play they make a big moment, easily recognized as one in the theatre . . . I . . . think that the suggestions of a fundamental horror in the play were meant to be prominent, whether you interpret them as some profound intuition about life or prefer to say, more simply, that the theme released a lot of real bad temper in [Shakespeare]. In any case, from the point of view of his immediate actors and audience, I submit, it was reasonable and not theologically suspicious to have this background of cosmic horror, because the play was about the huge evils which could follow from a false renunciation.

Where there does seem room for a religious view is through [an assumption] that . . . by being such a complete fool Lear may become in some mystical way superlatively wise and holy. It seems hard to deny that this idea is knocking about, and yet I think it belongs to the play rather than the character. The idea is already present, in its flattest form, if you think 'it is very sad, but after all I am not really sorry it happened, because it teaches us so much'. And the scapegoat who has collected all this wisdom for us is viewed at the end with a sort of hushed envy, not I think really because he has become wise but because the general human desire for experience has been so glutted in him; he has been through everything.

> We that are young
> Shall never see so much, nor live so long. □

(Empson, pp. 155–7)

Part Three: the New *King Lear*

In taking 'fool' as the 'key word' of *King Lear* Empson paved the way for the criticism and theatrical production of the early 1960s which over-turned (at least to this day) the perception of the play which saw it as effecting the redemption of its central character and the resolution of its deepest metaphysical conflicts. Remarking on the meaningless of the play's final act, Empson says:

■ the death of Cordelia, and the death of Lear in consequence of it, are different from those of any other Shakespearean tragedy in that they seem wilful; . . . The death is like a last trip-up as the clown leaves the stage; its shock and senselessness . . . are as far as Chekhov from normal tragedy. □

(Empson, p. 150)

And commenting on the blasphemies against the gods in the play, he argues that they ought to be understood not as 'pious ejaculations in favour of Christianity', nor as

■ specific attacks on it; they are not more shocking than the Book of Job. The point surely is that the world is a place in which good inten-tions get painfully and farcically twisted by one's own character and by unexpected events. □

(Empson, pp. 154–5)

Jan Kott, whose *Shakespeare Our Contemporary* was highly influential in the instigation of a new reading of the play in which destruction and despair were taken to be its dominant characteristics, does not mention Empson in his discussion of *King Lear*; some of his conclusions, never-theless, are strikingly similar to Empson's.

Kott opens his essay on the play by surveying the theatrical history of *King Lear*. The Romantics, he argues, conceived the play as a 'melo-drama . . . dealing with a tragic king' purified by suffering, whose 'fate was to arouse pity and terror, to shock the audience' (Kott, pp. 100–1). This was superseded by a 'historical, antiquarian and realistic Shakespeare' in which productions made efforts to set the play in a 'definite historical period', and in which 'Lear became an old druid' (Kott, p. 101); and then, at the beginning of the twentieth century, by an 'authentic' Shakespeare – an attempted return to the way in which critics assumed that the play would have been produced at the Globe, in Shakespeare's own time. But with this return, Kott argues, the play, and Lear himself, became ridiculous. 'The exposition of *King Lear* seems preposterous if one is to look in it for psychological verisimilitude', Kott maintains: 'regarded as a person, a character, Lear is ridiculous, naïve and stupid. When he goes mad, he can only arouse compassion, never pity and terror' (Kott, p. 102).

For Kott, this does not mean that the play is unimportant, nor unplayable, but that it needs to be understood differently, in terms which only the 'new theatre' can afford. For Kott, *Lear*'s cruelty is a 'philosophical cruelty' in which 'the tragic element has been superseded by the grotesque' (Kott, p. 103). The play, for him, bears more similarities to the drama of say, Brecht or Beckett than to nineteenth-century drama, for both invoke the grotesque to effect a new conception of tragedy. 'Both the tragic and the grotesque world,' Kott argues,

■ are composed . . . of the same elements. In a tragic and grotesque world, situations are imposed, compulsory and inescapable. Freedom of choice . . . [is] part of this compulsory situation, in which both the tragic hero and the grotesque actor must always lose their struggle against the absolute. The downfall of the tragic hero is a confirmation and recognition of the absolute; whereas the downfall of the grotesque actor means mockery of the absolute and its desecration . . . the grotesque is a criticism of the absolute in the name of frail human experience. That is why tragedy brings *catharsis*, whilst grotesque offers no consolation whatsoever. □

(Kott, p. 104)

For Kott *King Lear* is akin to the new drama in that both are absurd, offering a picture of the absolute as itself absurd, and charting a dramatic trajectory in which the mechanism of the tragedy is 'a trap set by man himself into which he has fallen' (Kott, p. 105). Such mechanisms, Kott claims, force the protagonist 'into a game in which the probability of his total defeat constantly increases' (Kott, p. 108): Kott compares the structure of this mechanism to a chess game against a computer which the protagonist must lose, and to a 'barrel of laughs' at a funfair, in which participants try to keep their balance whilst a barrel beneath them revolves. *King Lear*, he claims, is constructed around similar principles, and offers us a picture of the world in which the grotesque is ubiquitous. Thus in the opening section of his discussion of the play (not reproduced here), Kott reads the fall of Gloucester as a kind of grotesque pantomime, effected on an empty stage, in which 'there is nothing, except the cruel earth, where man goes on his journey from the cradle to the grave' (Kott, p. 116) and in which there are no gods who could make such a gesture meaningful, so that Gloucester's suicide becomes 'only a somer-sault on an empty stage' (Kott, p. 119). For Kott, the sensibility of *King Lear* is akin to the sensibility of Beckett's *Endgame*: grotesque, absurd, and nihilistic.

From Jan Kott, '*King Lear*, or Endgame' (1965)

■ The theme of *King Lear* is the decay and fall of the world. . . . In *King Lear* there is no young . . . Fortinbras to ascend the throne. . . . In *King Lear* there . . . is no one whom Edgar can invite to [a coronation]. Everybody has died or been murdered. Gloster was right when he said: 'This great world shall so wear out to nought'. Those who have survived . . . are, as Lear has been, just 'ruin'd pieces of nature'.

Of the twelve major characters one half are just and good, the other – unjust and bad. It is a division just as consistent and abstract as in a morality play. But this is a morality play in which everyone will be destroyed: noble characters along with base ones, the persecutors with the persecuted, the torturers with the tortured. Vivisection will go on until the stage is empty. The decay and fall of the world will be shown on two . . . different kinds of stages. . . . One of these may be called Macbeth's stage, the other – Job's stage.

Macbeth's stage is the scene of crime. . . . All bonds, all laws, whether divine, natural or human, are broken. Social order, from the kingdom to the family, will crumble into dust. There are no longer kings and subjects, fathers and children, husbands and wives. There are only huge renaissance monsters, devouring one another like beasts of prey. . . . The history of the world . . . is just action. These violent sequences are merely an illustration . . . and perform the function of a black, realistic counterpart to 'Job's stage'.

For it is Job's stage that constitutes the main scene. On it the ironic, clownish morality play on human fate will be performed. But before that happens, all the characters must be uprooted from their social positions and pulled down, to final degradation. They must reach rock-bottom. The downfall is not merely a philosophical parable, as Gloster's leap over the supposed precipice is. The theme of down-fall is carried through by Shakespeare stubbornly, consistently, and is repeated at least four times. The fall is at the same time physical and spiritual, bodily and social.

At the beginning there was a king with his court and ministers. Later, there are just four beggars wandering about in a wilderness, exposed to raging winds and rain. The fall may be slow, or sudden.

Lear has at first a retinue of a hundred men, then fifty, then only one. Kent is banished by one angry gesture of the King. But the process of degradation is always the same. Everything that distinguishes a man – his titles, social position, even name, – is lost. Names are not needed any more. Every one is just a shadow of himself; just a man.

> *King Lear*   . . . Who is it that can tell me who I am? –
> *Fool*   Lear's shadow. (1.4)

And once more the same question, and the same answer. The banished Kent returns in disguise to his King.

> *King Lear*   How now! what art thou?
> *Kent*   A man, sir. (1.4)

A naked man has no name. Before the morality commences, everyone must be naked. Naked like a worm.

> Then Job arose, and rent his mantle, and shaved his head . . .
>   And said, Naked came I out of my mother's womb, and naked shall I return thither. (*Book of Job*, I, 20–21)

Biblical imagery in this new *Book of Job* is no mere chance. Edgar says that he will with his 'nakedness out-face the winds and persecutions of the sky' (2.3). This theme returns obstinately, and with an equal consistency. . . . A downfall means suffering and torment. It may be physical or spiritual torment, or both. Lear will lose his wits; Kent will be put in the stocks; Gloster will have his eyes gouged out and will attempt suicide. For a man to become naked, or rather to become nothing but man, it is not enough to deprive him of his name, social position and character. One must also maim and massacre him both morally and physically. Turn him – like King Lear – into a 'ruin'd piece of nature', and only then ask him who he is. For it is the new renaissance Job who is to judge the events on 'Macbeth's stage'. □

(Kott, pp. 120–3)

And for Kott, the only character in the play with any access to the reality of the world it portrays is the Fool:

■ Lear and Gloster are adherents of eschatology; they desperately believe in the existence of absolutes. They invoke the gods, believe in justice, appeal to laws of nature. They have fallen off 'Macbeth's stage', but remain its prisoners. Only the Fool stands outside

'Macbeth's stage', just as he had stood outside 'Job's stage'. He is looking on apart, and does not follow any ideology. He rejects all appearances, of law, justice, moral order. He sees brute force, cruelty and lust. He has no illusions and does not seek consolation in the existence of natural or supernatural order, which provides for the punishment of evil and the reward of good. Lear, insisting on his fictitious majesty, seems ridiculous to him. All the more ridiculous because he does not see how ridiculous he is. But the Fool does not desert his ridiculous, degraded king, and accompanies him on his way to madness. The Fool knows that the only true madness is to recognize this world as rational. The feudal order is absurd and can be described only in terms of the absurd. □

(Kott, pp. 131–2)

Coincident with this reading of the play as an absurdist drama of annihilation and despair were theatrical productions of the text that emphasised in it those same qualities. I end this chapter with R. A. Foakes' description of Peter Brook's 1962 production of *King Lear*, a film version of which was produced five years later.

R. A. Foakes on Peter Brook's 1962 Production of *King Lear*

■ . . . The beginning of the text was cut, so that the film could open with Lear's great cry, 'Know that we have divided/ In three our kingdom . . .'; the long-drawn-out 'Know' brought out the pun on 'No', and negation became the theme. Further cutting removed most of the play's moralizing and words of comfort or consolation, and reduced the roles of Edgar and Albany especially. The film, set in a barbaric Jutland landscape where life is at best crude and primitive, emphasized desolation, loss, brutality. Lear's knights lay waste to Goneril's palace, and Oswald squeals like a pig when savagely killed by Edgar. Special highlighting was given to Gloucester's words.

As flies to wanton boys, are we to th' gods.
They kill us for their sport. (4.1.36-7)

These lines had been usually cut in productions of the play until the 1930s, as representing an unacceptable nihilism; by contrast, Brook kept them in and cut the remaining forty lines of dialogue between Edgar as Poor Tom and his father in this scene, as part of a deliberate attempt to remove any 'reassuring catharsis' in relation to either Lear or Gloucester.[15] □

Essentially, as we will see in the following chapter, it is this view of *King Lear* – one which sees in it no catharsis, no consolation, and most of all, no redemption for Lear himself, which remains the spoken or unspoken premise of most criticism of the play to this day.

CHAPTER FIVE

Contemporary Criticism of *King Lear*

THIS CHAPTER is constructed as an invitation to further reading (some more explicit advice on where to go is included at the end of this book's bibliography). The proliferation both of critical methodology and of sheer volume of critical production in the years since the early sixties is such that another volume the size of this would be necessary were I to attempt to provide anything like a comprehensive selection of the criticism on *King Lear* produced in these decades, let alone to explain the complex bodies of ideas which underlie the different literary theories – deconstruction, feminism, psychoanalysis, New Historicism, Marxism, amongst others – from which these treatments of the text variously emerge. For these reasons, and also because there already exists a number of good introductions to critical theory easily available to students of literature, I will devote as much as possible of this chapter to the reproduction of excerpts from essays, rather than spend any significant space on their explication.[1]

In extracting the material reproduced below, however, I have tried to let the critics themselves offer some sense of the different debates in which they participate, of the concerns which predominantly preoccupy them, and – to a lesser degree – of the methods which they variously adopt. For better or for worse, these concerns are primarily political ones: Shakespeare's negotiation of issues of class, gender, and power are the topics (almost universally) addressed in contemporary criticism, in stark contrast to the years before the 60s, when such considerations were (almost entirely) absent from discussions of the text; for better or for worse, the methodology adopted by critics of the early modern period has ever more increasingly moved towards historicisms of various kinds (again in great contrast to the criticism that preceded it).

From Stanley Cavell, 'The Avoidance of Love' (1967)

[Cavell is a philosopher by training, and his essay on *King Lear* first appeared as the concluding chapter of his *Must We Mean What We Say?*

(C.U.P., 1969). I include an extract from his essay here because his treatment of the play has been quietly but nevertheless significantly influential on later readings of the text (such as, for example, Coppélia Kahn's). Cavell's broader interests in Shakespeare revolve around his belief that many of Shakespeare's plays betray a scepticism as radical as that which was to be expressed some years later in Descartes' *Meditations*; for Cavell, 'the extreme precipitousness of the Lear story, the velocity of the banishments and of the consequences of the banishments, [figure] the precipitousness of scepticism's banishment of the world'.[2] In this excerpt from his essay on *King Lear*, Cavell takes issue with Paul Alpers' claim that the play's thematisation of vision has a purely literal role to play, and is not, as the then dominant New Critical reading contended, a metaphor for its characters' access to insight. Alpers had argued that 'the crucial issue is not insight, but recognition'; Cavell agrees with Alpers that moments of recognition are paramount in the play, but he sees these moments also as strategic, arguing that recognition of others is indivisible from recognition of the self, and that the avoidance of the eyes of others is a structuring principle of *King Lear*.]

■ In a fine paper published a few years ago, Professor Paul Alpers notes the tendency of modern critics to treat metaphors or symbols rather than the characters and actions of Shakespeare's plays as primary data in understanding them, and undertakes to disconfirm a leading interpretation of the symbolic sort which exactly depends upon a neglect . . . of the humanness of the play's characters.[3] . . . [Alpers] . . . begins by assembling quotations from several commentators which together compose the view he wishes to correct – the view of the 'sight pattern':

> In *King Lear* an unusual amount of imagery drawn from vision . . . prompts us to apprehend a symbolism of sight and blindness having its culmination in Gloucester's tragedy. . . . The blinding of Gloucester might well be gratuitous melodrama but for its being imbedded in a field of meanings centred in the concept of *seeing*. This sight pattern relentlessly brings into the play the problem of seeing and what is always implied is that the problem is one of insight. . . . It is commonly recognized that just as Lear finds 'reason in madness' so Gloucester learns to 'see' in his blindness. . . . The whole play is built on this double paradox. [Alpers, no page reference given.]

But when Alpers looks to the text for evidence for this theory he discovers that there is none. Acts of vision and references to eyes are notably present, but their function is not to symbolize moral insight;

rather, they insist upon the ordinary, literal uses of eyes: to express feeling, to weep, and to recognize others. Unquestionably there is truth in this. But the evidence for Alpers's view is not perfectly clear and his concepts are not accurately explored in terms of the events of the play. The acts of vision named in the lines he cites are those of giving *looks* and of *staring*, and the function of these acts is exactly not to express feeling, or else to express cruel feeling. Why? Because the power of the eyes to see is being used in isolation from their capacity to weep, which seems the most literal use of them to express feeling.

Alpers's . . . insistence upon the third ordinary use of the eyes, their role in recognizing others, counters common readings of the two moments of recognition central to the 'sight pattern': Gloucester's recognition of Edgar's innocence and Lear's recognition of Cordelia. 'The crucial issue is not insight, but recognition' (Alpers, p. 149): Gloucester is not enabled to 'see' because he is blinded, the truth is heaped upon him from Regan's luxuriant cruelty; Cordelia need not be viewed symbolically, the infinite poignance of her reconciliation with Lear is sufficiently accounted for by his literal recognition of her. – But then it becomes incomprehensible why or how these children have *not* been recognized by these parents; they had not become literally invisible. They are in each case banished, disowned, sent out of sight. And the question remains: What makes it possible for them to be *received* again?

In each case, there is a condition necessary in order that the recognition take place: Gloucester and Lear must each first recognize himself, and allow himself to be recognized, revealed to another. In Gloucester, the recognition comes at once, on hearing Regan's news:

O my follies! Then Edgar was abused.
Kind Gods, forgive me that, and prosper him!   (3.7.90–1)

In each of these two lines he puts his recognition of himself first. Lear's self-revelation comes harder, but when it comes it has the same form:

Do not laugh at me;
For, as I am a man, I think this lady
To be my child Cordelia.   (4.7.68–70)

He refers to himself three times, then 'my child' recognizes her simultaneously with revealing himself (as her father) [*sic*]. Self-recognition is, phenomenologically, a form of insight; and it is because of its necessity in recognizing others that critics have felt its presence here.

Lear does not attain his insight until the end of the fourth act, and when he does it is climactic. This suggests that Lear's dominating motivation to this point, from the time things go wrong in the opening scene, is to *avoid being recognized*. The isolation and avoidance of eyes is what the obsessive sight imagery of the play underlines. This is the clue I want to follow first in reading out the play.

If the blinding is unnecessary for Gloucester's true seeing of Edgar, why is Gloucester blinded? . . . Critics who have looked for a *meaning* in the blinding have been looking . . . for an aesthetic meaning or justification; looking too high, as it were. It is aesthetically justified . . . just because it is morally, spiritually justified, in a way which directly relates the eyes to their power to see.

> *Glou.*   . . . but I shall see
>   The winged vengeance overtake such children.
> *Corn.* See't shalt thou never.   (3.7.4-6)

And then Cornwall puts out one of Gloucester's eyes. A servant interposes, wounding Cornwall; then Regan stabs the servant from behind, and his dying words, meant to console or establish connection with Gloucester, ironically recall Cornwall to his interrupted work:

> *First Serv.* O! I am slain. My Lord, you have one eye left
>   To see some mischief on him. Oh!   *Dies.*
> *Corn.* Lest it see more, prevent it. Out, vile jelly!   (3.7.80-2)

Cornwall himself twice gives the immediate cause of his deed, once for each eye: to prevent Gloucester from seeing, and in particular to prevent him from seeing *him*. . . . The scene is symbolic, but what it symbolizes is a function of what it means. The physical cruelty symbolizes . . . the psychic cruelty which pervades the play; but what this particular act of cruelty means is that cruelty cannot bear to be seen. It literalizes evil's ancient love of darkness.

This relates the blinding to Cornwall's needs; but it is also related to necessities of Gloucester's character. It has an aptness which takes on symbolic value, the horrible aptness of retribution. . . . For Gloucester has a fault . . . and I cannot understand his . . . acquiescence in the fate which has befallen him . . . without supposing that it strikes him as a retribution, forcing him to an insight about his life . . . Not, however, necessarily a true insight. He has revealed his fault in the opening speeches of the play, in which he tells Kent of his *shame*. . . . He recognizes the moral claim upon himself, as he says twice, to 'acknowledge' his bastard; but all this means to him is that he acknowledge that he has a bastard for a son. He does not acknowledge *him*, as a son or a person, with *his* feelings of illegitimacy and being cast out. *That* is something Gloucester ought to be ashamed of; his shame is itself more shameful than his one piece of licentiousness. This is one of the inconveniences of shame, that it is generally inaccurate, attaches to the wrong thing. . . .

. . . Joking is a familiar specific for brazening out shame, calling enlarged attention to the thing you do not want naturally noticed . . . But if the failure to recognize others is a failure to let others recognize you, a fear of what is revealed to them, an avoidance of their eyes, then it is exactly shame which is the cause of his withholding of recognition . . . For shame is the specific discomfort produced by the sense of being looked at; the avoidance of the sight of others is the reflex it produces. Guilt is different; there the reflex is to avoid discovery. As long as no one *knows* what you have done, you are safe. . . . Under shame, what must be covered up is not your deed, but yourself. . . . Gloucester suffers the same punishment he inflicts: in his respectability, he avoided eyes; when respectability falls away and the disreputable come into power, his eyes are avoided. In the fear of Gloucester's poor eyes there is the promise that cruelty can be overcome, and instruction about how it can be overcome. That is the content which justifies the scene of his blinding, aesthetically, psychologically, morally.

This raises again the question of the relation between the Gloucester subplot and the Lear plot. The traditional views seem on the whole to take one of two lines: Gloucester's fate parallels Lear's in order that it become more universal . . .; or more concrete. . . . Such suggestions . . . leave out of account the specific climactic moment at which the subplot surfaces and Lear and Gloucester face one another . . .

Two questions immediately arise about that confrontation: (1) . . . Both the breaking through [of Lear's madness] and the reassembling [of his sanity] are manifested by his *recognizing* someone, and my first question is: Why is it Gloucester whom Lear is first able to recognize . . . and in recognizing whom his sanity begins to return? (2) What does Lear see when he recognizes Gloucester? What is he confronted by?

1. Given our notion that recognizing a person depends upon allowing oneself to be recognized by him, the question becomes: Why is it Gloucester whose recognition Lear is first able to bear? The obvious answer is: because Gloucester is blind. Therefore one can be, can only be, *recognized by him without being seen,* without having to bear eyes upon oneself.

Leading up to Lear's acknowledgment ('I know thee well enough') there is that insane flight of exchanges about Gloucester's eyes; it is the only active cruelty given to Lear by Shakespeare apart from his behaviour in the abdication scene. . . . Lear is picking at Gloucester's eyes, as if to make sure they are really gone. When he is sure, he recognizes him:

> If thou wilt weep my fortunes, take my eyes;
> I know thee well enough; thy name is Gloucester.   (4.6.178–9)
> . . .

This picking spiritually relates Lear to Cornwall's and Regan's act in first blinding Gloucester, for Lear does what he does for the same reason they do – in order not to be seen by this man, whom he has brought harm. (Lear exits from this scene running . . . not because in his madness he cannot distinguish friends from enemies but because he knows that recognition of himself is imminent . . .)

2. This leads to the second question about the scene: What is Lear confronted by in acknowledging Gloucester? It is easy to say: Lear is confronted here with the direct consequences of his conduct . . . he is for the first time confronting himself. What is difficult is to show that this is not merely or vaguely symbolic, and that it is not merely an access of knowledge which Lear undergoes. Gloucester has by now become not just a figure 'parallel' to Lear but Lear's double; he does not merely represent Lear, but is psychically identical with him. So that what comes to the surface in this meeting is not a related story, but Lear's submerged mind. This, it seems to me, is what gives the scene its particular terror, and gives to the characters what neither could have alone. In this fusion of plots and identities, we have . . . the double or mirror image, of everyman who has gone to every length to avoid himself, caught at the moment of coming upon himself face to face. (Against this, 'take my eyes' strikes psychotic power.) . . .

We now have elements with which to begin an analysis of the most controversial of the *Lear* problems, the nature of Lear's motivation in his opening (abdication) scene. The usual interpretations follow one of three main lines: Lear is senile; Lear is puerile; Lear is not to be understood in natural terms, for the whole scene has a fairy-tale or ritualistic character which simply must be accepted as the premise from which the tragedy is derived. Arguments ensue, in each case, about whether Shakespeare is justified in what he is asking his audience to accept. My hypothesis will be that Lear's behaviour in this scene is explained by – the tragedy begins because of – the same motivation which manipulates the tragedy throughout its course, from the scene which precedes the abdication, through the storm, blinding, evaded reconciliations, to the final moments: by the attempt to avoid recognition, the shame of exposure, the threat of self-revelation . . .[4] □

From Jonathan Goldberg, 'Perspectives: Dover Cliff and the Conditions of Representation' (1988)

[Dover, Jonathan Goldberg's deconstructive essay maintains, is initially invoked in *King Lear* as a 'counterforce' to the annihilative forces which consume its characters in the storm and its aftermath. But the vision of Dover that the play ends up by offering us is ultimately, and only, that encompassed in Edgar's description to his father of 'Dover Cliff'. 'Dover' in other words, emerges in the end as the 'place of illusion', the embodiment of the perception that the imaginary and the real collapse into each other and that all that is solid must melt into air. As such, Dover represents 'the limits of representation themselves'. The extract which follows reprints most of the opening of Goldberg's essay, and (following the ellipsis after Edgar's speech) most of the concluding paragraph of its second section.]

■ I. The Way to Dover

Act III of *King Lear* opens with a description that a nameless gentleman makes to the disguised Kent, a description of Lear blasted 'with eyeless rage' (3.1.8). Before we are offered the horrific spectacle of the king raging on the heath, we have this image of the king whom the storm would 'make nothing of' (3.1.9). And virtually simultaneously, before the full force of Lear's expulsion from Gloucester's home becomes apparent, the possibility that the movement of the play contains within it a counterforce is voiced by Kent. It crystallizes around Dover. Kent responds to the gentleman's annihilative vision; of his nothing he would make something, offering the hope of secrets to be revealed – the restorative forces of France, the return of Cordelia, the regaining of identity. Kent sends the gentleman, fortified with these hopeful words, with tokens 'to Dover' (3.1.36); as if to answer the blinding storm and its 'eyeless rage,' he assures him of the possibility that he will 'see Cordelia' (3.1.46) there. A compensatory pattern, initiated in this interchange and focused on the word Dover, continues in the scenes that follow.

Thus, just as we are offered *Dover* as the possibility of a happy ending before Lear's agony on the heath, the word appears again after Lear has endured the storm. Gloucester directs Kent to 'drive toward Dover . . . where thou shalt meet/ Both welcome and protection' (3.6.89–90). The king is borne sleeping to the place where he can escape the plots of death that threaten him. That direction and the reiteration of Dover, however, are even more forceful in the scene that follows, Gloucester's blinding at the hands of Regan and Cornwall. Shatteringly, the path of escape from 'eyeless rage' becomes the path to its realization. It is because Gloucester has sent the king to Dover that he suffers the inquisition of Cornwall and Regan:

Cornwall   Where has thou sent the king?
Gloucester   To Dover.

Regan	Wherefore to Dover? Wast thou not charged at peril –
Cornwall	Wherefore to Dover? Let him answer that.
Gloucester	I am tied to th' stake, and I must stand the course.
Regan	Wherefore to Dover?
Gloucester	Because I would not see thy cruel nails
	Pluck out his poor old eyes. (3.7.50–57)

The pathos of the escape to Dover emerges in the repeated question, 'wherefore to Dover?' Wherefore, indeed.

When Gloucester has endured what he would not see Regan sends him to 'smell/ His way to Dover' (3.7.9394). Gloucester's path, doubling Lear's, collapses the antinomy of 'eyeless rage' and the hope of recovery. Gloucester emblematizes, literalizes, and makes fully horrific a path of fulfilled desire – the desire not to see. The desire and hope constellated around Dover sickens. In the next scene, Edgar, disguised as poor Tom, meets his father with his bleeding eyes, and Gloucester asks him to lead 'i' th' way to Dover' (4.1.43). 'Know'st thou the way to Dover?' (4.1.55), he asks, and asks again, 'Dost thou know Dover?' (4.1.71). To Edgar's affirmative response, the old man describes the cliff that is his utmost desire, a verge from whose dizzying height he expects no return.

. . . [I]n these reiterations of *Dover*, the word names a site of desire, the hope for . . . repose, restoratives to answer 'eyeless rage,' or the final closing of the eyes in a sleep without end. Lear will awaken in Cordelia's sight, perceiving himself deprived that ultimate rest: 'You do me wrong to take me out o' th' grave' (4.7.45). Before that, Edgar will have fulfilled Gloucester's request in a way that as strongly undercuts any hope that Dover might embody. For, after Gloucester's reiterated questions to Edgar, the word *Dover* never recurs in *King Lear*. Instead of the place, we arrive at Dover Cliff only in the lines that Edgar speaks to his father in 4.6. . . . Dover Cliff exists only in Edgar's lines and nowhere else in the play. The refusal to allow the word *Dover* to arrive at the place it (apparently) names, the failure, in other words, for signifier to reach signified – the failure of the sign – establishes the place that *Dover* occupies in the text. It is the place of illusion – the illusion of the desire voiced by Kent or Gloucester, the illusion of recovery and the illusion of respite and end. Yet, to come to the central point that I wish to make here, Edgar's lines describing Dover Cliff establish themselves as illusion by illusionistic rhetoric. His description answers to a particular mode of seeing, and the limits that *Dover* represents in the text are the limits of representation themselves. Paradoxically, a speech that represents space in a realistic mode points to the incapacity of the stage – and of language – to realize what the lines represent.

II. Perspectives

Here are Edgar's lines:

> Come on, sir; here's the place. Stand still. How fearful
> And dizzy 'tis to cast one's eyes so low!
> The crows and choughs that wing the midway air
> Show scarce so gross as beetles. Halfway down
> Hangs one that gathers samphire – dreadful trade;
> Methinks he seems no bigger than his head.
> The fishermen that walk upon the beach
> Appear like mice; and yond tall anchoring bark,
> Diminished to her cock; her cock, a buoy
> Almost too small for sight. The murmuring surge
> That on th' unnumb'red pebble chafes
> Cannot be heard so high. I'll look no more,
> Lest my brain turn, and the deficient sight
> Topple down headlong.   (4.6.11–24)

. . . Hearing [Edgar's lines], Gloucester kneels, addressing the 'mighty gods', renouncing the world 'in your sights' (4.6.34–5). What is *our* sight at that moment? What is our perspective on the scene? Edgar has presented an illusion one must be blind to see, has disabled *at once* Gloucester's stage that depends on language and the stage that depends on pictorial illusion. The scene, summoning up the powers of representation, shows the limits of representation. Gloucester makes something out of Edgar's nothing, and Edgar's imagined Dover is a working out of illusion that rests on nothing: silences, invisibility, blindness. Pictorial space is founded on the meeting of the eye and the vanishing point. Acceding to this representation, Gloucester passes through the vanishing point and topples down headlong into double blindness, for he has agreed to see what cannot be seen – as we do when we refer to 4.4 as the Dover Cliff scene, or credit it with working miracles. The scene, however, insists that it is an illusion, and what it offers us is [an] anatomy of the techniques of illusion . . . upon which Shakespearean theatre depends. The 'eyeless rage' that beat upon King Lear's head and that would 'make nothing of' him is visited upon Gloucester and upon the audience to the scene. 'Nothing will come of nothing' (1.1.90), Lear had told Cordelia, and the anatomy of representation in 4.6 is spaced between the nothing of the vanishing point and Gloucester's assumption of Lear's 'poor old eyes' (3.7.57). This is the space of representation. By invoking these nothings as the condition of representation, 4.6 shows just what we accede to in seeing *King Lear*, and implicates the audience in its annihilative vision. . . .[5] □

From Kathleen McLuskie, 'The Patriarchal Bard: feminist criticism
and Shakespeare: *King Lear* and *Measure for Measure*' (1985)

[In this essay, McLuskie takes issue with earlier feminist criticism of
Shakespeare (of the 1970s and early 1980s,) which she sees as at fault in
two main respects: in its assumption of a stable female nature, which
persists unchanged under very different historical conditions, and in its
belief that Shakespeare was an essentially feminist writer, sympathetic to
the difficulties of the female characters he represents. For McLuskie, neither
of these is true; for her, moreover, tragedy is itself an inherently patriarchal
genre, the pleasures of whose experience are contingent upon its audience's
conscious or unconscious submission to its patriarchal, even misogynistic,
perspective. For McLuskie, *King Lear* is not merely misogynist, but in its
misogyny, a paradigm for the sexual politics of its genre.]

■ . . . The essentialism which lies behind Marilyn French's and Linda
Bamber's account of the men and women in Shakespeare is part of a
trend in liberal feminism which sees the feminist struggle as concerned
with reordering the values ascribed to men and women without
fundamentally changing the material circumstances in which their
relationships function.[6] It presents feminism as a set of social attitudes
rather than as a project for fundamental social change. . . . In
Shakespeare and the Nature of Women . . . Juliet Dusinberre[7] admires
'Shakespeare's concern . . . to dissolve artificial distinctions between
the sexes' (Dusinberre, p. 153) and can claim that concern as feminist
in both twentieth-century and seventeenth-century terms. She exam-
ines Shakespeare's women characters . . . in the light of Renaissance
debates over women conducted in puritan handbooks . . . [and] . . .
notes the shift from misogyny associated with Catholic asceticism to
puritan assertions of the importance of women in the godly household
as partners in . . . companionate marriage. . . . However her assertions
about the feminism of Shakespeare . . . depend . . . upon a mimetic
model of the relationship between ideas and drama. Contemporary
controversy about women is seen as a static body of ideas which
can be used . . . by dramatists whose primary concern is . . . simply
to 'explore the real nature of women'. By focusing on the presentation
of women in puritan advice literature, Dusinberre privileges one side of
a contemporary debate, relegating expressions of misogyny to the
fictional world of 'literary simplification' and arbitrarily asserting
more progressive notions as the dramatist's true point of view
(Dusinberre, p. 183).

A more complex discussion of the case would acknowledge that
the issues of sex, sexuality, sexual relations and sexual division were
areas of conflict of which the contradictions of writing about women

were only one manifestation alongside the complexity of legislation and other forms of social control of sex and the family. . . . Far from being an unproblematic concept, 'the nature of women' was under severe pressure from both ideological discourses and the real concomitants of inflation and demographic change. . . .

Tragedy assumes the existence of 'a permanent, universal and essentially unchanging human nature'[8] but the human nature implied in the moral and aesthetic satisfactions of tragedy is most often explicitly male. In *King Lear* for example, the narrative and its dramatisation present a connection between sexual insubordination and anarchy, and the connection is given an explicitly misogynist emphasis.

The action of the play, the organisation of its point of view and the theatrical dynamic of its central scenes all depend upon an audience accepting an equation between 'human nature' and male power. In order to experience the proper pleasures of pity and fear, they must accept that fathers are owed particular duties by their daughters and be appalled by the chaos which ensues when those primal links are broken. Such a point of view is . . . required and determined by the text in order for it to make sense. It is also the product of a set of meanings produced in a specific way by the Shakespearean text and is different from that produced in other versions of the story.

The representation of patriarchal misogyny is most obvious in the treatment of Goneril and Regan. In the chronicle play *King Leir*, the sisters' villainy is much more evidently a function of the plot. Their mocking pleasure at Cordella's downfall takes the form of a comic double act and Regan's evil provides the narrative with the exciting twist of an attempt on Lear's life. In the Shakespearean text by contrast, the narrative, language and dramatic organisation all define the sisters' resistance to their father in terms of their gender, sexuality and position within the family. Family relations in this play are seen as fixed . . ., and any movement within them is portrayed as a destructive reversal of rightful order (see 1.4). Goneril's and Regan's treatment of their father . . . is seen . . . as a fundamental violation of human nature . . . – as is made powerfully explicit in the speeches which condemn them (3.7.101–3; 4.2.32–50). Moreover when Lear in his madness fantasises about the collapse of law and the destruction of ordered social control, women's lust is vividly represented as the centre and source of the ensuing corruption (4.6.110–28). The generalised character of Lear's and Albany's vision of chaos, and the poetic force with which it is expressed, creates the appearance of truthful universality which is an important part of the play's claim to greatness. However, that . . . vision . . . is present in gendered terms in which patriarchy, the institution of male power in the family and the State, is seen as the only form of social organisation strong enough to hold chaos at bay . . .[9] □

From Coppélia Kahn, 'The Absent Mother in *King Lear*' (1986)

[Whereas McLuskie believes the play to be deeply misogynistic, Kahn reads its most profound outbursts of misogyny as both instrumental and instructive, and sees the play as charting its protagonist's progress from a misogynist rejection of the womanly parts within himself to a final acceptance of the presence within him of those more feminine qualities. In order to make this claim Kahn invokes both historicist and psychoanalytic strategies of reading: in the extract that follows she situates Lear's male anxiety in a historical account of the ways in which feeling has traditionally been represented as feminine, and a psychoanalytic reading of Lear which sees manifested in him the desire to be mothered by Cordelia.]

■ Fleeing Goneril's 'sharp-tooth'd unkindness,' Lear arrives at Gloucester's house in search of Regan, still hoping that she will be 'kind and comfortable,' although she was inexplicably not at home when he called before. He finds his messenger in the stocks . . . At first he simply denies what Kent tells him, that Regan and her husband did indeed commit this outrage. Then he seeks to understand how, or why. Kent recounts the studied rudeness, the successive insults, the final shaming, that he has endured.

For a moment, Lear can no longer deny or rationalize; he can only feel – feel a tumult of wounded pride, shame, anger, and loss, which he expresses in a striking image:

> O! how this mother swells upward toward my heart!
> *Hysterica passio*! down, thou climbing sorrow!
> Thy element's below.   (2.4 56–8)

By calling his sorrow hysterical, Lear decisively characterizes it as feminine, in accordance with a tradition stretching back to 1900 B.C. when an Egyptian papyrus first described the malady. Fifteen hundred years later in the writings of Hippocrates, it was named, and its name succinctly conveyed its etiology. It was the disease of the *hyster*, the womb. From ancient times . . ., women suffering variously from choking, feelings of suffocation, partial paralysis, . . . were said to be ill of hysteria, caused by a wandering womb. What sent the womb on its errant path through the female body, people thought, was either lack of sexual intercourse or retention of menstrual blood. In both cases, the same prescription obtained: the patient should get married. A husband would keep that wandering womb where it belonged. If the afflicted already had a husband, concoctions . . . were applied to force or entice the recalcitrant womb to its proper location.

In Shakespeare's time, hysteria was also called, appropriately, 'the mother.' . . . [L]ike anyone in his culture [Shakespeare] would have understood 'the mother' in the context of notions about women. For hysteria is a vivid metaphor of woman in general, as she was regarded then and later, a creature destined for the strenuous bodily labours of childbearing and childrearing but nonetheless physically weaker than man. Moreover, she was, like Eve, temperamentally and morally infirm: – skittish, prone to err in all senses. Woman's womb, her justification and her glory, was also the sign and source of her weakness as a creature of the flesh rather than the mind or spirit. . . . And the remedy – a husband and regular sexual intercourse – declares the necessity for male control of this volatile female element. . . .

A close look at the first scene in *King Lear* reveals much about lordliness and the male anxiety accompanying it. The court is gathered to watch Lear divide his kingdom and divest himself of its rule, but those purposes are actually only accessory to another that touches him more nearly: giving away his youngest daughter in marriage. While France and Burgundy wait in the wings, Cordelia for whose hand they compete, also competes for the dowry without which she cannot marry. As Lynda Boose shows, this opening scene is a variant of the wedding ceremony, which dramatizes the bond between father and daughter even as it marks the severance of that bond. There is no part in the ritual for the bride's mother; rather, the bride's father hands her directly to her husband. Thus the ritual articulates the father's dominance both as procreator and as authority figure, to the eclipse of the mother in either capacity. At the same time, the father symbolically certifies the daughter's virginity. Thus the ceremony alludes to the incest taboo and raises a question about Lear's 'darker purpose' in giving Cordelia away.[10]

In view of the ways that Lear tries to manipulate this ritual so as to keep his hold on Cordelia at the same time that he is ostensibly giving her away, we might suppose that the emotional crisis precipitating the tragic action is Lear's frustrated incestuous desire for his daughter. For in the course of winning her dowry, Cordelia is supposed to show that she loves her father not only more than her sisters do but, as she rightly sees, more than she loves her future husband; similarly, when Lear disowns . . . Cordelia, he thinks he has rendered her, dowered only with his curse, unfit to marry – and thus unable to leave paternal protection. In contrast, however, I want to argue that the socially-ordained, developmentally appropriate surrender of Cordelia as daughter-wife – the renunciation of her as incestuous object – awakens a deeper emotional need in Lear: the need for Cordelia as daughter-mother.

The play's beginning, as I have said, is marked by the omnipotent presence of the father and the absence of the mother. Yet in Lear's scheme for parcelling out his kingdom, we can discern a child's image of being mothered. He wants two mutually exclusive things at once: to have absolute control over those closest to him and to be absolutely dependent on them. We can recognize in this stance the outlines of a child's pre-oedipal experience of himself and his mother as an undifferentiated dual unity, in which the child perceives his mother not as a separate person but as an agency of himself, who provides for his needs. She and her breast are a part of him, at his command. In Freud's unforgettable phrase, he is 'his majesty, the baby.'

As man, father, and ruler, Lear has habitually suppressed any needs for love, which in his patriarchal world would normally be satisfied by a mother or mothering woman. With age and loss of vigour, and as Freud suggests in 'The Theme of the Three Caskets,' with the prospect of return to mother earth, Lear feels those needs again and hints at them in his desire to 'crawl' like a baby 'toward death'. Significantly, he confesses them in these phrases the moment after he curses Cordelia for her silence, the moment in which he denies them most strongly. He says, 'I lov'd her most and thought to set my rest/ On her kind nursery' (1.1.1234).

When his other two daughters prove to be bad mothers and don't satisfy his needs for 'nursery,' Lear is seized by 'the mother' – a searing sense of loss at the deprivation of the mother's presence. It assaults him in various ways – in the desire to weep, to mourn the enormous loss, and the equally strong desire to hold back the tears and, instead, accuse, . . . punish, and humiliate those who have made him realize his . . . dependency. Thus the mother, revealed in Lear's response to his daughters' brutality toward him, makes her re-entry into the patriarchal world from which she had seemingly been excluded. The repressed mother returns specifically in Lear's wrathful projections onto the world about him of a symbiotic relationship with his daughters that recapitulates his pre-oedipal relationship with the mother. In a striking series of images in which parent-child, father-daughter, and husband-wife relationships are reversed and confounded, Lear re-enacts a childlike rage against the absent or rejecting mother as figured in his daughters. . . .[11] □

From Stephen J. Greenblatt, 'The Cultivation of Anxiety: King Lear and His Heirs' (1990)

[In the opening of Greenblatt's essay (not reprinted here) Greenblatt reproduces a fascinating and lengthy account of an early nineteenth-century father's attempt to discipline his toddler into expressing to him both love and submission; he then proceeds to show the ways in which this account (left by the Reverend Francis Wayland) can elucidate our understanding of *King Lear*. Using an anecdote whose relation to the text at hand is at first sight unclear is a strategy typical of the New Historicist criticism which Greenblatt practises, and of which he was the principal pioneer; so too is an implicit refusal to hierarchise the interest of the different kinds of texts he discusses (in this essay, for instance, Greenblatt reads from Wayland to *King Lear*, and from *King Lear* to Wayland: each is used to shed light on the other). In the following extract, Greenblatt also makes use of more 'conventional' historicist strategies, in his comparison of the predicament of King Lear to those of medieval fathers who entered into 'maintenance agreements' with their children. The sensitivity and the generosity with which Greenblatt reads the different texts that he analyses, the brilliance of the connections that he establishes between them, and the humanity of his concerns are some of the reasons why one might claim Stephen Greenblatt to be the greatest contemporary critic of Renaissance literature.]

■ . . . Once a father had given up his land, he became, even in the house that had once been his own, what was called a 'sojourner'. . . .

Threatened with such a drastic loss of their status and authority, parents facing retirement turned . . . to the law, obtaining contracts or maintenance agreements by which, in return for the transfer of family property, children undertook to provide food, clothing, and shelter. The extent of parental anxiety may be gauged by the great specificity of many of these requirements – so many yards of woollen cloth, pounds of coal, or bushels of grain – and by the pervasive fear of being turned out of the house in the wake of a quarrel. The father . . . now has these children for his legal guardians. The maintenance agreement is essentially a medieval device, linked to feudal contractualism, to temper the power of this new guardianship by stipulating that the children are only 'depositaries' of the paternal property. . . . [T]he maintenance agreement can 'reserve' to the father some right or interest in the property that he has conveyed to his children.

. . . [*King Lear*] is powerfully situated in the midst of precisely the concerns of the makers of these maintenance agreements: the terror of being turned out of doors or of becoming a stranger even in one's own house; the fear of losing the food, clothing, and shelter necessary for survival, let alone dignity; the humiliating loss of parental authority; the dread, particularly powerful in a society that adhered to the principle of gerontological hierarchy, of being supplanted by the young. Lear's royal status does not cancel but rather intensifies these concerns: he will 'invest' in Goneril and Regan, along with their husbands, his 'power,/ Pre-eminence, and all the large effects/ That troop with majesty,' but he wants to retain the hundred knights and 'The name and all th'addition to a king' (1.1). He wishes, that is, to avoid at all costs the drastic loss of status that inevitably attended retirement in the early modern period, and his maddened rage, later in the play, is a response not only to his daughters' vicious ingratitude but to the horror of being reduced to . . . [being a supplicant for what was previously his]:

> Ask her forgiveness?
> Do you but mark how this becomes the house:
> 'Dear daughter, I confess that I am old;
> Age is unnecessary: on my knees I beg
> That you'll vouchsafe me raiment, bed, and food.'   (2.4)

His daughter, in response, unbendingly proposes that he 'return and sojourn' – a word whose special force in this context we have now recovered . . .

Near the climax of this terrible scene in which Goneril and Regan, by relentlessly diminishing his retinue, in effect strip away his social identity, Lear speaks as if he had actually drawn up a maintenance agreement with [his] daughters:

> *Lear*   I gave you all –
> *Regan* And in good time you gave it.
> *Lear*   Made you my guardians, my depositaries,
> But kept a reservation to be follow'd
> With such a number.   (2.4)

But there is no maintenance agreement between Lear and his daughters; there could be none, since as Lear makes clear in the first scene, he will not as absolute monarch allow anything 'To come betwixt our sentence and our power' (1.1), and an autonomous system of laws would have constituted just such an intervention. For a contract in English law implied bargain consideration, that is, the reciprocity inherent in a set of shared obligations and limits, and this understanding that a gift could only be given with the expectation of receiving something in return is incompatible with Lear's sense of his royal prerogative, just as it is incompatible with the period's absolutist conception of paternal power and divine power.

Lear's power draws upon the network of rights and obligations that is sketched by the play's pervasive language of service, but as Kent's experience in the first scene makes clear, royal absolutism is at the same time at war with this feudal legacy. Shakespeare's play emphasizes Lear's claim to unbounded power, even at the moment of his abdication, since his 'darker purpose' sets itself above all constraints upon the royal will and pleasure. What enables him to lay aside his claim to rule, the scene suggests, is the transformation of power into a demand for unbounded love, a love that then takes the place of the older contractual bond between parents and children. Goneril and Regan understand Lear's demand as an aspect of absolutist theatre; hence in their flattering speeches they discursively perform the impossibility of ever adequately expressing their love: 'Sir, I love you more than word can wield the matter / . . . A love that makes breath poor and speech unable; / Beyond all manner of so much I love you' (1.1.). This cunning representation of the impossibility of representation contaminates Cordelia's inability to speak by speaking it; that is, Goneril's words occupy the discursive space that Cordelia would have to claim for herself if she were truly to satisfy her father's demand. Consequently, any attempt to represent her silent love is already tainted: representation is theatricalization is hypocrisy and hence is misrepresentation. Even Cordelia's initial aside seems to long for the avoidance of language altogether and thus for an escape from the theatre. Her words have an odd internal distance, as if they were spoken by another, and more precisely as if the author outside the play were asking himself what he should have his character say and deciding that she should say nothing: 'What shall Cordelia speak? Love, and be silent' (1.1.). But this attempt to remain silent – to surpass her sisters and satisfy her father by refusing to represent her love – is rejected, as is her subsequent attempt to say nothing, that is, literally to speak the word 'nothing'. Driven into discourse by her father's anger, Cordelia then appeals not like her sisters to an utter dependence upon paternal love but to a 'bond' that is both reciprocal and limited. Against paternal and monarchical absolutism, Cordelia opposes in effect the ethos of the maintenance agreement, and this opposition has for Lear the quality of treason.

Lear, who has, as he thinks, given all to [his] children, demands all from them. In place of a contract, he has substituted the love test. He wants, that is, not only the formal marks of deference that publicly acknowledge his value, but also the inward and absolute tribute of the heart. It is in the spirit of this demand that he absorbs into himself the figure of the mother; there can be no division for Lear between authority and love. But as the play's tragic logic reveals, Lear cannot have both the public deference and the inward love of his children. The public deference is only as good as the legal constraints that Lear's absolute power paradoxically deprives him of, and the inward love cannot be adequately represented in social discourse, licensed by authority and performed in the public sphere, enacted as in a court or theatre. Lear had thought to set his rest – the phrase means both to stake everything and to find response – on Cordelia's 'kind nursery,' but only in his fantasy of perpetual imprisonment with his daughter does he glimpse, desperately and pathetically, what he sought. That is, only when he has been decisively separated from his public authority and locked away from the world, only when the direct link between family and state power has been broken, can Lear hope, in the dream of the prison as nursery, for his daughter's sustaining and boundless love.

With this image of the prison as nursery we return for the last time to Francis Wayland, who, to gain the love of his child, used the nursery as a prison. We return, then, to the crucial differences . . . between the early seventeenth- and early nineteenth-century versions of salutary anxiety, differences between a culture in which the theatre was a centrally significant and emblematic artistic practice, profoundly linked with family and power, and a culture in which the theatre had shrivelled to marginal entertainment. The love test for Wayland takes place in the privacy of the nursery where he shuts up his fifteen-month-old infant. In consequence, what is sought by the father is not the representation of love in public discourse, but things prior to and separate from language: the embrace, the kiss, the taking of food, the inarticulate moaning after the father when he leaves the room. It is only here, before verbal representation, that the love test could be wholly successful, here that the conditional, reciprocal, social world of the maintenance agreement could be decisively replaced by the child's absolute and lifelong love. And, we might add, the father did not in this case have to renounce the public tribute entirely; he had only to wait until he ceased to exist. For upon the death of Francis Wayland, Heman Lincoln Wayland collaborated in writing a reverential two-volume biography of his father, a son's final monument to familial love. Lear, by contrast, dies still looking on his daughter's lips for the words that she never speaks.[12] □

From Lisa Jardine, 'Reading and the Technology of Textual Affect: Erasmus's familiar letters and Shakespeare's *King Lear*' (1996)

[Like Greenblatt's, Jardine's account of the play proceeds through a method in which apparently disparate texts (in this case the play and Erasmus' *Letters*) are brought to bear on one another in order to chart historical changes in 'technologies' (Jardine's term) or 'strategies' (Greenblatt's) of affect.[13] Jardine argues that the representation of the exchanges of letters in *King Lear* betray the degree to which the 'technology of affect to "fabricate intimacy"' embodied in Erasmian epistolary instruction was, for Shakespeare, no longer available.[14] What in Erasmian pedagogy was offered as a model of desirable discourse 'which could combine the effective transmission of warmth of feeling, friendship and emotional sincerity with conventional techniques of logical persuasion to produce a compelling case for a particular course of action' (Jardine,

p. 89) is in *King Lear* 'demonised'; affect eventually being severed from its epistolary setting, and left to circulate, with catastrophic consequences, outside of the controlling structure of the written word.]

■ ... My ambition in this chapter is an attempt at a particular kind of historicised reading which reveals the textual construction of feeling in the early modern period. Historical approaches to Shakespeare's plays (including my own) have tended to concentrate on contextualising social and cultural practices ... We have not ... tried ... to contextualise the pivotal affective moments: the point at which emotion is intensified so as to structure the audience's and the reader's allegiance, and gain our assent to the unravelling or resolving of the action. [Here Jardine introduces a discussion of Erasmus' *Letters* which are, she argues, despite their apparent eschewal of all emotional contrivance, 'crucially affective', central to 'the Renaissance's construction of letter writing and reading as emotionally charged events'.] So influential was this pedagogical model of reading that the exchange of familiar letters could come to stand for the efficiency with which humanistic text skills could be used to alter an individual's social position and prospects. ... [T]he familiar letter ... organises feeling so as to manipulate its intensity at a distance ... enabling persuasion to a desired outcome.

... *King Lear* elicits our revulsion towards such efficiency by presenting us with the prospect of a world in which real affection is deprived of instrumentality ... precisely to the extent that a cynically operated technology of affect of warmth and intimacy generated by letters debases the heart's expressive resources, leaving 'nothing' to be said. [Here Jardine moves into her discussion of Erasmus' *Letters*.]

. . .

What we seem to have [in *King Lear*] is the demonisation of the persuasive technology of affect. . . . In this play, bastard sons and unnatural daughters conduct epistolary transactions which convince; plain folk and close kin are misled by letters, or betrayed by them. The most striking contrast here is that between the intimate letters which are exchanged between Kent and Cordelia in private (through the trusted intermediary of the gentleman), and the mirroring exchanges of letters which bring about Gloucester's downfall. In the first scene of Act 3, Kent sends letters to the French camp; in the third scene, Gloucester tells Edmund he has received letters thence:

> *Gloucester* Go to; say you nothing. There is division between the Dukes, and a worse matter than that. I have receiv'd a letter this night; 'tis dangerous to be spoken; I have lock'd the letter in my closet.   (3.3.8–11)

Challenged by Cornwall – 'Come, sir, what letters had you late from France?' – Gloucester tries to establish that these are familiar letters, not espionage:

> *Gloucester*   I have had a letter guessingly set down,
> Which came from one that's of a neutral heart,
> And not from one oppos'd.   (3.7.42–9)

But in the economy of this play, letters are written and received to incite mendaciously to action and to pervert the truth.

The two most vital exchanges of letter for the plot, however, are of course those which involve the treachery and duplicity of Edmund. At the beginning of the play, it is the forged letter . . . which convinces Gloucester that his legitimate son is a traitor. . . . In the final act, the intercepted letter from Goneril to Edmund, reminding him of their 'reciprocal vows' and inciting him to murder her husband, leads to the discovery of Edmund's general treachery. These are also the only two letters whose contents are divulged to us – both are banally instructive, without any kind of rhetorical embellishment. For Shakespeare's dramatic purposes, persuasive affect is located elsewhere. It is in the mouths of Regan and Goneril, contradicting their marriage vows in order to swear total love and duty to their father, and the mouth of Edmund, assuring his father of his trust at the moment he betrays him.

In the final section of this chapter I want to argue that this is significant: that Lear severs affect from its epistolary setting where it could be controlled, and leaves it circulating at large – on the Heath. Affect, let loose from its civilised setting in the familiar letter, is demonised as the trigger for social disruption and disturbance.

. . .

For Erasmus, the beauty of the familiar letter lay in its structuring and controlling emotional transactions, so that their moral value is enhanced. In Lear such controlled expression of feeling is apparently not available – it has been banished from the scene, and replaced by a version of epistolary artifice which distorts and misleads because it is in the wrong hands. . . . In consequence . . . the only emotional transactions to which true kin have access are uncontrolled and unstructured – are technically out of control. Cordelia cannot 'heave her heart into her mouth' to order for her father; she can only pant out verbal ejaculations of distress to represent her true feelings. . . . Throughout his companionship with Lear on the Heath and his compassionate guiding of his blinded father, Edgar utters not one word of comfort or consolation to either. Instead he contributes a sense of surreal dislocation of speech and action, which produces an almost intolerably emotionally meaningless commentary on the events as they unfold.

Such emotional dyslexia is meant, I think, to be a terrifying prospect. Lear and his party on the Heath, and Gloucester and the disguised Edgar at Dover Cliffs, are offered as appalling manifestations of helplessly uncontrolled feeling, damagingly circulating without motive or purpose, its moral efficacy terribly out of focus. When unnatural sons and daughters have taken control of the technology of affect for their own manipulative purposes, there is, it seems, no possibility of articulation left for the naturally caring members of the family. This is the play's catastrophe – its darkly nihilistic message, not its resolution.

Once we historicise the networks of feeling which form and reform the bonds of duty and friendship in *Lear* around the persuasive technology of letter writing and reading, we are bound, I think, to recognise that the 'natural' and uncontained versions of passionate emotion in the play are not available as a solution to the problems raised by Lear misconstruing his daughters' declarations of love. Raw emotion is not an attractive prospect for an audience which had placed its trust in Erasmus's promise that mastery of the familiar letter would enable humane individuals to persuade one another affectively to collaborate for a better, more Christian Europe. The spectacle of such 'civilised' technical skill working successfully on the side of deception and self-interest is disturbing and deeply pessimistic. Yet it is to precisely this vividly dramatised scenario that we, the modern audience, respond positively and intensely emotionally, because it is, of its essence, a representation of emotion unmediated by historicised social forms. The combination of horror and embarrassment with which we experience the spectacle of Edgar deluding the desperate Gloucester into casting himself down from a non-existent cliff owes nothing to Erasmus, or to humanist rhetoric, or to Renaissance philosophy. Like Gloucester and Edgar, we experience with immediacy that raw emotional intensity in a moral, social and historical void.[15] □

From Richard Halpern, '*Historica Passio*: *King Lear*'s Fall into Feudalism' (1991)

[Halpern's Marxist account of the play can be taken to indicate the degree of debate within as well as between discrete theoretical modes of reading. Halpern takes issue with earlier accounts of the play (Marxist and otherwise) which have read it as charting the transition from feudalism to capitalism; although Halpern agrees that the grand historical shift between these two modes of production underlies *King Lear*, he rejects the 'easy' association of particular characters (such as Edmund and

Kent) with the ideologies of particular modes of production (such as proto-capitalism and feudalism). For Halpern, there are divisions amongst these classes as well as between them; class struggle, moreover, need not necessarily proceed in an overtly oppositional manner, but can also manifest itself in the way in which up-and-coming classes appropriate the external signifiers of their class 'superiors' in an attempt to assimilate themselves into the class above them.]

■ In Act 2, scene 4, of *King Lear*, the sight of Kent bound in the stocks gives the king his first real taste of madness: 'O! How this mother swells up toward my heart;/ Historica passio! down, thou climbing sorrow!/ Thy element's below. Where is this daughter?' When the 'mother' rises up through Lear's body it seems to affect his Latin as well as his reason, for in the Quarto and the first three editions of the Folio he diagnoses himself as suffering from the hitherto unheard-of disease *historica passio*. By 1685, the year of the fourth Folio edition of the plays, Lear has apparently had time to bethink himself, for he now utters the 'correct' . . . phrase *hysterica passio*.

This small textual crux, lost perhaps in a play that has since been riven by such cruxes, nevertheless points nicely to a conflict of inter-pretative choices. What *does* Lear suffer from: hysteria or historia? Is the play to be read in a psychoanalytic, ethical, and personal register or in a political and historical one? (The term *passio* may be taken to invoke a third, bankrupt but nevertheless tenacious strain of readings: the religious . . .) Both approaches are partially satisfying, neither fully so; both leave a residue that resists critical totalization. Like hysterica/ historica, two terms fighting for the same textual space, each mode of reading has a certain claim to legitimacy, and neither manages fully to supplant or eradicate the other. This situation does not admit of happy pluralisms, however; as in Lear's kingdom, or as in his self-imagined anatomy, a sequence of painful displacements occurs as something is always trying to rise to the top.

One of the most insistent of the historical readings of *King Lear* was sketched out . . . by John Danby, who argued in 1952 that the play is poised between a 'medieval vision' of society and 'that of nascent capitalism'. For Danby, the historical malady that afflicts both Lear and the fictional world he inhabits derives from a conflict of histori-cally specific values. Characters such as Kent and Cordelia embody the old 'feudal' values of loyalty and honour, while Goneril, Regan, and above all Edmund are prototypes of the capitalist 'New Man' [*sic*]. Theirs is a society 'based on unfettered competition, and the war of all against all. Lear's is the feudal state in decomposition'.[16] . . . [Danby's] reading has appeared plausible to critics of a fairly wide range of ideological positions, in part because it responds to some salient aspects of the play. *King Lear* openly enunciates, at various points, an apparent nostalgia for a lost ideal of social order, an order represented largely by the 'feudal' ideals of loyalty, generosity, and military honour embodied in Kent and betrayed in various ways by Goneril, Regan, and Edmund. Yet the appeal of Danby's reading owes more than a little to its vagueness, which allows multiple and possibly contradictory constructions of such terms as *feudalism* and *new man*.

. . . *King Lear* is at least partly 'about' the transition from feudalism to capitalism. . . . Yet even in its most general and therefore most intuitively appealing formulation, the transitional thesis enfolds a number of implicit assumptions, many of them contestable. John Turner, for instance, has recently challenged the notion that Edmund represents a proto-capitalist 'type.' For Turner . . . 'the true subject of *King Lear* . . . is not an old order succumbing to a new but an old order succumbing to its own internal contradictions'.[17]

. . . Turner's reading of Lear attempts to . . . [situate the play's arena of ideological struggle] within feudalism rather than between two social formations. But whereas this strategy problematizes earlier 'transitionalist' readings, it shares with them certain assumptions about history and dramatic form, in particular the Lukácsian idea that dramatic agon among characters is a privileged or inherently fitting way of representing struggles among historical classes. Walter Cohen . . . explicitly adopts this Lukácsian assumption . . . Cohen sees *Lear* as a coherent analogical rehearsal of the class contradictions that would lead to the English Revolution – a revolution that 'at the level of social structure . . . reenacts the three-sided conflict of Shakespeare's tragedy'.[18] I shall return to this issue later to argue that there are some limitations to this 'agonistic' model both for understanding Shakespeare's experience of the historical situation of 1605–1610 and for tracing its representation in the play.

The agonistic model or assumption is, in fact, only one answer to a larger question: how can drama, which by its nature focuses on persons rather than transpersonal institutions, possibly represent historical processes . . .? One might reasonably contend that Shakespeare's Edmund is in some respects a . . . 'proto-capitalist' character, but certainly no one would . . . argue that *King Lear* portrays . . . proto-capitalism. Likewise, the play contains traces of feudal institutions but in no way . . . could aspire to represent feudalism as a social . . . totality. Rather, we speak of Kent as embodying certain feudal 'values,' by which we mean that his . . . beliefs, his actions, his manner of expression and quite possibly his costume recall those of the feudal knightly class. What drama has at its disposal as a means of historical representation is primarily a repertoire of such gestural manifestations of value. And insofar as drama manages to embody a historical vision of some sort, it does so largely by substituting these gestural *manifestations* for the social *production* of value. Historical . . . formations . . . are signified by dramatic persons; historical actants – collective or impersonal – designate themselves through dramatic agents . . . *Historica passio*, the bearing or enduring or manifestation of historical force through one's person and one's body, is thus a fundamental precondition of dramatic art. What Lear feels rising up within him . . . is that conversion hysteria which constitutes him as a dramatic character and invests his every gesture with . . . historical signification . . .

Dramatic agon, or confrontation, is one means by which a collision of social forces can be dramatically represented; it is one gestural embodiment of social values in conflict. But it does not exhaust the grammar of such gestures. This essay will situate the dramatic conflict of *Lear* within a larger framework of the gestural manifestation of value; and for *Lear* at least, agon is not necessarily the most important of these gestures. *King Lear* is indeed an explicitly 'transitional' play, but it represents the tension between feudal and proto-capitalist cultures in ways that circle around and even evade the play's dramatic conflicts.

. . .

The Order-Word[19] and the Consumption-Sign[20]

. . . One of the weaknesses of many historical readings of *Lear* is that they equate the collapse of the play's social order with the collapse of feudalism, whereas in fact the play collapses *back into* feudalism. Kent and Gloucester, the play's old men, may complain about the decay of knightly values, but it is Edmund who . . . reconstitutes a society in which those values can again have meaning. Edmund's dominant role in the play, then, is not to be midwife to capitalism; rather, it is to reintroduce the feudal war machine and thus fully reconstitute a baronial culture that had degenerated into ceremony and property rights . . .

Edmund the 'bastard' is thus the child of two very different ideological formations. If, on the one hand, he points forward to certain proto-capitalist values, on the other, he points backward to a more fully feudal conception of aristocratic rule and culture which predates the politico-military consolidation of absolutism. His structural role in the play is that of the donor who restores to the aristocracy its lost order-word, which had been confiscated and monopolized by the monarchy . . . *Lear* represents the decay of knightly values which result from the state's monopoly on military force, and the consequent transformation of an armigerous nobility into a class wielding only consumption-signs.

If Edmund evokes the Renaissance new man, then, he does so only for the purpose of driving it back into a culturally anterior form. . . . There *is* a new man in *King Lear*, however, and his name is Oswald. Oswald's symbolic importance may very well be underestimated because his dramatic role is relatively small. But this is precisely the point: he is clearly wheeled in solely as a foil to Kent, and his very existence is conjured up only to complete the play's set of 'social types'. . . . The mere sight of him provokes a kind of instinctive revulsion in Kent, who delights in beating him and burying him under piles of verbal abuse . . . Kent . . . needs Oswald to underpin his own existence: Oswald's artificiality secures Kent's authenticity; his effeminacy secures Kent's masculinity. . . . In short, his status as the 'new man' of the court secures Kent's status as the 'old man' of feudalism.

Kent's insults revolve around two conceptual centres: simulation and hybridization. The first of these pertains to Oswald's artificiality in general and to his pretensions to the status of gentleman in particular. Lacking a distinguished lineage . . . Oswald can only adopt the . . . *consumption-signs* of aristocracy. . . . Kent's taunts, intended to demonstrate Oswald's status as pure consumption-sign, nevertheless acknowledge the power of such signs to counterfeit aristocracy . . .

Related to the problem of class simulation . . . is Kent's assault on Oswald as a class and sexual *hybrid*. Oswald is, in Kent's rant, . . . 'the son and heir of a mongrel bitch'. Lear too refers to Oswald as a 'mongrel' [1.4.48]. . . . Although Oswald is perhaps the most explicitly and thoroughly hybridized character, however, he is hardly the only one. Edmund, of course, is a bastard, and Lear charges Goneril with being a 'degenerate bastard' as well. Both Goneril and Regan take on monstrously 'masculine' qualities in the latter stages of the play, and early on Goneril mocks Albany's 'milky gentleness' (1.4.340). And Lear, famously, expresses his own horror of female sexuality by describing women as 'centaurs' (4.6.121–30). Hybridized or mixed beings define and inhabit the play's realm of the sexually abject, and contribute strongly to Lear's 'image of that horror'. . . . But they also add to the play's confusions of social class. Lear as the beggar-king, Edgar playing Tom o' Bedlam, and Kent in the stocks are only three of the play's more prominent and grotesque class hybrids. Oswald thus concentrates a more global phenomenon in the play: the collapse of sexual and class boundaries. When Kent threatens, 'I'll teach you differences' (1.4.87), he attempts to secure the solidity of class and gender categories that Oswald disrupts.

Hybridization and simulation together represent the means of upward class mobility available to the gentry and merchant classes, who could assume only the consumption-signs of aristocracy. . . . [N]obles did what they could to secure the system of class difference through sumptuary laws and other such means, but they could not quite stem the encroaching tide of parvenus represented in *Lear* by Oswald. Even Oswald's effeminacy . . . impinges on this problem, for the aristocracy felt emasculated by conversion from a militarized to a consuming class. Thus Kent's formidable masculinity constitutes part of his class nostalgia, a last bulwark of heroic 'authenticity' which resists the simulating and hybridizing capacities of the consumption-sign. . . .

In *King Lear* . . . the strongest challenge to feudal values does not come from Edmund, who hates the current order; it comes from Oswald, who loves it in such a way as to debase it terminally. This is why the Lukácsian thesis fails for Lear: dramatic agon does not represent class struggle. In this play the heralds of bourgeois culture refuse to fight; they are, indeed, defined by the absence of military prowess or heroic pride. Their mode of assault is friendly, marked by hybridism and the simulating capacities of the consumption-sign. As a courtier, Oswald represents the limit of this assimilationist tendency; his dramatic function is to empty out the formal aspects of aristocratic class culture without offering anything in the way of a distinctively . . . bourgeois alternative. . . . The play does not offer presentiments of civil war; rather, it foretells a continuing debasement or dilution of ruling values in such characters as Oswald and 'the dukes of wat'rish Burgundy' (1.1.257).

Edmund occupies an ambiguous slot within the play's figurations of culture, for he cannot simply be opposed to Oswald. He is, after all, a bastard whom Albany addresses as 'half-blooded fellow' (5.3.82). He is a simulator who insinuates himself into an alien system of values. His aggressive upward mobility and desperate desire for aristocratic legitimation invoke the class wishes of a wide range of parvenus. The difference is that Edmund joins this configuration solely to drive it backward by assimilating it to the feudal war machine. His historical trajectory puts him in the roles of courtly lover, military commander, and finally, losing but valiant contender in a chivalric battle with his brother Edgar. That Edmund is in the end willing to dispense with his formal class privileges and 'answer an unknown opposite' (5.3.151–52) to defend his honour signals his choice of military or heroic prestige over mere titles of nobility. His effect on the world of the play is thus fully atavistic; he latches on to Lear's division of the kingdom and the subsequent decentralization of power to reestablish the hegemony of the aristocratic order-word. The fact and manner of his death attest to success in this project, not failure. . . .[21] □

APPENDIX: THE TWO VERSIONS OF *KING LEAR*[1]

3.6.11 *The History of King Lear* 1608 [Quarto version]

Lear	A king, a king! To have a thousand with Red burning spits come hissing in upon them!
Edgar	The foul fiend bites my back.
Lear	He's mad that trusts in the tameness of a wolf, a horse's health, a boy's love, or a whore's oath.
Lear	It shall be done. I will arraign them straight.
[*To Edgar*]	Come, sit thou here, most learnèd justicer.
[*To Fool*]	Thou sapient sir, sit here. No, you she-foxes —
Edgar	Look where he stands and glares. Want'st thou eyes at trial, madam?
[*Sings*]	Come o'er the burn, Bessy, to me.
Fool [*sings*]	Her boat hath a leak, And she must not speak Why she dares not come over to thee.
Edgar	The foul fiend haunts Poor Tom in the voice of a nightingale. Hoppedance cries in Tom's belly for two white herring. Croak not, black angel: I have no food for thee.
Kent	How do you, sir? Stand you not so amazed. Will you lie down and rest upon the cushings?
Lear	I'll see their trial first. Bring in their evidence.
[*To Edgar*]	Thou robèd man of justice, take thy place;
[*To Fool*]	And thou, his yokefellow of equity, Bench by his side. [*To Kent*] You are o'th'commission, Sit you, too.

Edgar	Let us deal justly.
	    Sleepest or wakest thou, jolly shepherd?
	      Thy sheep be in the corn,
	    And for one blast of thy minikin mouth
	      Thy sheep shall take no harm.
	Pur the cat is grey.

Lear	Arraign her first. 'Tis Goneril. I here take my oath before this honourable assembly she kicked the poor King her father.
Fool	Come hither, mistress. Is your name Goneril?
Lear	She cannot deny it.
Fool	Cry you mercy, I took you for a joint-stool.
Lear	And here's another, whose warped looks proclaim What store her heart is made on. Stop her there. Arms, arms, sword, fire, corruption in the place!

	False justicer, why hast thou let her 'scape?
Edgar	Bless thy five wits.
Kent	O pity! Sir, where is the patience now
	That you so oft have boasted to retain?
Edgar [*aside*]	My tears begin to take his part so much
	They'll mar my counterfeiting.
Lear	The little dogs and all,
	Trey, Blanch, and Sweetheart, see, they bark at me.

. . .

Lear	Make no noise, make no noise; draw the curtains. So, so, so. We'll go to supper i' th' morning. So, so, so.

Enter Gloucester

Gloucester [*to Kent*]	Come hither, friend. Where is the King my master?
Kent	Here, sir, but trouble him not; his wits are gone.
Gloucester	Good friend, I prithee take him in thy arms.
	I have o'erheard a plot of death upon him.
	There is a litter ready. Lay him in't
	And drive towards Dover, friend, where thou shalt meet
	Both welcome and protection. Take up thy master.
	If thou shouldst dally half an hour, his life,
	With thine and all that offer to defend him,
	Stand in assurèd loss. Take up, take up,
	And follow me, that will to some provision
	Give thee quick conduct.
Kent	Oppressèd nature sleeps.
	This rest might yet have balmed thy broken sinews
	Which, if convenience will not allow,
	Stand in hard cure. Come, help to bear thy master.
	Thou must not stay behind.
Gloucester	Come, come away.

Exeunt [bearing Lear. Edgar remains]

Edgar	When we our betters see bearing our woes,
	We scarcely think our miseries our foes.
	Who alone suffers, suffers most i'th'mind,
	Leaving free things and happy shows behind.
	But then the mind much sufferance doth o'erskip
	When grief hath mates, and bearing fellowship.
	How light and portable my pain seems now,

When that which makes me bend, makes the King bow.
He childed as I fathered. Tom, away.
Mark the high noises, and thyself bewray
When false opinion, whose wrong thoughts defile thee,
In thy just proof repeals and reconciles thee.
What will hap more tonight, safe 'scape the King!
Lurk, lurk.   [*Exit*]

3.6.11 *The Tragedy of King Lear* 1623 [Folio version]

Lear	A king, a king!
Fool	No, he's a yeoman that has a gentleman to his son, for he's a mad yeoman that sees his son a gentleman before him.
Lear	To have a thousand with red burning spits Come hissing in upon 'em!
Edgar	Bless thy five wits.
Kent	O pity! Sir, where is the patience now That you so oft have boasted to retain?
Edgar [*aside*]	My tears begin to take his part so much They mar my counterfeiting.
Lear	The little dogs and all, Trey, Blanch, and Sweetheart, see, they bark at me.

. . .

Lear	Make no noise, make no noise; draw the curtains. So, so. We'll go to supper i' th' morning.
Fool	And I'll go to bed at noon.

Enter Gloucester

Gloucester [*to Kent*]	Come hither, friend. Where is the King my master?
Kent	Here, sir, but trouble him not; his wits are gone.
Gloucester	Good friend, I prithee take him in thy arms. I have o'erheard a plot of death upon him. There is a litter ready. Lay him in't And drive toward Dover, friend, where thou shalt meet Both welcome and protection. Take up thy master. If thou shouldst dally half an hour, his life, With thine and all that offer to defend him, Stands in assurèd loss. Take up, take up, And follow me, that will to some provision Give thee quick conduct. Come, come away.

Exeunt [*bearing Lear*]

SELECT BIBLIOGRAPHY OF WORKS CITED

Alpers, Paul, '*King Lear* and the Theory of the Sight Pattern', in R. Brower and R. Poirier, eds., *In Defense of Reading* (New York: Dutton, 1963).*

Atkins, G. Douglas, and David M. Bergeron, eds., *Shakespeare and Deconstruction* (New York: Peter Lang, 1988).

Bamber, Linda, *Comic Women, Tragic Men: a Study of Gender and Genre in Shakespeare* (Stanford: Stanford University Press, 1981).*

Bate, Jonathan, ed., *The Romantics on Shakespeare* (Harmondsworth: Penguin, 1992).

Boose, Lynda, 'The Father and the Bride in Shakespeare', *PMLA* 97 (May 1982): 325–47.*

Bradley, A.C., *Shakespearean Tragedy: Lectures on Hamlet, Othello, King Lear, Macbeth* (London: Macmillan, 1950).

Cavell, Stanley, *Disowning Knowledge in Six Plays of Shakespeare* (Cambridge: C.U.P., 1987).

Champion, Larry S., *King Lear: An Annotated Bibliography* in two volumes (New York: Garland Publishing, 1980).

Cohen, Walter, *Drama of a Nation: Public Theatre in Renaissance England and Spain* (Ithaca: Cornell University Press, 1985).*

Coleridge, Samuel Taylor, in Thomas Middleton Raysor, ed., *Coleridge's Shakespearean Criticism*, vols 1 & 2 (London: Constable and Co., 1930).

Colie, Rosalie L., and F.T. Flahiff, eds., *Some Facets of King Lear: Essays in Prismatic Criticism* (London: Heinemann, 1974).

Danby, John, *Shakespeare's Doctrine of Nature: A Study of King Lear* (London: Faber and Faber, 1951).*

Danson, Lawrence, ed., *On King Lear* (Princeton: Princeton University Press, 1981).

Dickens, Charles, *The Examiner* (February 4, 1838) in Charles Dickens, *Miscellaneous Papers from 'The Morning Chronicle,' 'The Daily News,' 'The Examiner,' 'Household Words' 'All the Year Round.' 'Etc. and Plays and Poems'* in two volumes. Vol 1. (Gadshill edition of *The Works of Charles Dickens*. (London: Chapman & Hill, n.d.) Additional volumes. Volume XXXV), pp. 77–81.

Dusinberre, Juliet, *Shakespeare and the Nature of Women* (London: Macmillan, 1975).*

Eagleton, Terry, *Literary Theory: An Introduction* (Minneapolis: University of Minnesota Press, 1983).

Empson, William, *The Structure of Complex Words* (London: The Hogarth Press, 1985).

Everett, Barbara, 'The New *King Lear*' in Frank Kermode, ed.

Foakes, R.A., *Hamlet Versus Lear* (Cambridge: CUP, 1993).

French, Marilyn, *Shakespeare's Division of Experience* (London: Cape, 1982).*

Freud, Sigmund, 'The Theme of the Three Caskets', in *The Standard Edition of the Complete Psychological Works of Sigmund Freud*, trans., ed. James Strachey in collaboration with Anna Freud, vol XII(1911–13) (London: The Hogarth Press, 1958).

Goldberg, Jonathan, 'Perspectives: Dover Cliff and the Conditions of Representation' in G. Douglas Atkins and David M. Bergeron, eds.

Greenblatt, Stephen J., *Learning To Curse: Essays in Early Modern Culture* (London: Routledge, 1990).

Guizot, M., *Shakespeare and His Times* (London: Richard Bentley, 1852).

Halpern, Richard, *The Poetics of Primitive Accumulation: English Renaissance Culture and the Genealogy of Capital* (Ithaca: Cornell University Press, 1991).

Hazlitt, William, 'On Shakespeare and Milton' in Bate, ed.

Hazlitt, William, *Characters of Shakespeare's Plays* (London: Dent, 1906).

Hugo, Victor, *William Shakespeare*, trans. Melville B. Anderson (London: George Routledge and Sons, n.d.).

Jameson, Anna, *Shakespeare's Heroines: Characteristics of Women Moral, Poetical, and*

Historical (London: George Bell and Sons, 1905).

Jardine, Lisa, *Reading Shakespeare Historically* (London: Routledge, 1996).

Johnson, Samuel, endnote on King Lear, in volume VIII of *The Yale Edition of the Works of Samuel Johnson, Johnson on Shakespeare*, ed. Arthur Sherbo (New Haven and London: Yale University Press, 1968).

Kahn, Coppélia, 'The Absent Mother in *King Lear*' in Margaret W. Ferguson, Maureen Quilligan, and Nancy J. Vickers, eds, *Rewriting the Renaissance: The Discourses of Sexual Difference in Early Modern Europe* (Chicago: The University of Chicago Press, 1986).

Kamps, Ivo, *Materialist Shakespeare: A History* (London: Verso, 1995).

Kamps, Ivo, and Deborah E. Barker, eds, *Shakespeare and Gender: A History* (London: Verso, 1995).

Kermode, Frank, ed., *Shakespeare: King Lear: A Casebook* (London: Macmillan, 1969; revised edn., 1992).

Knights, L. C., *Some Shakespearean Themes and an Approach to Hamlet* (Harmondsworth: Penguin, 1966).

Knights, L. C., *Explorations* (London: Chatto and Windus, 1946).

Kott, Jan, *Shakespeare Our Contemporary*, second edition revised. (London: Routledge, 1967).

Lamb, Charles, 'On the Tragedies of Shakespeare, considered with reference to their fitness for stage representation' in Edmund D. Jones, ed., *English Critical Essays (Nineteenth Century)* (London: Oxford University Press, 1950).

LeWinter, Oswald, ed., *Shakespeare in Europe* (Harmondsworth: Penguin, 1970).

Marowitz, Charles, 'Lear Log', *Encore*, 10 (1963): 20–33, reprinted *Tulane Drama Review*, 8, no 2 (1963): 103–21.*

McLuskie, Kathleen, 'The Patriarchal Bard: Feminist Criticism and Shakespeare: *King Lear* and *Measure for Measure*' in Jonathan Dollimore and Alan Sinfield, eds., *Political Shakespeare: New Essays in Cultural Materialism* (Manchester: Manchester University Press, 1985).

Orwell, George, 'Lear, Tolstoy and the Fool', in *Inside the Whale and Other Essays* (Harmondsworth: Penguin, 1962).

Ryan, Kiernan, *King Lear*, New Macmillan Casebook, (London: Macmillan, 1993).

Schlegel, Augustus William, *Course of Lectures on Dramatic Art and Literature* trans. John Black (London: Henry G. Bohn, 1846).

Spurgeon, Caroline, *Shakespeare's Imagery and What it Tells Us* (New York: Macmillan, 1935).

Summers, Montague, ed., *Shakespeare Adaptations: The Tempest, The Mock Tempest, and King Lear* (London: Jonathan Cape, 1922).

Swinburne, Algernon Charles, *A Study of Shakespeare* (London: Chatto and Windus, 1880).

Swinburne, Algernon Charles, *Three Plays of Shakespeare* (London: Harper Brothers, 1909).

Tate, Nahum, *The History of King Lear*, in Summers, ed.

Taylor, Gary, and Michael Warren, eds., *The Division of the Kingdoms: Shakespeare's Two Versions of King Lear* (Oxford: Clarendon Press, 1986).

Taylor, Gary, *Reinventing Shakespeare: A Cultural History from the Restoration to the Present* (London: The Hogarth Press, 1990).

Tolstoy, Leo Nikolayevich, 'Shakespeare and the Drama' in LeWinter, ed.

Turner, John, 'The Tragic Romances of Feudalism' in Graham Holderness, Nick Potter, and John Turner, eds., *Shakespeare: The Play of History* (Iowa City: University of Iowa Press, 1987).*

Vickers, Brian, ed., Shakespeare. *The Critical Heritage*, vol 1, 1623–92 (London: Routledge and Kegan Paul, 1974).

Vickers, Brian, ed., Shakespeare: *The Critical Heritage*, vol.2, 1693–1733 (London: Routledge and Kegan Paul, 1974).
Vickers, Brian, ed., Shakespeare: *The Critical Heritage*, vol.4, 1753–1765 (London: Routledge and Kegan Paul, 1976).
Vickers, Brian, ed., Shakespeare: *The Critical Heritage*, vol.5, 1765–1774 (London: Routledge and Kegan Paul, 1979).
Vickers, Brian, ed., Shakespeare: *The Critical Heritage*, vol.6, 1774–1801 (London: Routledge and Kegan Paul, 1981).
René Weis, King Lear: A Parallel Text Edition (London and New York: Longman, 1993).
Wilson Knight, G., *The Wheel of Fire: Interpretations of Shakespearean Tragedy*. Revised and enlarged fourth edition (London: Methuen, 1949).

A note on further reading

The bibliography above lists the most substantial of the essays extracted in this book; it also includes several works (indicated by an asterisk after the entry) which some of the writers excerpted have used as their points of departure, as well as the books mentioned below. Readers will have their own ideas about what they wish to follow up, but were I to make suggestions to my own students, I would refer them in the first instance to the complete versions of any of the essays extracted in Chapter Five, and thence to further reading in criticism of the 1980s and 1990s.

Those who wish to pursue the issues raised in Chapter One might begin by looking at the Vickers volumes, which include a great deal more material on *King Lear* than I have been able to reproduce here, and whose introductions offer succinct but more detailed examinations of the critical preoccupations of the years covered in each volume. Jonathan Bate's *The Romantics on Shakespeare* would be a productive place to start for those who wish to follow through the material discussed in Chapter Two. The 'old' Macmillan casebook, edited by Frank Kermode, reprints a selection of mainly twentieth-century criticism up to the 1960s; Larry S. Champion's *King Lear: An Annotated Bibliography* offers synopses of more than 2,500 studies of the play published for the most part between 1940 and 1970 and summarises the changing critical concerns of those years in its introduction. Both of these would be good places to start further reading on the issues concerning the critics covered in Chapters Three and Four. For reasons of space, criticism of the Seventies is not represented in this book. Two anthologies, Lawrence Danson's *On King Lear* and Rosalie L. Colie's *Some facets of King Lear*, both reproduce a selection of essays from that decade. And for further reading in contemporary treatments of the play, the New Macmillan Casebook on *King Lear*, edited by Kiernan Ryan, is the best place to start (Ryan also includes an annotated bibliography, which takes in both recent writing on the play itself, and the theoretical standpoints from which this writing emerges, and of which it forms a part). A selection of deconstructive criticism on Shakespeare's plays can be found in G. Douglas Atkins' *Shakespeare and Deconstruction*. Ivo Kamps' recent anthology *Materialist Shakespeare* offers an excellent selection of historicist essays on Shakespeare; its companion volume, *Shakespeare and Gender*, edited by Kamps and Deborah E. Barker, reproduces an equally comprehensive selection of feminist essays on the texts.

NOTES

INTRODUCTION

1. Reprinted in Brian Vickers, ed., *Shakespeare: The Critical Heritage*, vol 2 (1693–1733) (London: Routledge and Kegan Paul, 1974) pp. 306–7.

2. Leo Nikolayevich Tolstoy, 'Shakespeare and the Drama' reprinted in Oswald LeWinter, ed., *Shakespeare in Europe* (Harmondsworth: Penguin, 1970) pp. 216, 217, 225–6, 252, 254.

3. See Rene Weis's introduction to his *King Lear: A Parallel Text Edition* (London and New York: Longman, 1993) for a much more detailed account of the nature of the differences between the two texts. On the question of the role of the Fool in each version, see John Kerrigan, 'Revision, Adaptation, and the Fool in King Lear' in Gary Taylor and Michael Warren, eds., *The Division of the Kingdoms: Shakespeare's Two Versions of King Lear* (Oxford: Clarendon Press, 1986). On the roles of Albany, Edgar, and Kent, see Michael Warren's 'The Diminution of Kent' (in Taylor and Warren, 1986) and his 'Quarto and Folio *King Lear* and the Interpretation of Albany and Edgar', in David Bevington and Jay L. Halio eds., *Shakespeare, Pattern of Excelling Nature* (Newark, Del 1978).

4. For a succinct account of the editorial history of the play, see Steven Urkowitz, 'The base Shall to th' Legitimate: The Growth of an Editorial Tradition' (pp. 23–43 in Taylor and Warren, 1986).

5. Gary Taylor, *Reinventing Shakespeare: A Cultural History from the Restoration to the Present* (London: The Hogarth Press, 1990) pp. 359–60.

6. Alexander Pope, preface to his edition of *The Works of Shakespeare, Collated and Corrected* (1725), quoted in Vickers, vol 2, p. 414.

7. Accounts of the rise of English as a subject of university study are offered by Taylor in *Reinventing Shakespeare*, and by Terry Eagleton in *Literary Theory: An Introduction* (Minneapolis: University of Minnesota Press, 1983).

8. I. A. Richards, *Principles of Literary Criticism* (New York and London: Harcourt Brace Jovanich, 1925) p. 114.

9. Stanley Wells, 'The Once and Future King Lear', pp. 1–22 in Taylor and Warren, 1986, p. 3.

10. R. A. Foakes, *Hamlet Versus Lear*, (Cambridge: CUP, 1993), pp. 1–2. To my shame, I read Foakes' book in the late stages of writing this one, and was initially horrified to find that he made a number of the connections I have made in his own introduction, sometimes phrasing uncannily similar to my own. On reflection, I decided to let my own introduction stand, but those interested in the questions that I try to raise should consult Foakes in the first instance for further reading.

CHAPTER ONE

1. From Ben Jonson, 'To the memory of my beloved, The Author Mr William Shakespeare: And what he hath left us', reprinted in Brian Vickers, ed., *Shakespeare: The Critical Heritage*, vol 1, 1623–1692. (London and Boston: Routledge and Kegan Paul, 1974) p. 24. Vickers' *Shakespeare: The Critical Heritage* series is a compendious resource for any student of the reception of Shakespeare over the period which this chapter covers, and I have made almost exclusive use of it in this chapter. Rather than giving separate footnotes for each extract, I shall only footnote individual volumes the first time that I use them; thereafter, I'll indicate within the text the relevant volume and page number.

2. Quoted by Brian Vickers in the introduction to volume 5 (1765–1774) of *Shakespeare: The Critical Heritage* (London, Henley and Boston: Routledge and Kegan Paul, 1979), p. 2.

3. The reliability of early editions of *King Lear* may be questionable, but it would be cumbersome to make this point every time I mention the text. Thus I will refer to 'the original *King Lear*', or 'Shakespeare's

King Lear' when I want to distinguish it from Tate's version of the text.

4. George Steevens, from 'Observations of the plays altered from Shakespeare', reprinted in Brian Vickers, ed., *Shakespeare: The Critical Heritage*, vol 6 1774–1801 (Routledge and Kegan Paul: London, Henley and Boston, 1981), p. 204.

5. Nahum Tate, *The History of King Lear*, reproduced in Montague Summers, ed., *Shakespeare Adaptations: The Tempest, The Mock Tempest, and King Lear*. (London: Jonathan Cape, 1922), pp. 180–4, 187–8.

6. Reprinted in Brian Vickers, ed., *Shakespeare: The Critical Heritage*, vol 2, (1693–1733) (London: Routledge and Kegan Paul, 1974) p. 258.

7. By 'catastrophe', these writers mean the 'outcome' of the play.

8. See Brian Vickers, *Shakespeare: The Critical Heritage*, vol I, p. 6. As Vickers dryly remarks, Tate 'cut both comedy and tragedy from the play'.

9. Aristotle' *Poetics* was the major classical text upon which Neo-Classical theoreticians drew, but it reached them by a circuitous route: they read him through their reading of French theoreticians such as Boileau and Rapin, who themselves took their Aristotle from the Italian critic Castelvetro (See the Introduction to Oswald LeWinter, ed., *Shakespeare in Europe* (Harmondsworth; Penguin, 1963)). Thus the Neo-Classical version of Aristotle bears only a mediated relation to the *Poetics*. As Schlegel was later to point out (see Chapter Two), Aristotle does not mention time and place, and is interested only in action.

10. By this Dryden means plot and sub-plot, especially if the subplot is comic.

11. See the appendices to Kenneth Muir's Arden edition of *King Lear* (London: Methuen, 1972) for extracts from possible sources for Shakespeare's play.

12. It seems hard to believe this of the poet of the Sonnets, but still.

13. I have left out the last two paragraphs of Johnson's endnote. The penultimate one refers to the debate over Lear's madness, which is covered below; the last

paragraph discusses the text's relation to a ballad entitled 'A lamentable Song of the Death of King Leir and his Three Daughters'.

14. Samuel Johnson, endnote on *King Lear*, reprinted in volume VIII of *The Yale Edition of the Works of Samuel Johnson, Johnson on Shakespeare*, ed. Arthur Sherbo (New Haven and London: Yale University Press, 1968) pp. 702–5.

15. One other topic upon which was expended a great deal of ink was the question of Shakespeare's classical learning, or lack of it. I have not covered this debate in this chapter because, frankly, it seems to me to be of very limited interest.

16. For two rather different eighteenth-century accounts of Lear's character see Aaron Hill (Vickers 3:33) and Richard Roderick (Vickers 4:342).

17. Thomas Davies, *Dramatic Miscellanies* (1783) ii, 267. Quoted by Maynard Mack in his *King Lear in Our Time* (London: Methuen, 1966) p. 14.

18. See Richard Roderick (Vickers 4:342)

19. Samuel Richardson, note to his post-script to *Clarissa* (1747–8) Harmondsworth: Penguin, 1985) p. 1497.

CHAPTER TWO

1. Victor Hugo, *William Shakespeare*, trans. Melville B. Anderson (London: George Routledge and Sons, n.d.), p. 289.

2. Augustus William Schlegel, *Course of Lectures on Dramatic Art and Literature* trans. John Black, revised by the Reverend A.J.W. Morrison (London: Henry G. Bohn, 1846), p. 21. Schlegel's lectures were originally delivered in Vienna, in 1808; they were published in 1809 and 1811.

3. M. Guizot, *Shakespeare and His Times*, (London: Richard Bentley, 1852), p. 138.

4. Charles Lamb, 'On the Tragedies of Shakespeare, considered with reference to their fitness for stage representation'. First printed in The Reflector, 1811, reprinted in Edmund D. Jones, ed., *English Critical Essays (Nineteenth Century)* (London: Oxford University Press, 1950),

pp. 81–101, this quotation pp. 91–2.

5. John Keats, 'On Sitting Down to Read King Lear Once Again', reprinted in Jonathan Bate, ed., *The Romantics on Shakespeare* (Harmondsworth: Penguin, 1992), pp. 198–9.

6. Reprinted in Bate, p. 78.

7. Victor Hugo, from the preface to *Cromwell* (1827) reprinted in Bate, pp. 226–7.

8. Samuel Taylor Coleridge, in Thomas Middleton Raysor, ed., *Coleridge's Shakespearean Criticism*, vol 2 (London: Constable and Co., 1930), pp. 73–4.

9. Samuel Taylor Coleridge, 'Notes on the Tragedies' reprinted in Thomas Middleton Raysor, ed., *Coleridge's Shakespearean Criticism*, vol I (London: Constable, 1930), p. 63. Most of Coleridge's criticism on Shakespeare appears in the form of notes and fragments, and was never collected together into coherent published essays.

10. Stendhal, *Racine and Shakespeare*, extracted in Bate, p. 218.

11. Reprinted in Bate, pp 41–3. Herder was writing before Romantic aesthetic theory had been elaborated; the relation between theory and practice is not direct.

12. For a brief account of Hazlitt's relation to Schlegel, see Bate's excellent introduction to *The Romantics on Shakespeare*.

13. Hazlitt, from 'On Shakespeare and Milton' (1818), reprinted in Bate, p. 182.

14. The following extracts come from volume I of Raysor's two volume edition of *Coleridge's Shakespearean Criticism*. The material in square brackets within Coleridge's text is Raysor's.

15. 'Here notice the improbability and nursery tale character of the tale prefixed as the porch of the edifice, not laid as its foundation.' [Coleridge's note to the text.]

16. Coleridge remarks elsewhere on the blinding of Gloucester: 'What can I say of this scene? My reluctance to think Shakespeare wrong, and yet –' and notes later that it is 'Necessary to harmonise their [Goneril's and Regan's] cruelty to their father'. (Coleridge, vol I, p. 66.)

17. William Hazlitt, *Characters of Shakespeare's Plays*, (London: Dent, 1906), pp. 118–36.

18. 'Not rain, wind, thunder, fire, are my daughters:/ I tax you not, you elements, with unkindness;/ I never gave you kingdom, call'd you children,/ You owe me no subscription: then let fall/ Your horrible pleasure' (3.2.15–19).

CHAPTER THREE

1. Macready had reservations about reintroducing the Fool, writing in his diary for January 4 that 'My opinion of the introduction of the Fool is that . . . in acting representation it will fail of effect; it will either weary . . . or distract the spectator. I have no hope of it, and think that at the last we shall be obliged to dispense with it'. The part was played by a woman, Priscilla Horton; as Macready relates the entry for the following day: 'Speaking to Willmott . . . about the part of the Fool . . ., I described the sort of fragile, hectic, beautiful-faced, half-idiot-looking boy that it should be, and stated my belief that it never could be acted. Bartley observed that a woman should play it. I caught at the idea, and instantly exclaimed: "Miss P[riscilla] Horton is the very person." I was delighted at the thought'. J.C. Trewin, ed., *The Journal of William Charles Macready 1832–1851* (London: Longmans, 1967), pp. 112–3.

2. Charles Dickens, *The Examiner*, February 4, 1838, reprinted in Charles Dickens, *Miscellaneous Papers from 'The Morning Chronicle,' 'The Daily News,' 'The Examiner,' 'Household Words' 'All the Year Round,' Etc. and Plays and Poems* in Two volumes. Vol I. (Gadshill edition of *The Works of Charles Dickens*. (London: Chapman & Hill, n.d.). Additional volumes. Volume XXXV), pp. 77–81.

3. I owe this observation to Tim Lustig.

4. Algernon Charles Swinburne, *A Study of Shakespeare* (London: Chatto and Windus, 1880) p. 223. Hereafter referred to in the text as Swinburne.

5. I am not here implying a simple cause/effect relation between the novel and nineteenth-century Shakespeare criticism. It would seem more likely that

both phenomena are refractions of larger scale differences in the ways that men and women experienced their world.

6. I do not know who coined the term 'fatal flaw'. As far as I am aware, Bradley himself does not use it.

7. Anna Jameson, *Shakespeare's Heroines: Characteristics of Women Moral, Poetical, and Historical* (London: George Bell and Sons, 1905).

8. Artemisia Gentileschi was an Italian artist who, raped in her youth, later painted a number of pictures in which women wreak terrible, and violent, revenge on the men who have done them injuries.

9. A.C. Bradley, *Shakespearean Tragedy: Lectures on Hamlet, Othello, King Lear, Macbeth* (London: Macmillan, 1950), p. 7.

10. This account of Bradley owes something to conversations I have had in past years with Neil Rhodes of the University of St Andrews.

11. Georg Wilhelm Friedrich Hegel, *The Philosophy of Fine Art*, extracted in Oswald LeWinter, ed., *Shakespeare in Europe* (Harmondsworth: Penguin, 1970) pp. 79–88.

12. G. G. Gervinus, *Shakespeare Commentaries*, trans. F. E. Bunnett. New edition, revised (London: Smith, Elder and Co, 1883), p. 615.

13. R. A. Foakes, *Hamlet Versus Lear* (Cambridge: C.U.P., 1993), p. 52.

14. Denton Snyder, *The Shakespearian Drama, a Commentary: The Tragedies* (New York: Ticknor, 1887) cited in R. A. Foakes, *Hamlet Versus Lear*, p. 48.

15. George Brandes, *William Shakespeare: A Critical Study* in two volumes, vol II (London: Heinemann, 1898), p. 134.

16. Shelley's remarks are reprinted in Frank Kermode, ed., *Shakespeare: King Lear: A Casebook* (London; Macmillan, 1969) pp. 46–7.

17. I have deleted here a comparison between Cordelia and Antigone, which underlies the rest of the paragraph, and exchanged for Swinburne's third person plural, the third person singular pronoun (in square brackets).

18. Hugo, as we saw in Chapter Two, was self-consciously and explicitly revolutionary, as was Shelley; Swinburne characterises Goethe and Gautier here as reactionary poets.

19. Algernon Charles Swinburne, *Three Plays of Shakespeare* (London: Harper Brothers, 1909), pp. 16–17. Hereafter referred to within the text as *Three Plays*.

20. Leo Nikolayevich Tolstoy, 'Shakespeare and the Drama', trans. V. Tchertkoff, reprinted in Oswald LeWinter, ed., *Shakespeare in Europe* (Harmondsworth: Penguin, 1970), p. 237. First published in England in Tolstoy on Shakespeare (The Free Age Press, 1907), pp. 7–81.

21. George Orwell, 'Lear, Tolstoy and the Fool', reprinted in *Inside the Whale and Other Essays* (Harmondsworth: Penguin, 1962), pp. 101–19, p. 105. First appeared in *Polemic*, no. 7 (March 1947).

22. See LeWinter's brief introduction to Tolstoy's essay in *Shakespeare in Europe*.

CHAPTER FOUR

1. A.C. Bradley, *Shakespearean Tragedy*, (London: Macmillan, 1950), p. 285.

2. G. Wilson Knight, *The Wheel of Fire: Interpretations of Shakespearean Tragedy*, revised and enlarged fourth edition (London: Methuen, 1949) p. 199.

3. Kenneth Muir, ed., The New Arden Edition of *King Lear* (London: Methuen, 1972), p. l, quoted by Barbara Everett in 'The New King Lear', for details of which see note 6 below.

4. L.C. Knights, *Some Shakespearean Themes and an Approach to Hamlet* (Harmondsworth: Penguin, 1966) pp. 79 (first sentence) and 101 (second sentence).

5. William Empson, 'Fool in *Lear*' in *The Structure of Complex Words* (London: The Hogarth Press, 1985), p. 150.

6. Barbara Everett, 'The New *King Lear*' reprinted in Frank Kermode, ed., *King Lear: A Casebook* (London: Macmillan, 1969) p. 185. Everett's article first appeared in *Critical Quarterly*, Winter 1960.

7. Jan Kott, *Shakespeare Our Contemporary* Second edition revised. (London:

Routledge, 1967) p. 116.

8. Another such manifesto is offered by G. Wilson Knight in his essay 'On the Principles of Shakespeare Interpretation', the opening chapter of *The Wheel of Fire*.

9. L. C. Knights, 'How Many Children Had Lady Macbeth?' in his *Explorations* (London: Chatto and Windus, 1946) p. 36. Hereafter referred to in the text as Knights, *Explorations*.

10. T. S. Eliot, introduction to G. Wilson Knight's *The Wheel of Fire*, p. xvii.

11. G. Wilson Knight, *The Wheel of Fire*, p, 15, quoted by L.C. Knights in *Explorations* (pp. 4–5).

12. Caroline Spurgeon, *Shakespeare's Imagery and What it Tells Us* (New York: Macmillan, 1935) p. 338.

13. Sigmund Freud, 'The Theme of the Three Caskets', in *The Standard Edition of the Complete Psychological Works of Sigmund Freud*, trans., ed. James Strachey in collaboration with Anna Freud, vol XII (1911–13) (London: The Hogarth Press, 1958) pp. 291–301.

14. The hypotheses upon which Empson proceeds in 'Fool in *Lear*' are laid out more explicitly in the essay on Erasmus which precedes 'Fool in *Lear*' in *The Structure of Complex Words*.

15. R. A. Foakes. *Hamlet Versus Lear* (Cambridge: CUP, 1993) pp. 58–9.

CHAPTER FIVE

1. The New Macmillan Casebook on *King Lear*, ed. Kiernan Ryan, reprints four of the essays I have excerpted below, sometimes in their entirety, sometimes differently extracted. See Ryan's introduction, in the first instance, for further elaboration of contemporary critical concerns.

2. Stanley Cavell, *Disowning Knowledge in Six Plays of Shakespeare* (Cambridge: CUP, 1987), p. 5.

3. Paul Alpers, '*King Lear* and the Theory of the Sight Pattern,' in R. Brower and R. Poirier, eds, *In Defense of Reading* (New York: Dutton, 1963).

4. Stanley Cavell, *Disowning Knowledge*, pp. 44–51, 57–8.

5. Jonathan Goldberg, 'Perspectives: Dover Cliff and the Conditions of Representation' in G. Douglas Atkins and David M. Bergeron, eds, *Shakespeare and Deconstruction* (New York: Peter Lang, 1988) pp. 245–8, 256.

6. McLuskie refers here to Marilyn French's *Shakespeare's Division of Experience* (London: Cape, 1982) and Linda Bamber's *Comic Women, Tragic Men: a Study of Gender and Genre in Shakespeare* (Stanford: Stanford University Press, 1981).

7. Juliet Dusinberre, *Shakespeare and the Nature of Women* (London: Macmillan, 1975).

8. Raymond Williams, *Modern Tragedy* (London: Chatto, 1966) p. 45 [McLuskie's note].

9. Kathleen McLuskie, 'The Patriarchal Bard: Feminist Criticism and Shakespeare: *King Lear* and *Measure for Measure*' in Jonathan Dollimore and Alan Sinfield, eds., *Political Shakespeare: New Essays in Cultural Materialism* (Manchester: Manchester University Press, 1985), pp. 90–1, 98–9.

10. Lynda Boose, 'The Father and the Bride in Shakespeare,' *PMLA* 97 (May 1982): pp. 325–47.

11. Coppélia Kahn, 'The Absent Mother in *King Lear*' in Margaret W. Ferguson, Maureen Quilligan, and Nancy J. Vickers, eds., *Rewriting the Renaissance: The Discourses of Sexual Difference in Early Modern Europe* (Chicago: The University of Chicago Press, 1986), pp. 33–4, 39–41.

12. Stephen J Greenblatt, *Learning To Curse: Essays in Early Modern Culture* (London: Routledge, 1990), pp. 95–8.

13. See the extract from Empson in Chapter Four for other associations between *Lear* and Erasmus.

14. Lisa Jardine, *Reading Shakespeare Historically* (London: Routledge, 1996), p. 84.

15. Lisa Jardine, *Reading Shakespeare Historically*, pp. 78–9, 93–4, 96–7.

16. John Danby, *Shakespeare's Doctrine of Nature: A Study of King Lear* (London: Faber and Faber, 1951) pp. 52, 138.

17. John Turner, 'The Tragic Romances of Feudalism' in Graham Holderness, Nick Potter, and John Turner, eds., *Shakespeare: The Play of History* (Iowa City: University of Iowa Press, 1987), p. 101.

18. Walter Cohen, *Drama of a Nation: Public Theatre in Renaissance England and Spain* (Ithaca: Cornell University Press, 1985), p. 352.

19. Halpern takes this term from Gilles Deleuze and Felix Guattari, 'November 20, 1923: Postulates of Linguistics', in *A Thousand Plateaus*, trans. Brian Massumi (Minneapolis: University of Minnesota Press, 1987). Halpern uses the term to designate a sign system in which signs are established as 'the effect and medium of (political) power'.

20. Here Halpern is using concepts elaborated in Jean Baudrillard, *For a Political Economy of the Sign*, trans. Charles Levin (St Louis: Telos Press, 1981). The term 'Consumption-Sign' designates a system of signs 'created by the consumption or destruction of wealth'.

21. Richard Halpern, *The Poetics of Primitive Accumulation: English Renaissance Culture and the Genealogy of Capital* (Ithaca: Cornell University Press, 1991), pp. 215–18, 234–5, 242–6.

APPENDIX

1. Reprinted from René Weis, ed., *King Lear: A Parallel Text Edition* (London: Longman, 1993), pp. 196–203. Unfortunately, it was not possible here to reproduce Weis' parallel format.

ACKNOWLEDGEMENTS

The editor and publishers wish to thank the following for their permission to reprint copyright material: Macmillan (for material from *Shakespearean Tragedy*); Cambridge University Press (for material from *Disowning Knowledge in Six Plays of Shakespeare*); The Hogarth Press (for material from *The Structure of Complex Words* and *The Standard Edition of the Complete Psychological Works of Sigmund Freud*); Peter Lang (for material from *Shakespeare and Deconstruction*); University of Chicago Press (for material from *Rewriting the Renaissance: The Discourses of Sexual Difference in Early Modern Europe*); Cornell University Press (for material from *The Poetics of Primitive Accumulation: English Renaissance Culture and the Genealogy of Capital*); Routledge & Kegan Paul (for material from *Reading Shakespeare Historically* and *Learning to Curse: Essays in Early Modern Culture*); Penguin Books (for material from *Inside the Whale and Other Essays* and *Some Shakespearean Themes and an Approach to Hamlet*).

Every effort has been made to contact the holders of any copyrights applying to the material quoted in this book. The publishers would be grateful if any such copyright holders whom they have not been able to contact, would write to them.

The editor would like to thank Ed Larrissy, of the English Department of the University of Keele, for reading and commenting on Chapter Two; Roger Pooley, also of Keele English Department, and always a supportive colleague; Keith, Patricia, Alison and Catherine Bruce, and Lori Maxwell, for their respective provision of other forms of support over the period in which this book was put together, and Tim Lustig, for being as valiant with the proof-reading at the later stages of the book's production as he was with childcare in the earlier.

Susan Bruce is Lecturer in the English Department of the University of Keele, and has also taught at universities in Italy, the USA, Switzerland and Scotland. Amongst her publications are articles on More's *Utopia*, Rochester's poems, and Swift's *Gulliver's Travels*.

INDEX